Tommy B

Bolton Wanderers

Ah'm
tellin'
thee

Biography by **Ian Seddon**
ex Bolton Wanderer

Published by Ian Seddon
Publishing partner: Paragon Publishing
© Ian Seddon 2012

ISBN 978-1-908341-93-8

Book design, layout and production management by Into Print
www.intoprint.net
+44 (0) 1604 832149

Printed and bound in UK and USA by Lightning Source

Dedicated in memory of Harold and Leah Seddon

Treasured memories of your deep love, affection and devotion are shared by your five children who will be forever grateful for their warm and happy childhoods.

All are thankful for being raised in a loving family and have tried to maximise the opportunities you gave us to follow our own paths in life.

Your grandchildren and great grandchildren have and are being taught the same priceless virtues to become decent citizens and also lead full lives.

Foreword

"I am delighted and very honoured to write a foreword for Ian Seddon's book "Ah'm tellin thee" regarding Tommy Banks."

When I signed for Bolton Wanderers in 1960 I was already a supporter of the club. My father had been at the same school as George Taylor, Bolton's Chief Coach in Ashton under Lyne, my birthplace.

I had seen their epic games all the way through to the '58 'Munich' F.A. Cup Final and in particular the semi-final victory over local rivals Blackburn Rovers at Maine Road, Manchester plus the classic quarter final game against one of the finest teams around, Wolverhampton Wanderers.

Tommy Banks gave every dressing room he entered his own special presence as a strong character and forceful leader. He was never frightened to speak his mind but that camouflaged the fact that he was also a very thoughtful and deep thinking quality defender in a defence that had the most fearsome reputation. Such was the reputation that great wingers of the day, Sir Stanley Matthews and Sir Tom Finney, always faced playing against Tommy with some trepidation.

It is no surprise that he featured for his country along with colleagues such as Eddie Hopkinson, Ray Parry, Dougie Holden, Dennis Stevens and the late great Nat Lofthouse.

As Chief Executive of the Professional Footballers Association I am very much aware of the crucial role Tommy played in the removal of the maximum wage. My predecessor Cliff Lloyd said how important it was to get the outstanding players of the day, players like Stanley Matthews to the meeting in Manchester at the Grand Hotel.

After some lengthy debate the delegate from Bury F.C. stood up to suggest that maybe strike action was not the best thing as his father worked down the pit for less than £20 per week. At this Tommy stood up...with the room in silence waiting for his reaction, he said,

"Yes, I hear what you say and I have every respect for your father's job as a miner because I have been down that pit and at that coal face."

" I know how difficult it is but just let me tell you one thing, you ask your Dad to come up out of that pit next Saturday afternoon and mark 'Brother' Stanley Matthews and see what he has to say ?"

At that Tommy brought the house down and Jimmy Hill and Cliff Lloyd had no problem in getting an unanimous vote of support for the P.F.A. in its actions which led to the removal of the maximum wage.

Today's multi-millionaire footballers owe a great debt to the son of Farnworth who might well have been formed out of the very coal pits which featured in that area as he was granite like, a great player, great person and a great character.

It is a privilege to know him and he was a very special personal guest when P.F.A. icons turned up at the Manchester Town Hall in January 2007 to celebrate the centenary of the P.F.A.

Gordon Taylor OBE
Chief Executive of the Professional Footballers Association

Accolades

Francis Lee (BWFC & Manchester City & England)

Tommy's a very bright clever guy who's always been there for his mates...if I was in the trenches he'd be my first choice to join me. He's a charismatic gent who was very popular in the dressing room and encouraging on the field plus he was extremely confident and an excellent all round footballer.

Tommy was astute and quick, wingers didn't like playing against him, he was belligerent, he would clatter them if required and he played mind games with them.

Dennis Stevens (BWFC)

I admire him, a gifted footballer he was also a leader, you could hear him all over the field roaring out instructions and praise.

He's no airs and graces to this day, a totally genuine man who was forever lifting spirits in the dressing room. Tommy was always laughing and never appeared to get upset, nothing bother him unduly. His personality gelled the lads together and he played a big part in generating a brilliant team spirit.

Sir Bobby Charlton (Manchester United & England)

Tommy has always been well respected and very popular with players... friend or foe.

He had a lot to say on and off the field but knew his football and was a master of his craft. Fast over the ground and hard as nails wingers didn't like playing against him. If you had any soft spot in your make up he'd exploit it, few if any got the better of him.

Every time I see him nowadays I always try to think of something funny to say but he always beats me to it, a lovely man.

Simon Marland (Bolton Wanderers secretary)

Unfortunately I never had the pleasure of seeing Tommy play as he had finished before my era began in the late sixties. His legend however was something that was evident to me from a young age growing up in Farnworth. It's quite amazingly that from our district we had two cup winners....World Cup winner Alan Ball and of course 1958 F.A. Cup winner Tommy. Stories were passed down from father to son of how the Wanderers won the cup. Information about the players themselves were something of legend to a youngster like me who by this time was getting used to seeing his team in the lower reaches of the old Second Division.

I have had the pleasure however of getting to know Tommy the man through speaking with him to get his recollections of his time in the game for updates on my Wanderers books. His words brought back those childhood memories passed down to me which allowed me to piece together what had been said in those formative years.

The stories of the gravel rash, the camaraderie and the togetherness of the team pulled together by the likes of Tommy are a million miles away from the current game but remain entrenched in our history. Perhaps the biggest compliment I can pay Tommy is to say that they certainly don't make 'em like Tommy Banks anymore.

Syd Farrimond (BWFC)

Tommy was a good footballer but he's also an intelligent, friendly and thoughtful man who was always willing to help other players with advice and usually had strong opinions on many issues.

He's extremely honest, told you how it was in his own words.... he would tell you straight if you'd played well or not, he was held with great respect amongst the lads.

It's quite easy to talk of players being legends these days but in Tommy's case there's no doubting the fact, he is a legend.

There's also no doubt that the mould was thrown away when Tommy was made, it's a great privilege to know him, his personality is infectious.

Andrew Dean (BWFC Promotions Manager)

Tommy's never changed over all the years I've known him, a thoroughly decent man who seems to have time for everyone.

He deserves immense praise after his football career for his ongoing contribution to charity, he's never really received any recognition for his efforts albeit organising or contributing.

Over many years Tommy's will do anything for you and never ask for anything.

Chris Chilton (Harper Green teacher)

Tommy's a sincere straightforward trusting and honest man with high moral standards. He's always upfront and leads from the front being prepared to do or say what he believes in.

Tommy possesses a warm canny character and he's great company.

He was a joy to talk with in building up a picture to enable a smooth production could be arranged of Harper Green's school musical in his honour in 1994.

Graham Cunliffe (BWFC)

The lads looked up to him he'd a heart of gold, a down to earth humble yet dignified guy he was our spokesman. He was forthright in his views but very loyal to the lads within the club. Tommy was a good clever footballer extremely comfortable on the ball with either foot yet also very gritty and passionate. He played with pride and his words of encouragement on the field were priceless, he always put the interest of the team before himself.

Off the field he thought anyone with a 'posh' car was flash.

Arthur Barnard (BWFC)

Tommy's ultra loyal, he's always there for you, no backwards step. One day in the 1980's whilst in a chip shop with Tommy waiting to be served a traffic warden wandered in to enquire about who owned a car (my car) which was just parked inside the yellow lines.

Tommy took up fighting my case like a high court lawyer.

When we had paid for our chips I said to him, thanks for your support I might not have received a booking and thus fine if you hadn't been so vociferous.

Like I say, "Allus theer fer thee"

Dave Hatton (BWFC)

Tommy's always been an extremely warm and approachable individual, a man of great dignity.

I first came across him from being around nine years old when he moved to live in the same street in the Moses Gate district of Bolton. I soon realised he was a down to earth man who'd time for a word with everyone. He was always walking in his clogs usually with a bucket in his hand but would stop and ask over my well being which I admired with just being a kid.

In later days when in the same Bolton Wanderers dressing room he was passionate and enthusiastic, a student of the game he still possesses a great love and knowledge of football.

If you ever wanted any advice Tommy was the man to turn to, he'd listen to you then give his opinion on the matter from his heart.

Acknowledgements

Tommy Banks's biography has been titled "Ah'm tellin thee" in keeping and with respect to Tommy's broad spoken word machine gun peppered with Lancashire dialect.

The sprinkling of "Lanky" phrases contained within stay true to some of his own "Tommyisms" to support his written story and portray this proud, dignified man in a fuller light. The dialect past down from Lancashire forefathers is nowhere near as apparent in everyday use by the public of 'Bowton' nowadays. The very loose translations (in brackets) should help maintain the flow of his story to the reader.

Heartfelt thanks are due to Tommy Banks for his hours of patience and brilliant memory in recalling amusing incidents and serious issues of days long ago.

Tommy's sons Dave and Lee for their total honesty in relaying how their formative years unfolded.

Many thanks to Lee's mate Nigel Howard for his interesting facts and warm gesture to be a sounding board. Doreen Ward for her eagle eye and attention to detail and my wife Pauline for her countless brews and ongoing support whilst I was writing Tommy's story.

Similar, thanks for the appreciative offers of assistance along the way from Bolton Wanderers F.C. via club secretary Simon Marland and Promotions Manager Andrew Dean.

The kindness of Gordon Taylor the Chief Executive of the Professional Footballers Association for his informative foreword and help in retracing the steps of Tommy's vital contribution to the union's campaign to abolish the Maximum Wage in 1961.

Worthy, tell tale contributions from former professional footballers relating incidents of yesteryears;

Francis Lee, Sir Bobby Charlton, Syd Farrimond, Dave Hatton, Dennis Stevens, Graham Cunliffe, Dave Lennard, Arthur Barnard and Jimmy Armfield.

Knowledgeable information received from former teacher Chris Chilton for depicting the scenes of the Harper Green school musical in honour of Tommy in 1994.

Valuable contributions of photographs to enhance and bring to life the world that Tommy, now 82 years old, knew in his youth, throughout his football days and later years via;

The Bolton News
The Professional Footballers Association
Rita Banks
Andrew Dean
Nigel Howard
Tim Cutress
Chris Chilton
Lee Seddon
Jamie Seddon
Jean Gallimore

A big thank you to Mark Webb of Into Print for all his help and guidance in ensuring this self publication made print.

Every effort has been made to trace the ownership of other illustrative items and apologies are given should copyright have inadvertently been broken.

Regards
Ian

Chapter 1

The Warm Up

It's the 1st March 1958, on a cold wet winter's afternoon at Burnden Park, former home of the famous Bolton Wanderers before their move to the Reebok Stadium in 1997.

The ground is bursting at the seams with almost 60,000 mainly flat capped spectators who have built a bristling boiling tinder box atmosphere as the "Trotters" take on the might of Wolverhampton Wanderers in the 6th round of the F.A. Cup.

This was in the days when football clubs had "grounds" not stadiums, each ground had its own individual characteristics, not the aesthetically sparkling sponsored stadiums of the Sky Sports era.

Indeed, Bolton's opponents that day Wolves played their home fixtures at Molineux similar in one aspect to Burnden Park that it featured a huge old 'kop' embankment from which almost 30,000 spectators would gaze down on the game urging on their heroes.

Burnden Park was blessed with a pitch surrounded by a gravel running track which encountered virtually a sheer drop of some three feet from the touchline to the trackside.

On days like these Burnden would be a cauldron, the crowd would be mostly male with a few women scattered amongst them. These hard working no nonsense Northerners were drawn from the mines and engineering factories that constituted the type of employment of the area. Work was predominantly mining, engineering and cotton...tough industries, tough times....and tough but fair people. These people flocked in their masses to these unique grounds to give their support.

People like Tommy Banks watching Tommy Banks who could identify with Tommy Banks...tough but fair.

The grounds, players, and everything associated with the national sport would be unrecognisable to today's young "fans" of the beautiful game. No blanket coverage, no Sky Sports panel of pundits telling you what you actually probably knew and a way of life which seems light years away. If you ever see any old footage from games of the era then the average spectator would be virtually identical in their clothing attire when at the match. A mackintosh coat, usually a flat cap the occasional trilby, a shirt with tie all appeared to be mandatory.

There was no stigma attached to smoking in the 50's and many men would supplement their image by having a branded or roll your own cigarette complete with untapped ash dangling from their mouths.

Nowhere in this crowd would you see a supporter wearing "this season's home shirt" complete with a player's name emblazoned on the back ... imagine..."Banks 3"?

Back to the game and a brief stoppage in play brings a slight lull in the fever of the crowd and a voice can be heard booming out from the pitch above the noisy chatter from the terraces.

"Roy,when thee's dun wi yon mon wilt chip im oer 'ere un ah'll si if 'ee leeks gravel rash?"

(Roy, when you have finished conducting your business with that gent please send him over to me and I'll ask him what he thinks of the gravel on the trackside.)

The indefatigable voice belongs to one Tommy Banks Bolton's fierce pint size bulldog left back whispering to his mate Roy Hartle (right back) asking about the current state of health of the Wolves left winger. Although it must be noted that to this day Tommy's "whispering" can allegedly be heard over three large fields!!

Lurid tales of this cinder track and hapless wingers being deposited onto it only tell part of the story.

Tommy Banks an ebullient Farnworthian was a hard man who used his muscle when needed to good effect on the football field. A working class hero hardened by coal bagging and labour under ground in all its vigorous glory he was also a fine all round footballer. Good control, genuinely two footed, and blessed with a touch of pace he would have prospered in the modern era as an overlapping full back on the carpets of today.

Messer's Hartle and Banks a lovable gruesome twosome had grown into cult status players in the eyes of Bolton's faithful followers over the years. Their no frills, no prisoners "seconds out of the ring" approach had made them the scourge of many an unwitting winger who dared to tease them with the ball along the touchlines. A lightening "friendly" sliding tackle implemented by either full back close to the touchline occasionally resulted in an opponent crashing over the whiteline and down the banking onto the harsh gravel track that surrounded the playing arena.

Roy originally from "down the country" and always the true gentleman would pick the unfortunate player up apologise and dust him down. However a repeat dose of medicine later in the game could find his opponent again sprawling on the trackside.

Local lad Tommy, a gritty, fiery yet gifted competitor would likewise sympathize in his own surly manner to any player grimacing on the track.

"Nethen owdlad downt thee tryter tek mi agen or else!"

(Now then my friend don't try to beat me again or the same fate may await you)

No wonder team changes regularly echoed from the loudspeaker as the man behind the microphone announced a surprise late pre match withdrawal. It was usually that of a famous visiting forward through a mysterious injury picked up en route to games at Burnden Park during the chilling Banks and Hartle era. Maybe it could have been travel sickness on the bumpy roads and rickety coaches (charabancs) of the day...or more likely it was indeed the thought of facing up to the "gruesome twosome"

Royston Hartle and Thomas Banks.

These were towards the dying ember days of clogs, pit ponies and dark satanic mills in the industrial north west of England where folk worked hard and played even harder....tough times...tough people.

Over this and previous decades those lucky enough to be blessed with football talent offered an opportunity. That being to escape the "cradle to the grave" working scenario of a Lancashire man's "future" in life was a chance willingly grabbed by the likes of Tommy Banks and other northern lads of a similar ilk.

Therefore there was a health saving to thankful individuals due to not breathing in coal dust to the lungs from the numerous pits in the district. Furthermore others retained their hearing not being subject to the endless uncompromising clatter of ongoing factory machinery to their ears.

The chance to escape the well trodden common work routes of men who had gone before brought fame and pride. Yes fame and pride but not fortune to a few grateful local youths...these being the lads who made the grade to become professional footballers.

Many memories, incidents, opinions and "Tommyisms" make up the life of Bolton Wanderers legend Tommy Banks but lets start with his formative years.....tough times.....tough people.

Chapter 2

Early Years

Over a period of days, late in October 1929, the Wall Street crash also known as the Great Crash occurred in New York. It had the most devastating effect on the stock market in the history of America causing twelve years of a great depression that filtered outwards. Western industrial countries were all affected, creating mass unemployment, and assisted the spawning of the rise of Fascism and one Adolf Hitler in Germany.

A month later on the 10th November 1929 almost on cue with the fallout from events in America Thomas Banks was born into this turbulent world at No 14 Tudor Avenue, New Bury, a small area of Farnworth, a suburb of Bolton.

The Bolton town crest contains the words "Supera Moras" meaning "overcoming delays" or another interpretation "overcoming difficulties" Tommy was to face many troublesome times battling gamely over all the obstacles and bouncing back from his tumbles along life's slippery slopes.

Called Tommy from an early age by all but his mother who always spoke to him by his birth name he was the final child of parents John and Catherine. John (known as Jack) Banks was a local Farnworth lad living some two hundred yards from Catherine Mannion prior to their marriage in 1908. They spent their early days together in a two up two down terraced house in Tonge Square, Farnworth.

The Mannion family had moved to the area from Golborne in Wigan seeking work around the turn of the century with the opening of Century Mill a specially built ring spinning mill in George Street, Farnworth. Mills of all shapes and sizes were plentiful in the various districts of Bolton with a bulk being in and around Farnworth and the Moses Gate area less than a mile away.

Cotton was king, in 1911 a Bolton census showed that over thirty six thousand workers were employed in the industry, mills were everywhere one turned or looked.

Children worked half –time, part school, part millwork, so by their thirteenth birthday the then end of their schooldays they were plunged into fifty five hour weeks.

The education system's academic studies of the era produced hordes of illiterate children and thus they became mere factory fodder for the clattering factories. Sadly these youngsters knew nothing better or different. Lip reading was a must not an option to workers, many individuals became stone deaf with the constant noise from the machinery. In some of these factories and mills everywhere you looked machines were in motion, steam was rushing and smoke was scowling, impending danger lurked for employees who always had to retain their concentration. Temperatures and humidity were kept high to prevent cotton thread breaking. The conditions were dreadful, cotton dust hung in the air causing a lung disease called byssinosis and many died young.

Compensation wasn't heard of in these desperate days, life was cheap.

The happy small hamlet of Bolton in the late 1700's had turned from a cottage cotton industry into a mighty 1900 industrial centre of filth and fumes with hundreds of high chimneys belching smoke forth and streams fouled with the chemical waste.

In the pursuit of profit it appeared the mill owners cared little about the welfare of their workforce.

Liverpool was the main port importing cotton for production to the spinners and weavers in the area. The ideal local climate for cotton was boosted by fast flowing rivers to power the mills and later the coalfields of the districts around Bolton, Leigh, Wigan, and Salford, ensured the steam driven engines ran relentlessly.

The mill owners were (in the main) ruthless by nature.

With employment legislation giving virtually no protection to the masses exploitation was rife, working conditions were desperate and the mill and factory owners indeed made vast profits.

Several of these owners in fact became the Roman Abramovich's of their times by being involved at board level at their local football clubs.

Did some treat the players in their employment just as disdainfully as the teenagers in their damp noisy factories?

In later years Tommy played a pivotal part in speaking out against the football establishment such was his dislike of the injustices of the then current footballer's contract.....but more of that later.

Thomas was the youngest of seven, four boys and three girls spanning 21 years between the first and last birth in the family.

John (Jack) (Father)	1888 + Catherine (Mother) 1890
Alice Ann	1908
John	1909
Annie	1911
Margaret	1912 died 1913
James (Jim)	1914
Ralph	1920
Thomas	1929

If his father Jack, had not served on the front line in the First World War fighting the Turks in Mesopotamia, which is now Southern Iraq and South West Iran, Tommy reckons there may have been a couple more additions to the Banks clan. Families tended to be bigger in those days often containing eight, ten even twelve children cramped yet surviving in small purpose built terraced properties for the workers.

Shortly after Tommy's birth, sister Alice Ann had married and eldest brother John soon followed suit, with both moving out of the family home. This prompted father Banks to seek a smaller lodging for his brood.

In the early 1920's the Banks family had been allocated a council house at Tudor Avenue due to outgrowing their original terraced house. After the end of the Great War the government, full of promises of a new era, put men to work building properties to provide shelter for the growing population. The New Bury estate of Farnworth where they now lived was relatively new and a mirror of what was happening nationwide in working class areas.

Father Banks now requested a three bedroom house from the council which would result in less rent to pay and a couple of more shillings in his pocket to spend in the pub each week.

Tommy's earliest recollections were, therefore, just around the corner once the family were installed at 104, George Street. Three bedrooms resulted in one for his parents, another allocated to his sister Annie with Jimmy, Ralph and Tommy in the other.

Tommy was about 2 years old when he left his cot and shared a double bed with his two older brothers. Unfortunately he kept falling out or was kicked out by accident in the scramble for a tad more sleeping space with him being so tiny in comparison to his siblings. With Jimmy now in his late teens and almost a man, Tommy found that new sleeping arrangements had been devised to ensure he was wedged between his brother Ralph and the wall to prevent anymore mishaps. It was for the best because the eldest in the bed

Jimmy was now earning a living and he was always the first to rise through necessity. Jimmy would roll out of bed on hearing the tapping on the bedroom window by the "knocker up" with his/her long pole and thus did not disturb the status quo sleeping positions.

Before the days of alarm clocks, mill workers and pitmen would pay a man or woman a few pence each week to ensure they were wakened early in the morning in time for their shift. Many men had a good hours walk to work so some of the "knocker ups" were out and about by 4.30am - 5am.

Tommy remembers that his grandma used to work as a knocker up and that she always smoked a clay pipe on her rounds. Some houses had such big families that started work at different times that she may return to knock on the same bedroom windows a number of times depending on the work schedules of the occupants.

"Eigh up theer, dustha' yermi, time thi wer clinkin' thee clugs" Tommy's grandma would often shout recalls Tommy.

(Hello, can you hear me, its time to set off for work)

Growing up as a kid back in Farnworth in the 1930's is a far cry from the borough the children of today would recognise. Technology was in its infancy and communications abroad were more pony express than internet.

If a comparison were to be made, then the "Facebook" of the day was 'clocking' folk in the vicinity and remembering their names whilst "twitter" took in the local grapevine.

Everyone knew the business of their neighbours due to virtually living on top of each other, many in their modest two up two down terraced houses with outside loos and no bathrooms.

There was a trust between families.... front and back doors could be left unlocked without enticing burglars. You will often hear from older folk who went through these hard times that no-one had "nowt."

"Nowt" meaning material acquisitions but they did possess bucketfuls of honesty, pride and decency plus a willingness to bring up their families with respect for others.

Most of Tommy's friends walked around in clogs from Monday until Saturday night which was bath night in an old tin bath in front of the fire. Sunday was the day to smarten up, put on your best togs, to attend church. Tommy was a regular, being an altar boy.

Clogs are always associated with the abject poverty endemic in the industrial towns of England and became the only footwear some children ever knew.

Clog uppers were cowhide, the soles wooden, 'irons' were optional and would be knocked a tad like shoeing a horse onto the outer soles to save use and thus prolong wear.

Clog makers were stationed all over Lancashire manufacturing in particular for coal miners and the thousands of mill workers throughout the county until the gradual demise of the industries. Indeed wherever it was damp or wet underfoot, clogs were the preferred footwear due to their cheapness (to buy and to repair) and their long lasting wear and comfort.

Lancashire is known for its heritage of clog dancing all over the world.

Cotton mill workers could emulate the sounds of the cotton looms with their "heel and toe" tapping and miners also partook in formal dance competitions at working men's clubs for monetary gain. Expert exponents of clog dancing would often become professional music hall dancers as a route out of the poverty and squalor of living in the crowded and polluted mill towns.

Father Banks did not go to church but Tommy's mother was a staunch catholic and took him to church every Sunday ensuring he was brought up under her love and direction.

"Mi mam purrer stamp un mi whilst ah wer littul" said Tommy.

(My mother instilled her ways in me whilst I was a little lad)

There was a vast age gap between first and last child, it appears Mrs. Banks was not really expecting to have any more children after Ralph was born. So with Tommy being a bit of a pleasant shock to her some nine years later when he came along she was keen to instil her ways and values of life into him during his formative years.

As stated earlier, earning a living was hard!

Industrial Bolton was a valley of smokestacks belching out fumes that served the numerous factories in and around the town. When viewed from Winter Hill high in the countryside north of Bolton in the district of Horwich it was virtually impossible to count them, there being so many.... however a survey in 1926 revealed there were 247 cotton mills and 24 dyeing and bleaching factories.

By 1979 there were just 8 left!

This was the life Tommy had been born into, the hand he had been dealt. Yes it was better than the turn of the century yet a long way off the social explosion and freedom of the 1960's.

Fashion had not arrived for the working man, shirt colours were either blue or white, symbolising grafters or pen pushers.

When braving the elements, most men wore a dour dark mackintosh with a flat cap known as a "nebber" and optional muffler (scarf of a sort) ideal for the smog ridden dismal days of the decade that seemed to envelop Bolton and associated districts on many a winter's day.

These were the days of whippet (small greyhound) racing on any spare bit of land where one man would bet on his dog against the rest over a chosen distance. There would also be the regular fly past of different flocks of pigeons over the row on row of terraced houses.

"Pigeon fanciers" somehow managed to cote their birds in the small backyards next to the toilet outhouse and coal bunker in these compact properties.

St Germaine Street in Farnworth was a quarter mile from the Banks home. It housed a big cinder football field where Tommy would hone his football skills whenever he could before retreating at dusk to enjoy a kick about under the gas lamps in George Street once they had been lit. Come the latter weeks of the local football calendar many of the finals were played on this pitch. Big crowds gathered to see the teams emerge from the changing room which was none other than the upper deck of an old tram bus nestling on the ground. Some tram windows may have been missing but the roof was still intact giving welcome relief from any severe or stormy weather. After the game, behind the half tram, a dousing with a cold bucket of water to remove any dirt was the best or worst any participants were likely to receive.

Tommy was only about four years old when his father was carried home after sustaining a bad injury whilst working in the pit. Across the heavy industries of Bolton, and the nation in general, an accident like this was not unusual.

Health and Safety rules were virtually non existent with both men and women working in intolerable dangerous conditions. Unfortunately he never worked properly again, another statistic lost amongst the profits of the pit owners.

A pittance of insurance was paid out which Tommy's mother claimed and marched father Banks down the road to buy a new bed.

During these early years Tommy did not receive any pampering or special treatment being the "baby" of the family. He was just usually given the same heavy hand, when it suited his father, like his older brothers and sisters had endured.

Tommy's mother somehow always managed to keep the wolf from the door.

This meant she was soon back grafting after giving birth to her children as did many of the women of the times. In fact she worked for 50 years at Century Mill before passing away in 1976 at almost eighty six years of age.

A proud man Jack Banks, he was not going to sit at home, in fact he knew Catherine with her strict values would not let him. However from hereupon he would eke out a living by any means he possibly could muster, a job here and there whenever an opportunity arose. The depression of the 1930's had cut deep, many men were unemployed and spent their day hanging around street corners shuffling their feet.

Dole money had been paid since 1911 under different titles but it was always only a pittance and by the mid 30's to receive any government benefits applicants had to pass a vigorous means test.

Tommy was too young to remember if his father was elegible but doubts he would have applied if it felt like he was begging. Jack Banks would have heard from others in a similar position of the depth of delving into a family's income and possible savings. Moreover it was the intrusion and insensitive nature of the officials who conducted the means test that caused the frustration and offended the unemployed.

The practice of "Off course" gambling on horses and greyhounds was illegal until 1961 but many bets were laid in shady hideouts by the underground world of "Bookie's Runners"

They were they said "fulfilling a service" to the workers, these men were the foot servants of the pioneers of today's bookmakers. If you will pardon the pun you can bet that many of today's multinational bookmakers were "born" thrived and ultimately prospered in those days.

No income tax, no betting tax, no books, just pure profit apart from the occasional odd quid to the local copper to keep him off the Bookmakers back. The back street bookie was a clever character who had to be sharp of mind and a runner quick on his feet.

These runners used to hang around outside the factories, on street corners, inside pubs, taking bets scribbled down on the back of cigarette packs or whatever came to hand. They would then rush to the backstreet "office" of the local "bookie" clocking in the bet to register the pre race time and so earn a small commission for their endeavours possibly returning later with winnings for any lucky punter.

A dangerous "career" carrying a few quid, they were forever looking over their shoulders to avoid likely muggers.

There was a degree of trust involved from punter through "runner" to bookie with the runner at the forefront. However it was not unknown for a runner with a substantial amount of money in his pocket from either party to go missing indefinitely; basically he'd done his own "runner".

In those days for two weeks in the summer the factories of the various Lancashire towns closed on their allocated weeks to give the workers a holiday.

Blackburn, Rochdale, Oldham etc. all had their own weeks these were known as "wakes weeks." When it was Bolton's stated holiday weeks the Banks family would always go to stay at Blackpool a popular Lancashire destination for northern factory workers.

The 1930's saw holiday making families tightly packed on the beaches like sardines in a can with the overworked Blackpool donkeys hard to spot in amongst the crowds.

Father Banks knew a local seaside bookie so for only these two weeks of the year he became a "runner." He knew plenty of the men who walked the Golden mile looking to place a bet because it appeared half of "Bowton" had camped in Blackpool.

Jack Banks reckoned it was his most profitable time of the year with men having a few extra pounds in their pocket to spare for a bet.

Blackpool hotels and businesses in this and other small towns on the seaside coasts of Britain enjoyed many prosperous summers. The bed and breakfasts, the chip shops, the dance halls, alongside the pubs and clubs had tills clattering....clattering with money from the rewards of the clattering factories.

This was of course until the birth and boom of cheap overseas package holidays in the mid sixties, the boom years of "No Vacancies" at Britain's seaside resorts had hit the rocks.

Jack did manage to find non physical work during the Second World War, son Jimmy who worked in a factory put his name forward for employment as a night watchman or firewatcher in this period. The law decreed that someone had always to be on factory site due to the possibility of fire.

The Luftwaffe at the time was pounding the docklands and factories of the north west of the country.

Hitler was well aware that in order to conquer Europe, he would first have to deal with the industrial North. The harsh realities of resisting "The Hun" sadly led to the deaths of many innocent men, women and children as wayward bombs found their way into the surrounding urban areas of Manchester and Liverpool. However the grim determination and characteristics of the indigenous population was something the Nazis did not allow for as the spirit of the people held up....despite desperate and horrible circumstances and conditions.

During the war period food was severely rationed and many day to day items became impossible to come by including olive oil.

Tommy's father a squat man who weighed over twenty stones used to buy thick pieces of fat off the butcher that he would cut up into chunks and put over the grill on the fire with a pot below to catch the dripping. He regularly dip his hand into the fat and chew on the bigger slower melting pieces considering it to be a delicacy, the rest would be used to cook with. Chips were a regular feature on the menu at the table of Catherine Banks.

Jack Banks like many of his friends was a diehard labour voter.

Subsequently the only two papers he allowed in the house were The Daily Herald (now defunct) and The People on Sundays. These two publications (allegedly) represented the views of the working classes. Any other newspaper like The Daily Express or Daily Mail would never find a way through his letterbox. These newspapers were seen as the voices of the Tories, they found no reader in the house of Jack Banks.

The Bank's home at 104, George Street was one of the two centre houses in a block of four. It featured a small archway alley running under the length of these two houses to give access to the tiny backyards. Tommy spent many an hour when the rain was falling kicking a ball under this alley virtually no wider than the width of a door.

Thinking back to his young days Tommy remembers the constant noise of the ball against the wall must have been very annoying. Old John Birtles, who lived next door, never complained even though he was in bed trying to sleep most of the time because he worked a night shift at the Century Mill.

Tommy's fledgling school years were spent at St. James's Primary School which was very close to his home under the control of headmaster Mr. George Bath.

Mr. Bath found him to be a bright pupil over the years and sent a letter home for the attention of his mother shortly before secondary school beckoned.

The letter recommended that Tommy sit an exam applying for a place at Farnworth Grammar School to finish his schooling. At the time Farnworth Grammar was an iconic educational establishment only for the "upper classes".

Tommy clearly remembers the conversation that decided his educational and academic path.

"What's this Thomas" said an alarmed Mrs. Banks reading the small print,

"You'll need a blazer, trousers, proper school shoes and a full P.E. kit"

"Sorry Thomas you might be cleverer than most but you've no chance, your father's not worked properly for years I can't find the money for these clothes"

Tommy often wonders if life would have turned out much differently for him should his parents have been able to afford him the opportunity of a grammar school education.

Who knows.... maybe even furthering his education via university.

Would he still have eventually worked in the pit, played professional football or grafted on the building sites?

For the working class children of the time it was very difficult.... for boys to escape the call of the pits or engineering works and a life around cotton machines enticing the girls...no...dragged them to the noisy mills once fourteen years of age beckoned.

Due to the opportunity of a Grammar School education not being possible Tommy attended Harper Green Secondary School.

The Second World War broke out in 1939 and a "Dig for Britain" campaign commenced across the country in 1940 with the aim of growing additional crops to feed the local communities and the troops. In the day anyone who had an allotment or pen where they grew their own food or kept chickens or pigs was a "somebody" within the local neighbourhood.

Harper Green school had an excellent football field but headmaster Mr. Halsall soon seconded it for the good cause.

Mr Halsall, who Tommy found to be an inspiring man, identified him to be a sturdy fit lad and he was one of a group regularly handed a spade to prepare the land for seeding. The school football team then played on a piece of rough common land near the school known locally as the "tip".

Tommy's sister Alice Anne was always very good to him from the day he was born. She would often act as a surrogate mother when Mother Banks was working in fact she was old enough to have been Tommy's mother. From just past toddler age until he left school at fourteen she would somehow find the money to buy him pairs of Mansfield Hotspurs football boots due to his love of forever kicking a ball.

The school also looked after a nearby crown green bowling surface for the pensioners with most of the younger men away at war. Due to Tommy always wearing his 'iron shoed' wood bottomed leather topped clogs (cheapest on the market) Mr. Halsall did not dare let him pull the roller for fear of denting the smooth grass top. Tommy always found a spade thrust in his hands come "Community Welfare" time.

Mr. Davy, who Tommy discovered to be a good history teacher, used to question him on "Where he saw his future".

Ah'm gooin t'bi a futbawler" replied an enthusiastic Tommy Banks.
(I'm going to be a professional footballer)
Mr. Davy replied, "You better had be I can see all you want is a ball, I hope you are really lucky in life and achieve your dream because there's nothing but the factory or pits around here for all your classmates," added the learned teacher.

In 1930 the first World Cup was held in Uruguay, with the host nation

24

taking the trophy, Tommy would have to wait another twenty eight years for his shot at glory on this stage.

Time and progression over the decades have changed much of the landscape of St James Street, New Bury. Grass now grows where the deep waters of Pikes Lodge once glided leaving no evident of events in Tommy's younger days.

Tommy's memory recalls the cold frozen winter days where he'd been involved in multi-side games of ice hockey on the lodge using sticks and a tin, a tennis ball if lucky. All the lads wore clogs and the iron on their soles increased speed resulting in many a hefty bump. People would wander by but strangely Tommy never remembers ever being chastised for skating on what he now recognises today to be such an obvious danger. They skated on this lodge for many long hours; people passed by, no one ever commented, most of the gang only returned home when they heard their parents shouting them in at twilight.

Tommy's mother did relate to him in his teens the lucky escape he had as a nipper on the same lodge.

Apparently mother was at work and aged about three or four years old he had wandered some hundred yards from home to the lodge with Sandy the family's Irish terrier dog trailing behind him. It was only the barking of the dog that alerted a passer by to drag him from the water he had somehow entered one cold winter's day.

Years later when he was playing for Bolton Wanderers a man who was about twenty years his senior approached him and after confirming he was Tommy Banks informed him that he had pulled him out of the water and his girlfriend a nurse had revived him.

He enjoyed school but over his time away from lessons Tommy engendered a love not only for football but also the sport of cricket which remains with him today.

In the summer, on a couple of evenings each week, after his tea, he would go down to the nearby Farnworth Social Circle Cricket Club and chase round the field 'mugging out' in his clogs collect loose balls during the net practice. The cricket club on Piggott Street soon became a place that would feature throughout his entire life.

Tommy played a few times at cricket for the school, in one game against St. Gregory's they bowled their opponents out for only nine runs. He picked up six wickets for three runs, whilst the other bowler took four wickets for two runs with their opponents top scorer with four being the extras. He never played cricket after leaving school, work and football were soon to become his main priorities.

By the time Tommy was twelve he had become a breadwinner for his family.

He was up before 6am and out on his boneshaker of a bike, one his dad had found at the local dump. He delivered the morning newspapers to the houses in the vicinity before nipping home for his breakfast about an hour later. A quick bite then off again to Eckersley's farm where he would help out on the farm milking or mucking out before jumping on and off the back of the cart delivering milk to the front doorsteps of houses on the established round.

If he was lucky he would make school by nine, if not he had to face the three tailed strap for being late. He was often late but never missed attending the next day. Tommy thoroughly enjoyed his schooldays despite the spankings he endured due to his early morning erratic time keeping.

He impressed the teachers with his willingness to learn in the classroom and his talent on the sports field. So much so that he became a school prefect but even this title did not prevent him having a constantly sore backside due to his erratic timekeeping 'earning his keep'.

After school he would call at the Journal Offices in Farnworth to collect fifty copies of the Bolton Evening News that were bound for letterboxes in the houses of his New Bury neighbourhood.

He worked all day Saturdays at Eckersley's farm prior to leaving school at fourteen.

Duties included helping milk the herd of some sixty cows, collect the eggs, feed the chickens, pigs, ducks and geese, although looking after the horses was always his preference.

He only turned out a couple of times in the school colours of the football team on a Saturday because much to Mr. Davy's dismay he was always working on the farm.

"Mi mam useter say wheers that munny,wor con do ?" Tommy remembers.

(My mother used to ask for my earnings if I hadn't handed them over to her)

Each week he gave his mother 27 shillings and 6 pence for his weeks endeavours;

15 shillings from Eckersley's for fulfilling his farm duties and milk deliveries.

12 shillings and 6 pence received for his Monday to Friday morning and evening paper rounds.

These were the 1940's, decimalisation in Britain didn't happen until 1971.

For those too young to remember here's a quick comparison;

20 shillings made £1

A shilling is worth 5p in today's (new) money

27 shillings and 6d is the equivalent today of £1-37 and a half new pence.

Those early years of Tommy's life were tough.

However he possessed a desire, strength of character and a larger than life personality that would overcome all kinds of challenges...and take a lad from Farnworth to Wembley with his beloved Bolton Wanderers and a World Cup wearing with immense pride an England shirt.

Chapter 3

Leaving 'Scoo'

Children could leave "scoo" at any of three points in the calendar year subject to when their birthday fell, Easter, summer, or Christmas. On leaving school at the end of the Christmas term in 1943, at just 14 years old, Tommy was hoping Eckersley's farm where he worked Saturdays whilst at school would employ him full time milking cows and generally turning his hand to whatever was needed. However the farmer had his own sons to employ and with jobs hard to find Tommy found himself unemployed.

Unemployment was not for long though, his Uncle Tom called round to tell him he had got him a job..........Coal Bagging!

Now Tommy loved horses engendered through his time spent at Eckersley's farm since he was 12 years old. As soon as Uncle Tom mentioned a horse was involved he jumped in with both feet although he suspected many days of hard graft were in front of him.

Tommy was given the job on Christmas Eve and started Christmas Eve.

He has no hesitation in saying he found it extremely hard tedious work, particularly with being just a young slip of a lad. Jimmy Hulme a local coal merchant employed him in a job that was to 'beef' Tommy up into the strong sinewy youth that the "Wanderers" came to know a few years later.

Scowcroft's a well remembered local coal merchant ran their business from Highfield Road, Farnworth. They were based just off the main rail line in the sidings where regular deliveries trundled in via wagons containing many tons of coal from the pits north of the district. Scowcroft's had their own business and employed workers delivering coal to the numerous factories that seemed to be around every corner in the districts of industrial Bolton. Scowcroft's also allowed the likes of smaller merchants like Jimmy Hulme to buy and collect coal from their premises.

At 7am in a morning Tommy would arrive with his horse and cart ready to commence a day that did not finish until his horse was fed, watered and bedded down for the night.

Tommy had often to get on top of the wagons to dig out the coal to fill his coal sacks. This was because the doors would not open due to the fact that the wagons were so full of coal. Digging into compact coal to then lever out was extremely hard on the arms, shoulders and legs particularly for a 14 year old. The intense daily graft eventually came to build his physique and stand him in good stead later in his professional football career. Twice daily he would fill 60 coal bags lifting them on his shoulders before transporting them onto a large open cart. The cart was about the size of the drays that the Breweries sent out pulled by horses to the public houses. Tommy's own horse Drummer was of mixed breed, strong and sturdy some 18 hands high but according to Tommy he was "reet gradely"(very good) natured.

Most of the streets were usually made up of cobbled stone and when the snow and ice came along the horse would often find it hard to keep his footing on the frozen surface. The horse could slip with his legs splayed out wide, it was not a pretty sight and not pleasant to see the animal in such difficulty. The only chance he had to get on to his feet was when the weight was taken off him by unhooking him from the cart and reins.

To try to prevent the horse from doing the splits a few nails were knocked into his plates which were left to protrude slightly to help assist him to get a grip when putting his feet down.

This was a trick also used by footballers when playing on frozen pitches. Each old worn down leather stud contained small nails which would have naturally protruded with wear and gave the player assistance in obtaining grip on the icy surface. Installing old studs into boots to play on such surfaces was a form of answer of the day before the invention of astra turf boots in the late 1960's.

It was very dangerous practice and Tommy knows that the boot inspections of today would have not got past referees because an opponent could be badly injured. Thankfully few incidents occurred and it helped players to keep their balance and stopped them looking awkward ....like Bambi on ice.

Tommy would endure all weathers and climates to ensure the coal reached Jimmy's customers around the streets of Farnworth and Kearsley. In the winter he could be soaked with the rain and snow, he would be freezing when he got home, however in the summer he was forever sweating with grafting in the warm weather.

If the empty coal sacks were wet at night in winter any overnight frost could see them practically standing up in the morning without any assistance.

His working day was as long as it took before eventually caring for his horse's needs at the night at the rented stable on Eckersley's Farm in Highfield Road, Farnworth.

Tommy worked Saturday mornings and could be found most of the weekend at the farm giving the horse his time to maintain its health although it played havoc with his emerging social life.

This tough full back has always had a soft spot for animals.

After playing football for Partridges on Saturday afternoons all Tommy's mates would be going out into Bolton or to a local youth club. Meanwhile Tommy would be by himself talking to Drummer, cleaning out his stable and generally looking after the horse's welfare.

Jimmy Hulme was very fortunate to have a worker so dedicated and promised Tommy the business when he retired. He had lost his sons in the war and he had no-one else to pass the legacy of his hard work onto. Tommy knew Jimmy was a good man with a big heart. However he did not see any future in being a coal bagger and soon decided it was not what he wished to do for the rest of his life.

Chapter 4

'Pitmon'

Tommy's dad had not been keen on him going to work down the pit with all the potential danger to life, limb and health and regularly made his opinion known.

When Jack Banks died in 1945 Tommy told his mother that the pit was the only place he knew where he could be guaranteed work and that was where he was heading.

Lads had to be 16 before they could go down the pit so Tommy spent the first year working on the top at Mosley Common Pit, a mile south of "Wogdin" (Walkden) town centre about six miles from Bolton doing every job thrown at him.

The pithead boss a Geordie came to him one day and passed comment,

"Where have you been all of my life, you've given me a lovely surprise, none of the young lads who we have previously employed had any desire to work hard."

Mosley Common Pit would today be right on the border of the postcode regions of Manchester (Salford) and Wigan. Men came from all over the districts including Bolton to earn a living although it was the guys from Leigh known as "lobby gobblers" due to their liking for corn beef hash and Wiganers (pie eaters) in particular who stuck in Tom's memory.

They were hard to understand, indeed Tommy thought he was a broad speaker but the dialect varied from district to district depending on where you lived.

For his first week in the pit Tommy thought every woman in Wigan was called Maud when the Wigan pitmen spoke about their wives or girlfriends. He quickly came to realised it was a term of endearment for their wife or girlfriend...regardless of the ladies' "real" names...they were all referred to as Maud.

Tommy threw himself into the work at the pit, although relatively small in height, he was very strong for his age mainly due to all that coal bagging he had endured after leaving school.

A year flew by and he soon found himself drafted down the pit to be employed close to the coalface. He worked on the transport arm of the workings of the pit at the top of the jig doing the essential job of "Lasher On." His role was to lash tub chains to haulage ropes to keep the tubs moving. Any rough working of the tubs around the jig section could cause a foul up and possibly take half a day to fix with lost production and loss of wages for the men.

The jig was an endless haulage system in which a self acting wheel with a brake allowed full coal tubs to go down a railed incline under gravity. Empty tubs were hauled up the incline by the weight of the full tubs going down to make a new supply of tubs readily available for filling.

Pits were dangerous places, miners had to be very alert and wary of any danger as these tubs were very heavy, weighing over half a ton, and constantly on the move. Fearful of tubs colliding or being derailed, safety holes for refuge were dug every few yards in the tunnel wall in which a miner could leap should an emergency occur.

It soon dawned on Tommy that not only was he doing an important job in keeping the coal moving from two coalfaces but he had also replaced two men who had gone to work at the "face" so he set about seeking a rise in his wages. The physical labour intensive days were initially draining on Tommy's young body but he soon acclimatised becoming adept at the role as he became accustomed to the daily demands of life below ground.

The ganger said forty men on the coalface gave another lad who was always full of coal dust looking after the loader three pence each because without him they would be held up and they could not pay Tommy as well. It was a kind of unofficial bonus paid to this lad as the coalface lads were earning better money thanks to his endeavour to keep things moving.

Always the negotiator Tommy then confronted the under manager who the miners had nicknamed "Isiah" because one of his eyes was higher than the other. Isiah was somewhat taken aback by his forceful approach at such a young age but admired his directness and promised to look into it.

Tommy then found his next wage packet ongoing contained an extra three shillings and nine pence on top of the standard three pound per week wage.

It was a long working day 7am until 4-30pm, the transport section of the pit always did an extra hour overtime to ensure everything was right for the next day. He was up at five o'clock in the morning to catch the 5-30am trolleybus from the New Bury district of Farnworth through to Little Hulton before jumping off at Walkden. Should Tommy ever miss the bus connection to Mosley Common from Walkden he then had to run in his clogs to prevent being late. Men had to make the last cage going down at 7am or else they were in danger of missing the shift because coal tubs then started to come up and these took preference. The cage used to drop at a rate of knots like a stone to the pit bottom. The miners had to walk short or long distances depending where the coalface was situated with only the light from their pit helmets to show the way.

The gaffers had the job well organised, the early shift extracted the coal, afternoon lads moved all the working tackle around ready for the early shift and the night men 'the road makers' blew the face and propped up the roof with iron girders to make it safe.

By 1945 all his brothers and sisters had left home so Tommy was now the only young adult in residence to look after his mother. His concern for his mother was the reason why he did not take up any of the apprenticeships that were offered to him on the first day he started at the pit. His best mate Alf Lee, who was a tad older, had started as a Fitter and his cousin Bill Hinks was well on the way to becoming an Electrician. Apprenticeships meant studying one day a week at Worsley Technical College for a few years alongside learning the trade daily on the job until the lads became qualified. Tommy realises he should have attended day release to gain a qualification in a trade but if he had he would have been stopped a day's pay.

Sons followed fathers down the pits working side by side in some cases and friendly rivalry existed between families in production records. There was a tradition of a good team spirit between the pitmen. It was a dangerous way to make a living but everyone helped each other by work or deed, the job forged a togetherness that was difficult to beat.

There was nothing good about the pit apart from giving men a living.

Many suffered ill health due to all the coal dust swirling around and some who worked at the coalface also had trouble with their hands caused by the vibration from drilling.

Men contracted a range of lung diseases often later in life, silicosis and pneumoconiosis were prevalent and some former miners died painful lingering deaths traced back to their time in the pit.

Caged canaries were used down the pits as the precursor to the evidence of odourless gases like carbon dioxide and carbon monoxide. Should the canary show distress or stopped its usual non stop singing the men knew it was time to evacuate quickly from that area before they passed out. Men also carried Davy Lamps that assisted in detecting methane gas, whilst the threat of roof falls, explosions and flooding were ever present in this dark and damp location.

Pitmen earned every last penny they received!

It was because of the harsh conditions down the pit that Tommy started to chew tobacco a habit that has stuck with him throughout his life, although he did manage to kick it into touch in 2009.

The dangers of cigarettes were not as common to the public back then and many miners rolled their own although smoking down the pit was forbidden. Partly because of this rule, miners would carry in their pockets cheap twist tobacco. Chewing on this dark fired leaf to alleviate their craving for a smoke also offered some relief against the unhealthy choking conditions near the coalface. The pitmen would bite into these thick chunks of congealed tobacco and chew in an effort to nullify the dust and dirt lodged in their mouths and throats before ejecting the spittle of pure nicotine.

"Tha fust taste o' raw nicotine in thi throat stays wi thee forever" said a forlorn Tommy.
(It was a truly awful never to be forgotten taste)

Tommy recalls it was putrid but for some unknown reason he, like a lot of other pitmen, took another bite and slowly became addicted admitting all these years on he recognises it was best never to start.

On "vesting day" the 1st January 1947 the pits in Britain which numbered over 1400 were nationalised and the control came under the statutory corporation the National Coal Board. Coal had become a very political issue due to the conditions under which colliers worked and the way they were treated by the colliery owners.

Coal mines had been taken under government control in both world wars and Labour were determined to "put people before profits."

In 1950 the NCB employed over 700,000 with the vast majority members of the National Union of Mineworkers.(NUM).

The dismal history of the coal mines between these wars and need for coal in post war Britain made nationalisation of the British Coal industry almost inevitable after the election of a Labour government under Clement Attlee in 1945.

In September 1950 just short of Tommy's 21st birthday anyone fortunate enough to own a television would have been able to watch the first ever televised "Come Dancing".

Tommy signed as a full time professional for Bolton Wanderers on his 21st birthday in November 1950, having justified his playing ability and "footballed" his way to freedom out of the pit. Within weeks of commencing his new career, the dreaded letter conscripting him to compulsory National Service dropped through the Banks's letterbox in George Street, Farnworth.

From January 1951 he would not be showing his "quickstep" on the Burnden Park dance floor, he would most probably be indulged in a "military two steps" routine down at the Army barracks at Oswestry. The following two years in the army he found to be a very tedious "slow waltz" in time when all he really wanted to do was "jive" to the noisy beat of Bolton Wanderers' regular 30,000 swaying spectators.

Chapter 5

In Demand

At 15-16 years Tommy could be found playing football regularly for Partridge's in the Bolton Boys Club League. Every side in those days took the name of the guy who had formed the team and Syd Partridge was the originator of this Farnworth team.

Boys Clubs were only just in their infancy after the war and to be a team you had to have a "room." In reality this was somewhere that you could say was the "home of the team," a kind of base camp where all the players and officials could meet.

For Syd and his lads there was an old gentleman's club in Hall Lane, Farnworth behind a pub containing a room that housed a snooker & table tennis table. Syd obtained permission to use this room and Partridge's became affiliated and were soon up and running winning football matches in and around the Bolton districts.

Lads of a similar age had for a number of years made up Great Britain teams for other recognised youth organisations of the regular services.

The Army Cadets/Navy Sea Scouts/Air Training Corps (Cadets) had for years held there own triangle competition sponsored by the London Star newspaper with the ATC usually the successful team. The Boys Clubs of Great Britain had become recognised and were asked to make up a fourth team, thus the chase was on to identify the best talent available in the island.

Tommy was starting to make his name one to remember on the field of play, he had already been spotted locally and signed amateur forms for Bolton Wanderers. He had made such strides that he played for the Under 18's Bolton Boys Federation representative team at the tender age of 15 years and again the following season before turning part time pro. Bolton team mate in 1958 Nat Lofthouse and fellow Farnworthian Tommy Lawton (Everton F.C.) who was some ten years Tommy's senior were local amateurs who had also graced the Bolton Boys Federation on route to full international illustrious fame for England.

Amateur forms in 1945 did not tie him to Bolton should a better offer present itself, so he was still looking to the future to impress scouts. He was selected for the northern trials at Leeds to compete for a place in the Great Britain's Boys Club team.

A former Army Major who was now one of the selectors for the Boys Club approached him after the trial saying he would like to pick him but due to a previous trial held in the south of England some positions had already been filled. One of these was the left back berth, but so desperate to include Tommy was the Major, that he asked him if he would play wing half.

"Wing heawf's awe reet, owt tha weeshes, ah'll play in gall if thee wannts" said Tommy.

(I will play wing half if that's your wish, I will even play in goal if you would like me to.)

Up stepped proud team owner Syd Partridge who had travelled across to Leeds with his young protégé.

"He is a left back if he does not play there he does not play" roared Syd.

The Major was not used to straightforward northern talk and caved in with Tommy taking the left back spot in the Great Britain Boys Club team against the young cream of the other forces. More importantly for Tommy and his future, the games were played in front of a wealth of football scouts.

In the first game at Chelmsford against the ATC the Boys Club triumphed 6-5 after extra time to send the favourites out. In the final the Boys Club ran out easy winners over the Army Cadets, however it was the venue rather than the game that put a gleam in young Tommy's eye.

Tommy was very honoured to play on Stamford Bridge and this was an experience he was not going to forget. He recalls thinking this is the life.... I cannot wait until I am back here with a professional club to play Chelsea.

Tommy then went on to captain England Boys Clubs against Wales and then Scotland Boys Clubs at Bloomfield Road the home of Blackpool Football Club.

Leeds United representatives had witnessed the early Boys Club trials in Yorkshire and were so impressed with Tommy that they asked him there and then to sign amateur forms with them. Leeds at this time were a second division team and Tommy thanked them but reckoned he would stick close to home with Bolton Wanderers and work in the pit.

Later in October 1946 Tommy was fast approaching his 17th birthday, the age when lads could sign professional forms with football clubs and found he was very much in demand.

Returning home from a pit shift one Friday tea time he was told by his mother that as she arrived home from shopping a gentleman was sat in a big posh motor car outside their house. This well dressed man spoke in a Scottish accent and was wearing a wide rimmed hat pulled well down over his forehead.

The gentleman asked her if Tommy would like to go through to Manchester United a week on Saturday for a chat and to watch a Division One match.

Cars were hard to find in the working class district of Farnworth at the best of times more so just after the war. Almost everyone relied on the rattling trolley buses that serviced the main roads of the district, a motor car being a desirable few could afford.

So the sight of such a big "posh" vehicle in the backstreets would certainly have had the eyebrows raised and the gossip rife.

"Werrit Matt Busby?" enquired Tommy.

"Not sure, I was a bit overawed and did not quite catch his name, it might have been but I was too busy watching the neighbour's curtains twitching to really take it all in" said Mrs Banks.

Tommy decided not to travel to Manchester and never did find out exactly who did call that day. The Banks's did not possess such a luxury as a house telephone so his mother could do little but passed on the verbal message she had received.

Wolves, Arsenal, Burnley and Portsmouth also all made it known to Tommy that they would like his signature. However with his brother Ralph being already signed up by the Trotters his beloved hometown team were a big pull.

George Taylor, a man Tommy would come to know well in the future, also approached him and uttered a few words regarding coming to the Wanderers.

"Now don't be shy Tommy we think a lot of you, sign for Bolton you won't regret it."

"Ah'm gooin t' sign fer Bowton" son said to mother, "Tha towd mi t' pless misell"
(I am going to sign for Bolton, you told me to make my own mind up.)

Walter Rowley, the then 1946 Bolton secretary/manager, who had also played for the team back in the 1920's and 1930's approached him to discuss a contract.

"Nethen Walter wor art thi offrin?"
(Now then Walter what are you offering.)

"£6.50p a week in the season £4 in summer is the best I can do" said Walter.

Now this was a reasonable offer for a young lad, the top players in the country, Finney, Lawton, Lofthouse, Matthews were only on £10, with £8 non playing wages in the summer. This was the maximum allowed payable by the country's football powers that be.

Tommy's brain was racing contemplating his best negotiating reply!

He knew that there was no guarantee that he would make the first team grade although he never doubted his own self belief regarding his ability. The timing of the offer was not the best, many pre war players were returning to their clubs after the end of the Second World War.

The Football League stated that they should be given a year's paid contract to try to attain their previous playing standard if possible. Tommy knew there would be numbers challenging for places so he thought he would hedge his bets. The pit, although it was extremely hard graft, was giving him a steady income to look after his mother. Thus he backed himself... due to his fitness to work underground whilst learning his football trade and get paid on both fronts if acceptable to Bolton. Tommy had done his sums in his head very quickly and responded to Walter Rowley's offer,

"If thee'll pey mi £6 fer part time pro. ah'll jeyn up"
(If you will pay me £6 for playing part time I will sign up.)

Tommy had reckoned that if he carried on in the pit for awhile it would give him time to gain some professional football experience. With his three pounds three shillings and nine pence pit money added to his part time pro. money from Bolton he would only be sixteen shillings and three pence worse off per week than the England stars!

This proved acceptable to Mr. Rowley, the deal was done.

Bolton also gave him a £10 note, this being the mandatory signing on fee for all lads up and down the country who were turning professional. On reflection Tommy struck himself the deal he wanted without the aid of an agent, how times have changed!

He took it home to his mother who was so surprised to see Tommy in possession of a ten pound note that could be the weekly pay packet of three or four men. Catherine Banks was an honest woman and needed a complete explanation as to how her son had managed to acquire this ten pound note.

"Mam owdonabit wilta purritin yor purss, bey thisell summut neece" said Tommy.

(Mother hold on a while will you put it in your purse, buy yourself something nice.)

After his mother had settled down and accepted the ten pounds had been received legally Tommy thought he had better tell her the rest of the details of his meeting with Mr. Rowley.

It appears Walter Rowley also had another job!

He worked part time for the Refuge Insurance selling various policies to all and sundry. The ink was not dry on the part time professional forms Tommy had signed before Walter Rowley spoke to educate him about the need to look to tomorrow for when his playing days were over.

Even in those days everyone knew that despite the glamour and accolades (but not the money) that professional football is a very short career. Here was Tommy at the tender age of just seventeen and some pin striped pen pusher was pitching to him about an insurance fund payable on his retirement from football. The same man was talking to Tommy but with a 'different hat on' than that as the manager/secretary of Bolton Wanderers Football Club.

Tommy had just signed his first contract and had not yet kicked a ball for the club in anger and the manager was discussing his retirement!

Somewhat bemused Tommy agreed to pay a shilling a week out of his wages ongoing into a long running Insurance Policy which would hopefully bear fruit in time. In the early 1960's shortly after he had left the 'Trotters,' Tommy to his surprise, received a cheque for around a couple of hundred pounds. Bearing in mind he had almost forgotten all about this policy once he had signed on for Bolton this was a pleasant surprise.

On reflection in later years he readily acknowledges he should have invested in additional insurance during his football days to cover for the three decades he would be earning a living of another kind. There was no guaranteed pension at the end of a player's football career in those days however it was difficult saving for the possible 'rainy days' ahead on the low wages paid at Bolton.

A few lucky lads were granted testimonials after ten years service but it was not mandatory and always at the club's discretion.

Tommy took his missed chance of saving via insurance policies on the chin, he realised the opportunity had passed him by but stayed upbeat. The cheque was an unexpected bonus and put to good use for the family. The holiday that summer was exceptional, for once he had a few extra pounds in his pocket.

Chapter 6

Now a Wanderer

At first little changed once Tommy signed as a part time professional with Bolton Wanderers in November 1946 at the age of 17. He was still up at 5 o'clock in the morning catching trolley buses, before putting in a gruelling five day week down the Mosley Common pit south of Walkden.

Tuesday and Thursday nights each week he was training in the evening at Burnden Park with other part timers and local amateurs. These amateurs were desperately trying to show their ability and earn a professional contract.

Tommy always used to wear his clogs travelling directly from the pit to evening training at Burnden Park he had no need to get dressed up because he was not going out later into Bolton's town centre. After training his itinerary would revolve around a quick bite and bed ready for an early start down the pit.

Night training sessions in the winters were dull and very repetitive, ideas for training sessions were still very much in the dark ages plus facilities were limited. Small somewhat inadequate floodlights had however been rigged up on the spare land behind the Burnden Stand. Here small sided games took place on a cramped 60 x 40 cinder surface area which was known to the full time professionals as "The Gravels."

However most of the time the training the lads did in the evenings involved running around the gravel track that "moated" the pitch. Tommy reckoned, tongue in cheek, that the track was level with the football field when he joined the Wanderers, five years later after endlessly pounding out countless laps at night he had worn it down by approximately three feet.

Tommy laughs about it today but he found it was very boring and he would have relished working more with the ball to fine tune his touch to show his ability rather than the endless slugging. He knew (as did knowledgeable football fans come to realise) that apart from the hard uncompromising Tommy Banks here was a gifted footballer. He could pass the ball well, was reasonable in the air and he could read a game of football. It was a man's game back then, his unquestionable ability sadly often being lost in translation due to his physical approach.

In reality the raised pitch is a nagging question that no-one seems to know the true answer to?

Pictures show that up to around 1915 the pitch was flat with a running cum cycle track around the pitch which would have given the ground a totally different look. The Burnden Park pitch was the widest in the league at the time and had such a camber that if you stood on one touchline you could not see the other. The camber was later levelled a tad to help viewing plus terracing dug into the disbanded running/cycle track to raise the pitch and also improve drainage. The approximate three feet "moat" drop was somewhat unique in the professional game; other grounds may have been raised slightly but nothing to match the high banking around Burnden Park.

Many a visiting winger a few years later came to shy away from a Tommy Banks or Roy Hartle full blooded challenge from fear of being jettisoned onto the gravel below.

At evening training Tommy said he first met up with a lad called John Higgins who eventually came to be a team mate and a big buddy making the first team centre half position his own for a spell. John was something of a foreigner and not impressed with Bolton at first.

A native of Buxton in Derbyshire, and a grammar schoolboy to boot John told his dad after the first session that he was not going back!

John stated that "This night before training there were many lads with panda eyes and arms and legs full of muck."

He was adamant he was not going back!

It was a bit of a culture shock to John, these youths had been grafting in the pits and factories all day, after training the communal bath was thick with scum from coal dust or oil grim.

Lads with an ounce of ability aged sixteen upwards were eager to move into the world of professional football. They strove to prove their football worth to the club and thus obtain a professional contract. They yearned to spend their working days training in the fresh air rather than toiling half a mile or so down in the bowels of the earth or caged in the factories.

Changing his mind John Higgins did return to train at Bolton and attend training the next week, and the next. Eventually he moved through the club's football ranks to play in the "1958 team," apparently he said they were the best set of lads he ever came to know.

Sadly John passed away in April 2005.

John's son Mark played many games for Everton from 1976 onwards before a serious injury forced his premature retirement in 1984. Against all odds he made a comeback playing a handful of games for his new club Manchester United in 1985 plus good spells at Bury and Stoke before retiring by choice in 1990.

In the mid-late 1940's 1st Division clubs carried big full time playing staffs.

Therefore gaining a playing contract, even part time, was always going to be a mountain too high to climb for most amateurs. Clubs like Bolton would have full time professionals playing in the A and B teams below the reserves. They also ran a colt's team, a form of trials team for likely lads who came and mostly went back through a non stop revolving door.

Lads who were professionals prior to the start of the war had lost over six years of their playing careers although some had "guested" occasionally for other professional clubs in friendly matches whenever possible during the war years, 1939-45.

In 1945/46 for some of the older lads around 30 plus it was a big "ask" after years of little football through service to the country to finely tune their bodies back to the personal playing standard that had originally earned them a living. Clubs paid any former professional player a year's wages once he returned from service to give him every opportunity to train and hopefully make the required grade again. Although many years had been lost from football by individuals in some ways these were the lucky guys.

Former club captain Harry Goslin was killed in action in December 1943, his final place of rest being at the Sangro River War Cemetery in Italy.

On the 8th April 1939 with war seemingly inevitable Harry addressed the assembled 22,692 football crowd from the Burnden Park pitch prior to the kick off in the game against Sunderland. He said that after the game the entire Bolton team would all be attending the local Territory Army hall to sign up. Imagine what coverage Sky TV would create today should such an event take place on Super Sunday!!

Fifteen players signed up in April and thirty two of the thirty five pre-war professionals at Bolton saw action on the British forces front line. Harry was not the only Wanderer who did not make it back to these shores.

In the November of 1944 another player Walter Sidebottom lost his life when the ship he served on was torpedoed in the English Channel.

Football in England 1945/46 season was slowing working its way back to full action with a number of matches organised between the professional clubs of the Football League, furthermore the F.A. Cup had been reinstated. To make up for the lack of quality football being played, a decision was made regarding the F.A. Cup. Matches, from Round 1 up to and including the quarter finals were to be played over two legs, home and away affairs.

The war had ended, people wanted to be entertained and one of football's top entertainers of the period Stanley Matthews was in town, Stoke City being his first club. With no pre match tickets in 1946 spectators paid on the gate with both sets of fans mixing happily together.

So on the 9th March 1946 Bolton played Stoke at Burnden Park in the second leg of the quarter final....amidst much anticipation nobody could have imagined the events that would transpire.

During the war Bolton's ground had been used by the Army to stock sensitive equipment under and in the large Burnden Stand on the far side of the ground.

Large stocks still remained and thus this stand could not be utilised by the paying public taking out about a quarter of the ground's capacity. Burnden Park featured behind one of the goals a vast part of the ground named,

"The Embankment End"

It was a huge gothic like rise behind the goal, uncovered and open to all the elements. The "castle wall" that ran at the back was reached by steep unruly steps that were in no set design and negotiating them even on a "quiet" match was never easy. Randomly dotted in no particular order across this area were safety barriers of unknown strength. Perched at the top of this "castle wall" sat the score box. This large black and white structure stood on four elongated legs with a staircase on one side and adjoined the railway signal box behind. In this score box sat a man who would put up the half time scores via alphabet letters corresponding to fixtures listed in the club's programme, information had been phoned in from around the leagues.

A regular sight would be a slow chugging or temporary motionless train on top of the embankment...the signals always seemed to be on red judging by the time trains appeared to stop for lingering minutes giving a view of the game.

Back to the match...the ground was full to burst apart from the Burnden Stand mentioned earlier.

It appears that when the turnstiles on the Embankment End registered a certain intake of spectators they had to be closed. According to reports at the time, one turnstile was illegally opened and non paying fans on hearing this spilled in. Many others climbed over the boundary wall and it was not long before the inevitable happened. Quite simply there were too many spectators in a confined area and a surge apparently took place in this corner of the Embankment terraces. Due to the sheer numbers in attendance, barriers which people were pressed against collapsed in this area of the ground.

Sadly 33 people died in the crush with more than 400 people injured....the darkest day in the history of Bolton Wanderers Football Club

Quite unbelievably the game was played and Tommy Banks was a paying spectator at the opposite end of the ground behind the goal in the Lever End. Few individuals so far away realised the severity of the incident before the match was completed.

Mrs. Banks was stood in the street as Tommy arrived home that evening and raced to embrace him, in tears she blurted,

"Thomas I am ever so glad to see thee" throwing her arms around her bewildered son.

Mrs. Banks like many other mothers had learnt of the tragedy on the radio and with no previous means of communicating with Tommy she was so desperate to greet him that night.

In 1946/47 the Football League returned to normal but players threatened to strike if weekly wages were not increased from the maximum £10 to £12 per week.

No strike action occurred and the truly significant change in players' wages was still away off.....happening in 1961 with the scrapping of the £20 maximum wage payable to professional footballers in The Football League.

Tommy continued to shine on the field and became the regular fixture at left back for Bolton reserves through the 1947-48 season. On the 24th April 1948 at 18 years old he was given his Bolton league debut...unfortunately a 1-0 defeat against Wolverhampton Wanderers at Molineux.

It was also the F.A. Cup Final day at Wembley between Manchester United and Blackpool with United triumphant 4-2. The league fixtures ran on the same day as the final which seems strange in the course of football today. There was not the same hype in football back then, television schedules did not control the fixture dates. If you wanted to watch a professional game you paid your money at the turnstiles every Saturday afternoon.

Arriving home one Friday evening in October 1949 from his daily stint in the pit Tommy's mother relayed a message from the Wanderers. It was an instruction for him to be at Burnden Park the next morning at 10am sharp.... he was playing at Blackpool.

"Nar mam tha's geet message wrung, fust teems oer ut seaside, ah'm tellin thee awe'm deawn ti play wi ressies agen Blackpu ut wom " said Tommy.

(No mother you've got the message wrong, the first team are at the seaside, I'm saying I'm picked to play for the reserves against Blackpool at home.)

First & Reserve team league fixtures back then were played wherever possibly on a vice versa basis on the same day against the same opponents. Tommy's mother was adamant she had heard correctly and told him repeatedly. So still muttering to himself off Tommy trooped the next morning walking the mile or so from his Farnworth home to Burnden Park. His mother was correct, not only was he picked as left back in the 1st team he found his immediate opponent on the Blackpool team sheet was none other than the wing wizard Stanley Matthews.

The home team were soon on the offensive and had a perfectly good goal from Stan Mortensen disallowed because the referee thought Morty's close range cannonball shot had hit a post rather than one of the steel back stanchions that used to support the bar and uprights. Newspapers reported that Mortensen hit the ball so powerfully it would have travelled a long way into Blackpool town centre if he had missed the goal stanchion he struck it so sweetly.

According to the press of the day Tommy had a good game but his efforts could not stop Blackpool who ran out 2-0 winners at Bloomfield Road. Later that evening, after returning home Tommy immediately apologised to his mother for doubting her.

Tommy enjoyed pitting his wits against Blackpool's finest;

"Ah wernt fazz'd agen yon lad, ah metave bin a pitmon but Mr. Matthews soon feawn eawt who Banky wer"

(It didn't bother me playing against him even though I still worked full time in the pit, Mr. Matthews soon realised he had a challenge on his hands with me.)

Tommy reckoned that over the seasons Sir Stanley was the quickest player he would ever face over the first five yards. Matthews was alleged to conduct his own weekly training sprinting session on the beach wearing army boots so on Saturday his boots felt that light he could have been wearing ballet shoes.

Over the seasons from 1953 onwards as Tommy established himself as Bolton's first choice left back he came up against Matthews on a number of occasions and he had the utmost respect for him on and off the field. Tommy speaks kindly of Matthews who he knew was a pleasure to converse with after the game. Matthews was the best corner taker he witnessed, he could drop those heavy balls anywhere he wanted in the penalty box.

All that said Tommy more than held his own that day in his first encounter with the great Stanley Matthews.

One-to-one winger-full back tussles were more prominent in the football of the late 1940's-50's era than in today game, defensive duties were never expected from the likes of Matthews. Wingers were out and out wingers often waiting near the half way line to receive the ball from team mates rather than drop back and defend from the front like today's teams.

Matthews, he had his own way of playing he was a creator of goals!

He liked to slow the full back down then use his dribbling ability and rapid acceleration to pass him on the outside to reach the dead ball line and pull the ball back for the other forwards. With Tommy being a natural left footer and quick he reckoned Matthews style suited him. Never other than totally honest Tommy knew he never had a bad game against the Blackpool maestro and although acknowledging Matthew's ability he always relished the challenge.

Both players had a healthy respect for each other which continued long after they had both finished their playing days.

However the 1953 F.A. Cup final found Tommy viewing from the Wembley stands whilst his brother Ralph did battle in the number 3 shirt with Sir Stan..... a shirt that was later to become Tommy's.

Chapter 7

National Service

At the outbreak of war on the 3rd Sept 1939 the government installed a system of wartime conscription between 1939-1948 called Military Service. Men between 18-41 years were conscripted, subject to medicals, whilst others in essential services, the pits, farm work and the merchant navy, would be spared conscription by playing their part in helping the country by supplying fuel and food. Provision was also made for conscientious objectors to justify their position at tribunals with powers to allocate these applicants to specific civilian work or non combatant corps such as the Royal Army Medical Corps.

In the midst of the war in 1942 the government increased the age of enrolment to fifty one years of age.

After the war those already in the armed forces were given a release classification determined by length of service and age. In practice, releases began in 1945 with the last of the war time conscripts not being "freed" until 1949.

After the war young men were still being called up for Military Service as peacetime conscripts from 1945-1948 before a bill was formalised by the National Service Act of 1948 with the new title of National Service.

It was clear in the immediate post war political landscape that Britain had considerable obligations and only a limited number of men were still in service. There was Germany to be occupied with over 100,000 troops, and Austria. In the Middle East Palestine needed policing, Aden to be protected, issues with the Suez Canal zone, Cyprus, Hong Kong, Singapore and other military bases needed staffing.

From January 1949 healthy males between 18-21 years were expected to serve in the armed forces for eighteen months and remain listed for four years. Men were exempt from National Service if they worked in one of three essential services; Farming, the Merchant Navy and Coal Mining.

In this period over 2 million were conscripted with almost 6000 being called up every fortnight. This continued right through to 1960 almost the birth of "The Beatles" pop group and the decade that changed the face of life in Britain.

To many youngsters National Service was a case of Get in, Get out and Get away.

Young people were basically putting their ambitions, desires and to a degree personal lives on hold for this period in order to comply with the law of the land.

Compulsory National Service may sound strange to the youths of 2012 but possibly not so if they chat to their grandfathers, even fathers in some cases.

Many people today still believe in the fundamental principle that the idea of bringing back National Service evokes.

Their belief being that it installs a level of personal discipline and pride which would go a long way to combat the growing problem of anti social behaviour amongst today's youths. Most people forget that millions of young boys were conscripted soon after the Second World War into National Service in much tougher times. Once "groundhog day" beckoned the army owned them lock stock and barrel for two years.

No amount of government propaganda could stop youngsters complaining about the disruption to their lives caused by National Service. It affected those individuals with further educational aspirations and prevented young boys less academically inclined from starting apprenticeships they had been promised. Many wives and girlfriends were faced with the prospect of their beloved disappearing with only occasional leave.

The only escape...... or so it seemed, was failing the medical which was easier said than done.

In 1948 Tommy Banks was 18 years old working full time in the Mosley Common coal mine and playing as a part time professional footballer when he made his debut for Bolton Wanderers away at Molineux the home of Wolverhampton Wanderers.

Tommy's mind was set on progressing his football career into a full time profession with his immediate aim to put more 1st team games under his belt as soon as possible and thus prove his worth to the Bolton management.

He knew that whilst he worked in the pit he would not be called up for National Service. However he also realised that that eventuality would arise sometime in the future if he left earning a crust underground. He could be called up anytime in the foreseeable eight years after he left the pit, this was the rule for men working in the three essential services.

His ambition was not proving easy after a single football league appearance in the following 1948-49 season and only three more early in the 1949-50 season. At the start of the 1950-51 campaign Tommy felt this might be something of a make or break season if he was going to achieve his ambition.

Three enterprising early season appearances in the first team number 3 shirt found a full time professional contract being promised to Tommy on his 21st birthday in November 1950.

Tommy's dreams were somewhat shattered when a few weeks into his life as a professional a letter arrived in a government stamped envelope. He found himself called up and so six weeks after signing professional football forms with Bolton he reluctantly enrolled for National Service. That January day in 1951 over 200 other young lads enlisted alongside him for the 17th Training Regiment. The 17th were based at the Regional depot which also housed three other regiments at the expansive headquarters at Oswestry in Shropshire.

To make matters worse in 1950 for the unwilling conscripts, a decision was made to extend the period of National Service from 18 months to two years. This was in response to Britain's involvement in the Korean War and the growing Soviet threat against the west.

Every conscript faced a medical, it was a ritual preformed like everything the military did, strictly according to king's regulations. The medical still etched in Tommy's memory only ending when the dreaded moment came and the lady doctor asked him to drop his trousers and cough!

The country had summoned him, he found himself at the mercy of the military but soon came to realise, a little later on, that in this scenario his background in professional football had come to his assistance.

Once they had been head shaved and kitted out within a few hours of arrival the conscripts all looked almost identical even though back in the barracks every man was without any shadow of doubt still his own man... no-one more so than the character... Thomas Banks.

The arena for the 'breaking in' of these young men was to be many hours spent on the parade ground. In squads they learned how to obey orders instinctively and to react to a single word of command by coping with a torrent of abuse from the sergeants and drill officers.

"Come on you mangy lot you are in the army now.....quick march"

"We are your mothers and fathers here, we will take care of you!" was another favourite jest that was not appreciated by the reluctant conscripts. The look of gloom, doom and despondency on most young faces showed that the barking bellowing sarcasm of the Sergeant Major had fallen on unreceptive ears.

During one session of the six weeks of basic training Tommy was pulled up by the Lance Corporal in charge of teaching the marching on the drill field who roared at him.

"Banks why are you always laughing and put your feet together when you address me"

"Owdonabit wilta,teech thum t' march, ast thee nar notic'd tha heawf o'um cawnt wakk proper" gibbed Tommy
(Hold on a moment will you, teach them to march, have you not recognised that half of them cannot walk properly)

None of the recruits had any idea where they were going to be eventually based when they had passed out. When the Sergeant said the Army was always struggling for Paratroopers he then asked for volunteers to train. This was an unusual step by the powers that be; actually asking rather than telling came as a surprise to the cadets.

Tommy had always fancied jumping out of a plane so he thought he would give it a go. He did not know what the other options were so thought he would take his chance with the Paratroopers.

A week later, a Staff Sergeant wandered into the barracks of the 17th and he began eyeballing and weighing up the new recruits.

"Who is Banks" he asked.

"Ah'm tha' mon" said Tommy.
(I'm that man)

"Just who are you?" retorted the Staff Sergeant.

"Ah'm no-body, why dust thi ax?" Tommy replied.
(I'm nobody why do you ask?)

"You have got to go to Brigade H.Q. to report to the Major." said the man with the stripes on his arm.

Tommy was escorted into a plush office and the Major ordered two teas and fancy cakes and explained the reason for seeing him.

"We do not get many cadets wanting to join the Paratroopers, most are gang pressed into it, so I need to be sure you have volunteered without any pressure although I cannot stop you if you really want to go"

"Aye thee's reet ah did pur mi hond up" qualified the new recruit.
(Yes you are correct I did volunteer)

The Major continued "I know you are a professional footballer, do you realise the paratroopers are more rugby orientated?"

"Banks, I would like you to stay here and represent the 17th against the other battalions and other services at football."

"Have you any other army stationing preferences" said the Major

"Ah'd leek t' stay fit sumheaw fer mi futbawl con thi geet mi inth' gym" said a somewhat bemused Tommy.

(Somehow I would like to stay fit for my football can you get me a role in the gym)

"Right leave it with me you can be a Physical Training Instructor and keep the rest of us in shape for your two years with us." said the Major with a smile.

Tommy still did all the other compulsory training but did not go to the Welsh Hills for gun trials, or rifle shooting, and thus did not go to the Korean War like most of the other recruits who had been conscripted alongside him at the same time....Tommy never knew if they returned.

Such a twist of fortune definitely saved his career and possibly his life, in retrospect it was one of the definitive moments in Tommy's life. Just imagine if the Major had not loved his football, life, let alone the England team may never have beckoned for Tommy in 1958.

It was during his time in the army that Tommy first met up with Roy Hartle who initially became and still is a good friend. A few years later Roy won the right back spot at Bolton and this duo formed a formidable and legendary Wanderers partnership due to their tough tackling and uncompromising approach.

Roy from Bromsgrove had signed as an amateur for Bolton just prior to being enlisted, so straight away they had a common interest...... to stay fit!

Roy was also fortunate to be a P.T.I. and had served approximately a year when Tommy joined the Army base at Oswestry. At six feet plus of muscular build Roy always had an imposing present and had a gift for teaching most sports, particularly basketball, but he was not built for gymnastics. Roy always left demonstrating how you do a forward roll to Tommy being such a big lad it was not one of Roy's better physical training examples.

Tommy recalls being stern but fair with the new recruits, if they were trying he would encourage them, any slackers though would receive his full wrath. Once he had educated the lazy lads into the benefits of physical fitness he would boost their morale and self esteem by challenging them to keep improving to give them an aim.

Due to his regular physical training schedules Tommy stayed fit and captained the 17th Regiment throughout the country. Tommy guided his Army team (each team allowed a maximum of five registered football professionals) to cups against virtually all challengers. He enjoyed his football whilst in the Army but if he was given the slightest opportunity he headed for his Bolton home whenever possible.

The recruits only received twenty five shillings a week (£1.25p in today's money) from the army and Tommy sent his mother fifteen shillings.

If Tommy could get a two day pass, Bolton Wanderers would pay him £6 for turning out for the reserves, so he was chomping on the bit every time the opportunity arose. Roy Hartle who at this stage had not played a game for any of the Bolton junior teams helped Tommy out when he could. Roy would forego his leave handing it to Tommy and thus ensuring his mate could return to his northern roots.

Tommy had also married his Maggie in February 1952 so it was going to be a long last year down at Oswestry with only the occasional visit to see his wife who was still based with her family back home at Little Hulton near Bolton!

He went home whenever possible and all things taken into account he reckoned army life was the worst two years of his life. He was sick of eating "pom" (mashed potatoes) and being restricted in what he could do... even harder to stomach was what he could say. Generally keeping his opinions to himself Tommy did as his character dictates, he knuckled down to the job in hand. His endeavour must have impressed his army superiors because they selected him to put recruits through a training session for the eyes of Field Marshal Montgomery himself.

He was also told that if he would sign on for three years after his compulsory two years he would soon make the rank of sergeant.

"Tha' wor?" bellowed Tommy
(I beg your pardon)

"Ah'm tellin' thee ah'm gooin wom cum tha midneet heawr in January 53"
(I am going home as soon as my time is up)

Tommy could not wait to finish his time in the army and true to his word on the day of his release he was on the early morning train to Manchester on route to Bolton to recommence his football career.

Two years National Service had been a nuisance...it could have been a lot worse and Tommy fared much better than most of his contemporaries from the parade ground.

That said there was no doubt…National Service had stalled the momentum of his life and his professional football career. A career Tommy was now determined to put into overdrive and show the football world his talent and personal mettle…tough times endured and behind him…tough times ahead.

Tommy Banks (age 14) & mother at Blackpool in 1944.

Bolton Boys Federation Inter League team 1945; Tommy 2nd right on ground.

BWFC 1939 Team enlist at the Territorial Army for the World War II (Harry Goslin, 3rd right in the crombie coat).

Burnden Park 9th March 1946 Bolton v Stoke cuptie; The scene in the corner of the Embankment End just prior to the disaster and loss of 33 lives.

Mosley Common Colliery 1948; today nothing remains, all housing sites.

Part of Mosley Common Colliery; railroads infrastructure.

Clocking off; A typical view of a pit head yard at the end of a work shift.

*Images of the times;
A view over part of
Bolton 1949, chimneys
galore.*

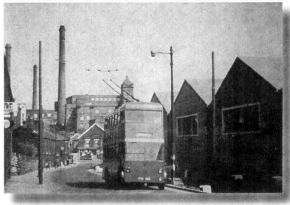

*Trolley bus leaving
Tyldesley, near Leigh.*

*A woman's pride; clean steps
& pavement outside home.*

Clog Makers.

Western Command Team 1952, Tommy back row 4th right.

1951–53 Army Physical Training Instructors, Tommy back row 1st left.

1950 BWFC 1st Team, Tommy & Ralph (brother).

BWFC 1953;
  Back row l-r; Wheeler, T.Banks, Barrass, Hanson, Hartle, Bell.
  Front row l-r; Pilling, Moir, Lofthouse, Hassall, Webster.

Burnden Park 1950.

Burnden Park 1953, chugging train overlooks the match.

Tommy & Maggie.

1958 Tommy & young son Dave feeding their chickens.

1958 Tommy & friend; similar to his coal bagging carthorse in 1944.

Chapter 8

Married

Tommy had married Maggie in 1952 whilst a Physical Training Instructor in the Army during his two years compulsory National Service down at Oswestry. However it was only on his demob in January 1953 that they secured the premises of 45, Thorne Street, Moses Gate, Farnworth.

Prior to his marriage and National Service, Tommy used to give his mother his weekly pit wages, with his part time money from his football with Bolton resting deep in his own trouser pocket.

House prices were reasonable in 1953 so he had just enough money to put down a deposit. Brother Ralph lived in this street and he had tipped Tommy off about the possibility of grabbing a bargain if he purchased this two up two down terraced house which was situated a mile or so from Burnden Park.

The couple soon settled down to married life once Tommy had accustomed himself to recommencing his football career without a staff sergeant constantly barking into his ear.

Since their marriage Maggie had remained at her family home in Little Hulton so the peace and quiet of their own home was a new experience for both husband and wife.

These were still the days of "donkey stones" where the lady of the house would use a type of scouring block to regularly clean and glean her front door stone step. Some ladies even extended their scrubbing duties to include the pavement immediately outside their terraced houses. The blocks were often given by rag and bone men in exchange for a few bits of old clothing. Seeing who could obtain the best decoration on the stone step became a bit of a competition between some housewives.

How and where did the pair initially come to court and marry?

Just prior to the army in his late teens, Tommy used to turn out at weekends with four or five mates touring the temperance bars of Farnworth, occasionally on Saturdays watching the films at the local Savoy picture house.

Sunday was the main social "parade ring" for "coppin off."

Market Street the long main road in Farnworth was filled with young men and women in their best togs continually walking up and down eyeing each other up with the odd comment to break the ice. It was like "promenading" at Blackpool but the roar of the sea had been replaced towards pub closing time by the blare of the trolley buses alerting many a stumbling drunk on the road to the bus's right of way.

Tommy's not quite sure how he met Maggie when he was out on his Sunday jaunt. Maggie was a girl from a big family who lived in the next district and she was a couple of years his senior. He might have 'pushed the boat' out by asking her if she would like a "99" ice cream, the "99" being the top of the range choice from Powell's ice cream shop.

Maggie warmed to Tommy's straight talking with a hint of charm and he remembers rather bluntly asking her for a date,

"Dust thee wannt gi owt"
(Can I escort you on a night out?)

He then told her he would be taking her to the Odeon cinema in Manchester city centre.

Tommy was picked by Bolton that following Saturday to play against Manchester United reserves at Old Trafford so thought he would 'kill two birds with one stone' and save himself having to travel back home again. He told Maggie she would have to make her own way to Manchester via the No. 8 bus, no taxi, very romantic like, and he would meet her after the game outside the Odean cinema.

Just to emphasise how popular football was after the war, 12,000 watched this reserve match although back in 1947 Tommy said the attendance for a second team game away at St. James Park, Newcastle numbered 22,000 plus when the legendary 'wor' Jackie Milburn was returning from injury.

At the end of the Second World War in 1945 life in Britain was starting to return to normal, rationing on certain foods was decreasing and reconstruction taking place within the island. Generated by a general all round uplift in spirits the nation had a new spring in its step, the population wanted to be entertained, professional football was such a vehicle to bring the public out onto the streets.

TV viewing, for those fortunate to own a set, was still somewhat in its infancy and coverage of the game England invented was minimal. If fans wanted to watch football on a regular basis they had to pay at the turnstiles of the 92 Football League Clubs ....pay they did, they turned up in their droves.

Tommy and Maggie soon became a regular couple which helped him focus on his future so that he stayed on the straight and narrow road to further his football ambitions. He had tasted first team action and knew he wanted more and to achieve his ambition he would have to channel his young life along dedicated ways.

Tommy had turned full time professional on his 21st birthday in November 1950. Just prior to leaving for his Army stint the Banks' brothers had on three occasions filled Bolton's first team full back berths; Tommy at left back with Ralph taking the number 2 shirt.

Unfortunately two years of his career had now past him by, putting him down the pecking order for the first team No. 3 shirt but he was determined to make the most of his football opportunity. He had made up his mind, much as he respected the brave men who worked there, he didn't want to return to earning a living in the pit.

Tommy was keen to have another weekly income to supplement his football money, he only received slightly above a working man's wage and knew it was a short career. Also at the end of each football season a compulsory decrease was bestowed in the non playing summer months. This was entirely legal under the football contracts at the time all tilted heavily in favour of the clubs. A player's money was reduced in the off season and to make up the shortfall which may have been the difference in paying or not paying a house mortgage the lads asked all and sundry for a couple of months full time employment.

He had experienced farm work, since the age of 12, and decided to take this path renting an allotment behind Norris's which was a local factory relatively close to Moses Gate.

Tommy invested in hens and pigs, and with breeding he soon had an income selling eggs to the local people with the odd pig sale every so often turning a handsome profit.

The eldest son of Eckersley's farm had by now taken over the running of his father's farm and knowing what a good worker Tommy was in his early teens approached him to employ him again, on a part time basis. A deal was struck and early in the mornings Tommy would cycle the mile or so back to his New Bury roots to become an extra pair of hands, milking the large herd of cows or mucking out on the farm. A swift dart home for a quick bite then out to his allotment to feed his hens and pigs before setting off to meet the ten o'clock rendezvous at Burnden Park for training.

Depending on time he would hail a bus, walk or pedal cycle although at least once a week, usually a Thursday, he would definitely cycle.

This was the day with a bucketful of eggs and egg cartons on his handlebars he'd carefully pedal still wearing his clogs down the road into the ground. He'd dismount once inside after entering via a side entrance that led onto a tunnel which ran beneath the Manchester Road stand between the seats and terracing.

He'd park his battered bike anywhere under that tunnel.

Nobody ever sought to steal such an old fashioned contraption but he had to hide the bucket containing the eggs under a seat in the press box until training was over to ensure he 'brought his goods to market.'

Once the session had finished Tommy would do a roaring trade selling his home range eggs at slightly discounted prices to his team mates.

Dave Hatton recalls Ray Parry informing Tommy he didn't require any eggs one week,

"Nethen, art sure o'that Raymondo, theers mon feightin t'jump queue tha noes"

(Are you sure Ray, think carefully, I'm overwhelmed with requests for eggs I just can't meet)

"Bukkit wer allus empty, even Bill Ridding geet a few now un agen once mi regulars wer sort'd"

(I'd no problem selling the eggs, the price was right, once my regulars were served it was open house, even Bill Ridding occasionally purchased subject to availability)

The home team dressing room was no place for anyone with claustrophobia.

It was situated under the main stand with no natural passage of light until you walked through the boot room into Bert Sproston's physiotherapy enclave viewing the welcoming sky through small windows.

Players were allowed one pair of boots each and had to visit Albert Ward's Sports Shop in Bolton to choose their footwear. It was here also where a chitty was kept, carefully monitored by the financial powers at Burnden Park and Frank the shop manager who would pull out a "bargain range" of boots to view. If any of the lads dared to ask about any others in the more elite section they were told the budget given him by the club only ran to a couple of pounds per pair and they must pay the extra cost.

Training kit was expected to last a week and it always seemed to be in short supply.

Monday morning was an army like routine when each professional would receive an unmarked tee-shirt, shorts, socks, occasionally track bottoms plus the only items that carried each individual's initials a regimental thick jumper plus their pumps.

Facilities for training were somewhat restrictive and limited activity. The club gym wasn't constructed until 1960 so the dressing rooms often doubled for stretches and exercises prior to going outdoors to extend their legs. Physical endurance was a key part of the team's training sessions, Burnden Park was notorious for being a heavy sapping surface so track work played a big part in building stamina.

Once outside the players trained in all weathers which in the depths of winters in Bolton usually resulted in a soaking.

Later on the players would retreat to the warmth and sanctuary of the home dressing rooms for a brew of tea. They would place their sweaty often wet kit on the labyrinth of thick pipes which were situated in the adjoining drying room. The humidity in this facility was high and the room always had an odd whiff in the air!

This practice ensured there was always dry kit ready for the next day.

Come the morning many of the shirts and socks would have dried crusty and stiff with a smell bordering on bad eggs! This odour became progressively worse as the week went on. Notwithstanding this it still did not deter the "earlybirds" each following morning from handpicking clothing thus mixing and matching the most attractive of the jumble sale attire.

Always on the last minute due to his early morning endeavours Tommy knew it was "first up best dressed" come Tuesdays onwards.

On one such morning Tommy found that not only were there no shorts, socks or pumps.... someone had hidden his pumps in a typical prank.

Tommy wasn't fussed....the lads had set him up and they were looking for a reaction so he gave them one.

He came out of the tunnel bare footed running onto the track wearing only his basic underwear and thick jumper!!! The gravel was very painful on his feet so he soon jumped up onto the grass to the merriment of the staff.

Bill Ridding must have heard the lads laughing, he came out shaking his head and looking disgusted, he certainly didn't see the funny side.

"Ah ses,Bill unstitch thee trowser pokkets un dig deep thee met find a couple o'tanners fer sum new kit," Tommy commented.

(I asked the manager if he'll look closely if the club could afford to buy some new training kit)

There were two young modern dressers in the team.... Dennis Stevens and Ray Parry.

They decided to opt out of this desperate kit scenario taking their Monday kit home to be washed and dried ready for each and every day, they had a reputation to protect.

In 1955 the eldest of his two sons Dave arrived, with Lee being born five years later, both whilst living at Thorne Street. One of Dave's first recollections of life was in 1960 when he had just started primary school.

Bolton's European tour that season had finished in Seville in Spain although the early games were played in Germany against Stuttgart and Borussia Dortmand.

It appears Tommy had been quite taken by the fashion worn by the male youth of Germany and on his return handed over a present to Maggie.

"Dave con weer thum short britches fer scoo" he said to Maggie handing over a green pair of lederhosen (leather) pants complete with braces and drop down flat top fronts.

(Dave can wear these short trousers to attend school)

Dave knew no different at five years old and he set off for school in what his father said he should wear but soon realised he definitely stood out from the crowd!

Lederhosen is often viewed with a hearty smile by the British. Television and the media have created stereo type visions of German men in these outfits performing a sort of "clap and slap" dance something the majority of Brits wouldn't dare engage in.... never mind wear such strange outfits!

"Around this time Mum told Dad that I was going through shoes like there was no tomorrow" said Dave,

Tommy replied "Geet 'im sum clugs"

Dave remembers, "I was then being kitted out in red clogs for a couple of years and I must have looked a bonny sight in these and my green lederhosen, attracting laughable comments from other kids."

"It was a good job I could fight!"

Whilst on the subject of clothes Dave recalls his first day at St. James's secondary school in 1965.

"No boy ever went to secondary school in short pants in those days, two did in my year group, one lasted a week and I wore them for a year, I wasn't happy but Lee and me did what we was told."

Lee said, "When Dad was not working he would take me into Bolton town centre and with being very young I was amazed at men shouting there's Tommy Banks and coming up to Dad and shaking his hand."

"I asked Dad after who they were, he didn't know them, it baffled me everyone I spoke to I knew but these guys were complete strangers to him, it was only in later life that I learnt of Dad's football fame"

"If I was in Bolton and told Dad I need a toilet he'd point me to the nearest grid in the road, I got used to the passengers on the passing No. 42 and 43 buses gawping as I had a wee from the towns pavements."

Lee remembers around 12 years of age in 1972 when long hair was all the rage greeting his Dad coming home from work and regularly being told.

"Geet thee 'aircut"
(Get your hair cut)

"But Dad it doesn't need cutting," said Lee.

"It duz,caw inth' barbers on thi wey wom fro scoo"
(It does call at the barbers on your way home from school)

"Can I have a square neck" pleaded Lee

"Nar,sithers all o'er,tell yon barber thi father ses sithers allo'er"
(No, get it cut short all over, make sure you tell the barber to cut it close, 'scissors all over' that's what your father instructs)

Lee said, "We'd get the odd clip behind the ear if Dad thought we were getting a bit lippy or up to a tad of mischief."

"I'd often be sat in the car for what seemed ages eating crisps and drinking pop, Dad had left me whilst he disappeared, I never found out where he went?"

"On his return he'd switch the engine on and give me a clip around the ear when the windscreen wipers began rotating and indicators started clicking he knew I had been messing."

"Littul lads shudbi sin un nar 'eard un kepp theer honds t'thimsells"
(Little lads should be seen and not heard and keep their hands to themselves)

"We did as we was told, whilst in Thorne Street Dad would whistle us when it was time to come in like a shepherd controlling his dogs, we'd immediately stop playing, Dad ruled." said Dave.

Dave recalls having some good days out in Blackpool with Dad and his brothers Ralph and Jimmy and associated families.

"We would play cricket on the sands and Dad would walk us up and down the promenade like he was back in the army. We would be cajoled along the Golden Mile by being told to breathe deeply, in through your nose out through our mouths and constantly reminded to put our shoulders back."

"We holidayed in Cornwall in 1962 but it rained for two weeks and Dad said that is the last time in this country, true to his word we had some great holidays. In 1963 Majorca, 64 Torremolinos and a place that was to become a favourite of the Banks families.... Sitges near Barcelona in 1965."

Although still a nipper Lee fondly remembers Sitges,

"Dad used to stay late on the beach with us every day then take us for tea whilst Mam and Ralph's clan went back to prepare for going out in the evening. Come 8pm as soon as we hit the pillow we would be gone, apparently Dad would run upstairs every hour to the apartment to check on us."

"Early to bed early to rise, so by 6am I was shaking and moaning at him to get up although I could see he'd usually enjoyed one too many drinks the night before."

"Sithee Uncle Ralph" Dad would mutter from under closed eyes so off I'd trundle to bang on his door.

"'Come in love' Ralph would say weary eyed and I'd drag him off to the beach where I'd play in the sand leaving him to snore on a beach bed as the sun was starting to warm the new day."

In the early sixties very few working class families ever went on holiday's abroad to such glamorous resorts. Tommy was an overseas holiday pioneer keen to search outside the English coastlines. He always returned back home with stories of wall to wall sunshine, cheap drinks and a thoroughly relaxing leisurely time. His words enticed many Farnworthian acquaintances to obtain a passport and explore new horizons for themselves.

Over the years Sitges and particular one bar owned by a Spaniard called Cisco became a favourite haunt of half of the members of Farnworth Social Circle Cricket Club. Well known "Circle" devotees made it their local bar, lads such as Big Bob Brabin, Barry Stansfield, Stuart Hipwood and legendary drinker "Bean" began a yearly trip to this growing resort.

Maggie was the backbone of the family always there for the lads with Tommy working long hours on the building sites after his footballing days. He handed over his wages on a Friday just like he'd done with his mother with his regular weekend overtime being his spending money.

Tommy always seemed to be working even Sundays although before bolting through the door on his way out he would trust Maggie to make sure the lads attend church. She saved up for their holidays and if a meal whilst away or bill at home needed paying she would tell Tommy not to worry they had sufficient money to cover it.

A few years down the line Tommy thought he would treat Maggie one Christmas by buying a long gold chain with his 1958 F.A. Cup medal installed as the centrepiece.

Maggie was no wag though and although sparing his thoughts wondered where she'd be going to carry this ton weight around her neck. She'd rarely attended matches and never interfered in football that was/had been Tommy's job.

Maggie ran a stable ship the boys grew up balanced with respect for everyone including themselves and their father.

Tommy was always strict although fair with his sons, he did not "eff and blind" and has never swore and as long as they told him the truth any dubious situations were soon forgotten, he didn't keep harping on to them.

Their biggest fear if they were up to something "iffy" was folk saying,

"I know your dad, I'll tell your dad" everyone seemed to know Tommy and the fact that they were his lads.

He used to take them on the Farnworth fair that came around once a year and every Friday they would visit the pictures, eventually Tommy would not take Lee because he always fell asleep. Dave grew up a John Wayne fan due to these picture trips and now possesses virtually every cowboy film on CD that "The Duke" starred in.

"He wanted us to grow up normal with not a worry in the world and to make our own way, have fun and be proper lads. He didn't mollycoddle us, never told us what to do as we were getting older although expected respect for the family name" said Dave.

A couple of Tommy's favourite sayings Dave repeats today to his teenage daughter if she's going out,

"Remember, down't leet side dawn"

"Down't brin any trouble wom"

(Behave yourself, don't bring any trouble home)

Diet didn't play any part in a footballer's life back in the 1950's many young players would be told by the club that they needed beefing up and to get some good old fashioned grub down them. Some lads could be found after training each day in the cafe across the road from the ground tucking into steak pudding chips and peas with lashings of butter on a few rounds of bread washed down with a big mug of tea....not Tommy.

Maggie did though always make Tommy a hefty fry up breakfast on home match days but the saving grace was he ate before 10am with no dinner. Match day breakfast were the real deal, a proper fry up it could have sunk the Titanic. However Tommy would walk to the ground on Saturdays when Bolton had home fixtures, this helped his meal to digest.

Graham Cunliffe remembers that Tommy was forever generating a laugh by words or deeds taken in good stead by the receiver, he found young reserve team winger Frank Briers to be a lad who would always rise to his bait. This lad was pretty quick over the ground so Tommy said to him,

"Thi fancies theesell as a bit of a runner dusant thee"
(You fancy yourself as a sprinter don't you)

"I'll beat you over any distance up to 100yards" came the winger's reply

"Thee's gam ah'll gi thee tha,worrabeawt mi gi'in thee 25 start oer 100" enquired Tommy.
(You are very positive I like that, how about me giving you 25 start over 100 yards)

"Pay me now I'll run blindfold with that start" Briers replied

"Nar downt thi geet cocky thi must drink a mug o' watter before thee starts"
(Now do not get big headed, you'll have to drink a mug of water at the starting post)

The rest of the players stood around the track after training waiting for the contest to begin although Tommy had gone missing collecting the water. Tommy emerged from the dressing rooms with a mug and marched up to Briers on the 25 yard mark.

He thrust the mug into Frank's hand whilst pointing to the steam rising from the boiling water he had just poured out of a kettle.

"Theer thee goes Frank gerrit deawn thee"
(Here's your water Frank have a good drink)

With the watching players noisily encouraging the contestants twenty seconds later the tortoise passed the stationary hare who was blowing his cup awaiting his first gulp!

72

Tommy was forever tending 'his sheep' no matter what the cause or where the situation arose, he liked to see the young lads make their way in the game.

An overnight stay in Brighton prior to a game found half a dozen of the regular first team lads seeking a barber's shop to kill a bit of time.

Young Syd Farrimond had travelled down as the 12th man in case of illness and Tommy beckoned him,

"Aye Farry thi con cum if thi wannts, thou wi may need t'owd thee hond when yon mon wi sithers sez thi 'air"

(Syd come with us, brace yourself, you look like you're in need of a proper haircut)

When Syd took his turn in the chair Tommy immediately stood up and told the barber,

"Nah mind what 'ee ses ah'm tellin' thee iz'airs leek bloody straw geet it awe'l off reet deawnter wood"

(He will tell you different but I'm telling you his hair is a mess and he needs a short haircut)

Syd said, "The barber seemed in awe of Tommy's stern approach and before I could speak my 'teddy boy quiff' had been lopped with his scissors, it was the only time in my youth that I was given a crewcut without asking."

Syd Farrimond originates from Hindley near Wigan but there must have been something in the Farnworth tap water of the 40/50's because a host of local lads found themselves signed up by the Wanderers.

The boy who became the most famous was 1966 World Cup winner Alan Ball who lived on the Farnworth / Walkden border and spent time at the club as an amateur before Bill Riding decided against signing him professional because he was so diminutive. Everyone makes mistakes, Ball moved on to Blackpool and with a spurt of growth and a sharp gain in strength he soon became a non stop all action individual.

However no wrong decisions occurred regarding Charlie Cooper, Arthur Barnard, Ernie Phythian and particularly Roy Greaves who became a Bolton stalwart in the 1960/70's with over 500 games. In 1962 Phythian who had mainly been the reserve centre forward since 1958-59 moved to Wrexham being something of a make weight in a £20,000 plus player transfer deal that brought a young Wyn (the leap) Davies from The Racecourse Ground to Burnden Park.

Dave Hatton who went on to represent the Wanderers in over 250 games in the early 60's lived a few doors from Tommy in Thorne Street and he must also have acquired a taste for the tap water. Born in 1943 Dave was around nine years old and in his formative years when Tommy moved in. A house key to let Dave in from school whilst his parents were working was always left with Ralph's family, a sign of the friendly neighbourly times.

"Hatto" as Dave in his fledgling Wanderers days later became know to Tommy remembers he and his mates used to play football and cricket in Thorne Street without a murmur of discontent from any household. There was also a nearby street adjacent to an eight storey factory they nicknamed "White Lane" which was laid with concrete and possessed four tall lamp standards situated in close proximity that made for an excellent floodlit small side football pitch on dark nights. Playing night and day on White Lane they would take their sandwiches with them and come "half time" sit on the "warmer" in the cold of winter. The "warmer" was a metal grid that must have been above the factory boiler room and oozed gushes of warm air at intervals like a relief valve.

Dave's gang were forever eagle eyed on the look out for large delivery trucks that would disrupt their matches. Whenever they heard Tommy clinking down the road in his clogs carrying his bucket it was the cue to increase the tempo and try that extra trick with the ball.

Tommy would stay, spending time joining in the game with words of encouragement.

"Art awe reet lads,heaw thee gooin on"
(Hello there lads how are you going on)

School holidays Dave and his mates would be out at dawn and home at dusk, this was the 1950's children had freedom. They learnt themselves about success and failure with responsible parents siding with the law if their kids caused trouble.

Teachers threw blackboard rubbers at them if they were not concentrating with a rap on the knuckles with a ruler or a gym pump across their behind never far away.

A letter to Australia took weeks to arrive nothing akin to the press of a send button instantly delivering a text on a mobile phone, no play stations, nintendo's or DVD's many families did not have televisions. Only girls wore ear-rings and tattoos for the young in households were taboo only visible on the bodies of the male teenage workers on the visiting fairgrounds.

They built "bogeys" out of old prams without any brakes, breaking bones when they fell out of trees and tripped over pavements without any lawsuits. They would collect old bottles and return them receiving cash at the local corner shop. Takeaways were limited to fish and chips, no ready meals or fast foods....not even pizzas, hamburgers or fried chicken.

They ate white bread with real butter and drank cows milk and soft drinks containing sugar but few were overweight.....they were always outside playing.

These were the days before lawyers and government regulated our lives, health and safety was down to yourself, human rights was a punch up if you failed to agree.

"Hatto" says that Tommy and Ralph were very popular in the street, great mixers with no edge. Open the local pub door and they could occasionally be found having a swift pint and a game of dominoes in the Egerton Arms at night. If not footballers they would have been setting off for the factories or pits alongside their previous evening "bones" partners the next morning.

"Both brothers were down to earth individuals and completely modest, unless they were asked they never brought up their football lives," said Dave.

Tommy was married to Maggie for 25 years until 1977 when sadly she passed away.

Chapter 9

1953-1958

On returning to Bolton Wanderers in January 1953 Tommy was free; free from the army, free from the pit. He knew that what he wanted most was a proper professional football career which was now his for the taking. He also knew that with hard work, and application, that he had every chance to succeed. He was determined to achieve his goal.

Tommy found Bill Ridding had been the team's manager for almost two years after serving a few months trial period very late in 1950/early 51.Tommy had little recollection of Bill's role as a trainer since 1946 with the club, but remembered his title associated him more with looking after the welfare of players in the medical room.

"Eewer a gud rubber deawner 'ee wark'd wonders"
(He was a good physiotherapist because, looking back, the equipment was antiquated)

George Taylor was appointed Chief Coach in 1951 with George Hunt his assistant.

Both men had given excellent playing service to the professional game and unfortunately their careers suffered due to the Second World War. George Taylor played for Bolton from 1930 right through until 1939 and also in the wartime friendly games, whenever he was allowed time home from National Service retiring in 1945.

George Hunt had been a prolific goal scorer for Tottenham from 1930-37 with 138 goals in 198 games earning him three England caps. A transfer to Arsenal followed and then 24 goals in 45 games for Bolton 1938-39 also turning out for the Trotters during the war.

Although the Bromwich Street training ground, accessed via a short trek down the valley behind the Burnden Stand and over the River Croal stepping stones had just been purchased from the police, facilities were still limited. George Taylor did everything he could to vary the training with the resources that were available. Bolton players spent many sessions on fitness training generally around the gravel track that ringed Burnden Park, occasionally running in their pumps along the streets of Bolton.

Much of Bolton's training was based on pure physical fitness with little time devoted to improving individual skills. The players recognised the hard graft was necessary to enable them to be able to handle some extremely heavy pitches notably at Burnden. With nil to little technical work Monday to Friday, the lads who were comfortable on the ball, like Tommy, were always glad to see the "big round thing" come match days. Bill's theory apparently was to starve the players of a ball during the week which would make them hungry for it on the Saturday.

Bert Sproston the former Leeds, Tottenham, Manchester City and England full back had been installed as the club's trainer-physiotherapist in the 1951-52 seasons freeing up Bill Ridding to devote more time to his manager-secretarial duties.

Tommy had plenty of time for Bert, who he regarded as a nice guy, although for some personal reason he was "frecken o'ees own shadow" (frightened of his own shadow) he would be on pins jumping up every time the dressing room door opened!

Bert had been a top class right full back who made his Leeds United 1st team debut at Christmas 1933 at nineteen years old. The following campaign he became a regular and was selected for England at 21, his talent was recognised by all who saw him play.

At the time Leeds needed money and sold him to Spurs in 1938 but he never settled in the capital and requested a move back north. Manchester City came in with a bid and he signed for the Blues on the day before they were due to play each other.

The next day he travelled north on Tottenham's team bus in the morning and wore the Sky Blue shirt of City to face his old team mates that very afternoon at Maine Road!

Bert was a talkative well mannered gentleman who loved to remind the 1950's Bolton players of his past and, although grateful for his job was partial to a moan. If not busy administering physiotherapy he was always eager to join in with the players' banter. He could be found rubbing the players' backs down with a towel when they returned to the dressing room from the communal bath. One day with sparks flying from his towel in full flow on Graham Cunliffe's back he commented wryly

"You should consider yourself very honoured 'Cunny' having this pandering treatment because I have got caps!"

Tommy Banks who was sat nearby had heard it all a million times before shouted;

"Bert,thee wannts t'geet thum look'd ut bi doc?"
(Bert, let the doctor have a look at your complaint?)

Bert was a confidant the players trusted, they would often off load their worries about anything and everything to the former England international whilst receiving treatment. On football, he tried to help by passing on his opinions from the experience he had gained over many seasons playing in the English 1st Division with little comments particularly to midfield players like,

"Don't think you've always got to be on the move, if you think you're on to receive the ball don't leave a good position for a bad one"

He played 11 times at full back for England between 1936-38 and was famous for a quote he made whilst talking with Stanley Matthews after an international against Germany in Berlin in 1938.

"I know nowt 'bout politics and t'like, all I know is football, but way I see it yon Hitler fellow is an evil little bugger"

How right Bert was!

George Hunt would at times be designated to conduct many of the endlessly boring running sessions around the perimeter of the track. For a change of scenery he would send the players up and down the terraced steps and striding between the upturned seats in the Burnden Stand, building up stamina that was vital on the notorious heavy playing surface.

"Hunty why's it allus four laps, four sprints, moest scoo's teech thee to start countin fro one." was a question Tommy asked.

(George always said four laps or four sprints, I asked him why he had not been taught at school to start counting from one)

Four this or four that suited George, he always needed time to think what his next activity would be, he did little football coaching but usually looked after the footballs and transported the training equipment.

George Taylor used to bond the players with games and challenges and recognised that George Hunt was a character the lads loved to have a bit of fun with, therefore involving him wherever possible.

G.T. gave Hunty (then in his late 40's) about a third start of a full circuit of the gravel track around Burnden Park against Tommy Banks. For those who remember Burnden Park Tommy started at the playing tunnel entrance with Hunty at the far corner behind the Lever End goals running anti clockwise. In his playing days George Hunt was a very quick player and having never lost his competitive spirit he set off like a train.

"Ah thout ah'm nah gooin t'catch this mon" said Tommy
(I thought I'm not going to catch this man)

However near the home turn coming off the Embankment end, George's fondness for cigarettes appeared to find him out and he ran out of breath. He now looked like he was carrying a sack of coal on his back....... Tommy just made the winning line.

George Hunt was never short of a woodbine hanging out of the side of his mouth even when conducting training. Hunty was easy going a very likeable man with a dry sense of humour, the lads took to him and nothing riled him.

Former Wanderer Dave Lennard was a 15 year old schoolboy attending training during the Easter holidays when he first encountered Tommy Banks. Teams were listed on the notice board to alternate between competing on "The Gravels" in the newly built gym or fitness work around the track, 'Lenny' and Tommy were named in the same side. Tommy took exception to a decision George Hunt made in the game in the tight gym area, picking him up by the scruff of his neck lifting him a foot off the floor.

Dave said "I froze to the spot, not realising until later after the session when all the pros were laughing and joking that me and a couple more kids who were on trial had been set up to see how we reacted"

Burnden Park was never allowed to be utilised for training apart from when the temperature dipped and the ground froze. Allowance was however made towards the end of season when the surface became worn, grassless and bone dry. With soil dust blowing off it and windswept litter representing prairie grass it was more akin to portraying a scene from a gun draw in one of Clint Eastwood's famous cowboy movies.

If Saturday's game was in serious doubt, due to the frost in winter, the ground staff would light large braziers on the nights leading to the weekend. These were dotted all over the pitch in an effort to soften the surface and allow the match to take place.... under soil heating was a remedy for the future.

From November to March the playing surface was generally very heavy caused by the seemingly endlessly rain to the region and even though the pitch was considerably raised above the track with a pronounced crown it was prone to hold water. Any individual wandering onto the ground before dinnertime on a match day may have spotted a couple of the ground staff lads pulling a roller to flatten the mud prior to the referee inspecting the pitch around one o'clock. It was often cosmetic treatment, twenty minutes into a game it looked like a posse of horses not footballers had ploughed through the surface.

These often desperate conditions were quite standard and Bolton's players trained Monday to Friday to be ready to cope with ninety minutes of hard graft. In comparison to the magnificent pristine playing surface today at the Reebok and most other grounds further down the football ladder the pitches then looked more geared to rugby than football.

The footballs were made of leather and laced until around 1960, they held the water and were extremely difficult to propel through the air, bending a free kick usually was not an option. Boots with knocked in leather studs were strong, somewhat heavy and cumbersome in appearance they were never going to win any fashion awards. They did though help to provide adequate protection against injury with few players sustaining the ligament injuries that seem to be prevalent today by rolling an ankle.

The never to be forgotten match day smell, owing to lads massaging liniment into their muscles, oozed out under the dressing room doors. They applied cream known as wintergreen which was hot, and to be avoided at all costs, to private parts.

The shin pads worn by the players were bulky and looked more like the yellow pages had been stuffed down their socks. Players competed honestly being too embarrassed to "dive" on the field to win free kicks.

Treatment on the field took the same form no matter the injury ...one size fits all...an ice cold "magic" sponge down the back of a player's neck soon brought him to his feet ready to rejoin the battle with the physio's words "Run it off" echoing in his ears.

Some teams appeared to seek an advantage; when Bolton played over the Pennines at Barnsley's Oakwell ground players recall on kicking their footballs that their feet and legs felt like they were trying to move a medicine ball. Rumour had it that Barnsley put two bladders into the ball before it was laced up. Barnsley's players apparently trained all week with heavy balls, it was a way of giving them an 'edge' to assist them in trying to win their home matches.

The players of today just do not know how lucky they are to address the modern lightweight balls that have now evolved...... footballs that can be manoeuvre with ease around or up and over defensive walls. Balls goalkeeper Eddie Hopkinson would have preferred, because he could hardly reach the half way line with his goal kicks back in the late 50's often leaving the chore to Hartle or Banks.

Bill's managerial role in those days was the same as the majority of his contemporaries up and down the country.

A non coaching role, never to be seen in a tracksuit, he did not work with the players. He was occasionally partial to pushing salt and pepper pots around a table to explain his tactical views during a Friday morning pre game discussion. He was old school, his manager secretary duties were similar to that of his predecessor Walter Rowley who had left due to ill health, although Bill's trade outside football was physiotherapy not selling insurance.

He was the manager of the club rather than the team, the club's front man, the man the newspapers would consult for information. The man the players discussed a contract with, the man who took his team selection to be ratified by the board, the man who would wheel and deal in the transfer market. Also, he was the man who told players if they were hired or fired at the end of their contract.

Indeed a man who wore many hats...not all of them very comfortable at times.

He was the buffer between the players and the board, having to juggle the views of the players, whilst carrying out the club's policy dictated by the directors. Bill Ridding was anxious to justify the faith the directors had placed in him and hoped he could retain the player's confidence in his judgement and impartiality. He knew that the club's future success was very much in his hands and that the club held all the aces contract wise. Contracts of the day due to their wording were strongly in favour of football league clubs with the players somewhat at their mercy.

A difficult situation, possibly working under constraints from above yet wielding power over the players below, respect from the playing staff would be hard earned.

He was in no-man's land, he could not win either way, not a director nor one of the lads.

Players were all on different wages within the club, usually staggered by their years of experience in the game. The maximum allowed payable by the rules of the football league being £20 in 1960, about £14 in 1953. Many of the Bolton lads were paid slightly above the national average for a working man back in 1953 of around £9 per week.

Every contract increase, even a couple of quid per week a player had to virtually fight tooth and nail for with Bill. The players thought the hard bargaining was wrong with the clubs pulling in excellent revenues of cash from the large gates.

If the team was not playing well, and the crowds were small, the low wages would have been more understandable. Bolton were a distinguished and competitive first division side (premier league today) triumphing regularly against the top teams of the day... the Manchester Uniteds and Wolverhampton Wanderers of this world.

Football crowds were up throughout the country with Bolton averaging 30,000 at Burnden Park come hail or high water. Fans turned up in their droves to be entertained on bleak and dreary wintery Saturday afternoons and it was the players who they cherished that the locals came to support. The players only wanted a fair slice of the cake, they were regularly playing in front of these large crowds at Burnden Park and pleased their success on the field was generating a lot of money for the club due to these excellent attendances.

Though professionals they were men the fans could relate to, they could have been their next door neighbours. Home was more often than not, a two up two down terraced house with no recognised bathroom and outside outhouse toilet facilities.

The vast majority did not own a car throughout their careers catching the bus or train to and from home. Players were normal everyday men who could possibly be seen and approachable to chat with if enjoying a pint after a game in a local hostelry.

One also has to realise that the life span of a footballer is relatively short... 10 years being a good innings as injury could, and did, curtail promising careers. Many hoped to leave with a few bob in their pocket just enough to give them a start in a business of some kind once the club told them they no longer required their services.

Tommy soon realised that taking the full picture into account Bill was a decent man, he worked hard for Bolton.

He was good at organising and delegating to ensure the smooth running of the club, this was his forte... the football side was George Taylor's domain. Bill would keep a very firm grip on the clubs wealth, if players asked for a pay rise he'd bring out reams of papers showing unemployed professionals seeking clubs.

Tommy knew Bill was a tough negotiator who also had a habit of holding up his hand to show what pay rise he was prepared to offer a player.

"Trouble wer ee'd louwst heawf o'one finger ona hond," Tommy remembers.
(Trouble was Bill had lost half a finger on a hand)
Therefore Tommy was never sure if it was a £3 or £2.50 pay rise he had been given when he left the room.

Gateshead, a then football league third division side, had been that season's cup giant killers and hosted Bolton in the F.A. Cup quarter final tie at their Redheugh Park ground on the 27th February 1953. However in a see-saw match a single Nat Lofthouse goal saw the "Whites" progress into the semi finals. Tommy did not play at Gateshead but a few days later he found himself back in the 1st team number 3 shirt for a league game against Liverpool. A goal less draw away at Anfield was closely followed by another outing in a midweek home win over Manchester City in front of almost 40,000.

He retained his place for the next match, a trip to Cardiff City but personal disaster struck when he sustained an injury pulling a hamstring and finished the game on the wing at Ninian Park. This game was shortly before the semi final against Everton F.C. which was to be staged at Maine Road, a ground capable of holding high capacity crowds. Although he had recovered in time, he was told he would not be risked for the semi, substitutes were still in the far and distant future and the club erred on the side of caution.

Bolton faced Everton at Maine Road on the 21st March before a crowd of over 72,000 with a youthful Roy Hartle now looking like he had made the right back position his own. Goals from Dougie Holden, Willie Moir and two from "Lofty" put Bolton into what looked like an unassailable lead at half time. Everton hit back with three second half goals but Bolton hung on by the skin of their teeth to make their first final since 1929.

A reserve game at home to Newcastle, just before the final, once again saw Tommy looking to impress to make the Wembley team. The local Bolton Evening News scribe Hayden Berry known under his reporting pseudonym "The Tramp" beckoned him at the entrance leading into Burnden Park.

The Tramp said he had heard a whisper from within the club's higher inner circles that a good performance today could see him in the number 3 shirt for the final against Blackpool!

Tommy doubted the words related from the newspaper hack, he had not been measured up for a Wembley suit for the day and could not see the club forking out to buy another at this late stage.

The two Banks brothers who had last formed a family full back pairing at Wolves in a league match back in 1950 were sweating on whether one, neither or both of them would make the final team. George Higgins had played the bulk of the league matches wearing the left back shirt up to March late that 1952-53 season. Tommy's had dislodged him before his own injury had brought Ralph's quest for a final shirt to the fore with ten games on the bounce. Ralph was some nine years older than Tommy and had like many others lost a big chunk of his promising career due to the war and National Service.

Sure enough despite a personal solid reserve team performance against Newcastle Tommy was not in the twelve that left for Wembley a few days prior to the final.

Sadly neither was his big mate Roy Hartle who had been left out of the team a couple of games earlier after an indifferent display in a league match at Sheffield Wednesday. Although he had played in every round of the cup on route he also would not be in the Bolton line up at Wembley. Roy had made his debut on New Years Day 1953 and established himself with a run of 24 league and cup games.

These were the days before realistic man management skills had been born, the sensitivity of the player did not appear to matter one jot. There was no arm around a shoulder and a comforting word on breaking the news of their non selection.

Tommy and Roy brutally found out via the team sheet pinned on the dressing room notice board a few days prior to the final.

John Ball was restored to the right back spot and Tommy's brother Ralph had been picked on the other flank giving him the ominous task of containing the well published threat of England international Stanley Matthews.

There was also a decision made to include Eric Bell who had declared himself fit in the left half position after a few weeks on the sidelines with a hamstring injury. Tommy thought it a very dubious call picking Bell!

Tommy had been in an identical situation himself prior to the semi final with a similar injury which was difficult to shake off and he had been omitted from the team at Maine Road on cautionary grounds. Similar injury, Bell was an established professional who had played many games over the seasons so had the Wembley final choice been based on his vast experience against Tommy's non semi final selection due to only a dozen or so first team games under his belt?

At Wembley Bell lasted 18 minutes before hobbling onto the left wing with the Bolton team re-jigged to compensate for his injury re-occurrence. Bolton went 3-1 in front with Bell somehow managing to climb high to head the third goal and the "Trotters" looked home and dry.

Twenty minutes from the end Blackpool finally managed to bring Matthews more into the game, up to this point Ralph had been able to keep his well renowned ability in check.

Matthews started to weave his magic along the touchline and by-line creating a number of chances for other Blackpool forwards. They were gleefully twice accepted by Stan Mortensen although a ricket from goalie Stan Hanson assisted and a last minute winner from Bill Perry sealed their fate.

Known as the "Stanley Matthews final" even though Stan Mortensen had scored an hat trick, it was Matthews' third final and third time lucky to win the much coveted trophy after losses in 1948 and 1951... the 4-3 defeat left Bolton to surmise what might have been ....

Bolton Wanderers;
Hanson; Ball; R.Banks; Wheeler; Barrass; Bell; Holden; Moir;
Lofthouse; Hassall; Langton

Blackpool;
Farm; Shinwell; Garret; Fenton; Johnston; Kelly; Matthews; Taylor;
Mortensen; Mudie; Perry

This was the beginning of the end for the majority of Bolton's Wembley losers which saw the gradual break up of the team as the bulk of the players where allowed to drift away over the coming seasons, mainly on free transfers.

Ralph Banks had played his last game for Bolton and at 33 years of age was given a "free" allowing him to follow his instincts and choose his own path. Ralph was a "salt of the earth" cheery character, a funny guy but not as loud as Tommy...he joined Aldershot a few rungs down the leagues ladder which resulted in the upheaval of moving house to pastures new. Aldershot was better known for its connections with the Army being one of the biggest bases in the country.

"Ah sez wor duz thee wannter gi deawn theer fer" asked Tommy,
(I asked Ralph why he wanted to go down to Aldershot)

Ralph explained he liked being a full time professional and wanted to stay in the game, plus Aldershot were paying him their top money of £14 per week.

He could have earned a better wage working as a bricklayer and playing as a part time professional in the non leagues but chose to stay full time. Tommy thought Ralph would have to make sure he played well for the "Shots" otherwise they may send him down the road to join up with the Army again.

Tommy was saddened to see his brother depart, naturally due to being a close family member, but also on a football level.

The pair had only embraced a few short months together as full professionals at the club due to Tommy's enforced National Service from 1951-53.

Short but sweet.... they had occasionally donned boxing gloves trading punches to give the dressing room a pre training laugh with blows below their considerable high belts not welcomed.

Ralph eventually played a couple of seasons for Aldershot before picking up his bricklaying trowel full time whilst moving again to enjoy part time football with Weymouth.

The summer's break in 1953 saw Tommy's introduction to the gruelling role of hod carrying. For those unfamiliar with this "profession" it involves transporting bricks, blocks and mortar in a specific carrier called a 'hod.' These materials are delivered as close as possible to the desired position near the build to make life workable for the bricklayers. In effect the 'hod carrier' is a donkey carrying the essential materials for the more skilled tradesmen...the bricklayers. It is hard physical graft and not for the weak or faint hearted.

Bolton had just played the F.A. Cup Final at Wembley yet the substantial drop in out off season wages saw Tommy seeking work in summer to make ends meet. At this stage in his life any stop gap job would have filled the void but he jumped at the chance of outdoor work on a new building site for a local company. Tommy thought that hod carrying would build his muscles up and also keep him fit during the off season.

He reported to site expecting to start day one on the hod only for the site foreman to tell him a number of deep footings were required due to building in the close proximity of a railway cutting. Tommy and another new starter were informed that sorting out these footings was their job for that week. By the following Saturday Tommy could see the mixer in his sleep he never stopped loading cement, sand and cinders to make cindercrete. The cinders helped save on cost plus added strength to the mix but it was heavy going transporting and dragging the cindercrete around the footings and with his hands bleeding the cement seemed to find every cut.

Reporting for work the following Monday morning to the site cabin high up on the railway banking Tommy asked the foreman if his mate from last week would be turning up?

"That lazy bugger finished Friday I sacked him you were carrying him" explained the foreman who could survey the site from his lofty perch.

"What's more I am giving you a pay rise you will be by yourself this week"

A week later Tommy eventually "made his debut" on the hod and as the houses progressed he was carrying materials up 36 foot 32 rung ladders which was some challenge for a novice. It did not faze Tommy he was back for more the next two summers although in "56" and "57" the wages Eckersley's Farm were paying for haymaking gazumped the building site money. He might have been better off wage wise but he certainly earned it, the hours in the field were long from seven in the morning until dusk at night.

Tommy was expecting to start the 1953-54 in hold of the 1st team left back shirt so it came as a big surprise to him when the team sheets were pinned up for the opening day of the season, "Banks" was in the "A" team. Somewhat bemused, he was informed via the underground football grapevine by a newspaper reporter that very weekend that Wolves who had tried to sign him on amateur forms in his mid teen years were extremely interested in his current team selection misfortune.

What was Bill Ridding trying to do by picking him in the 3rd team, were his days numbered at Bolton or was the manager trying to show him who was boss?

Had Wolves put a bid into Bolton for Tommy Banks?

Tommy was now a fully fledged accepted member of the dressing room, a character all the lads could trust. He was always first with the banter that is notorious within the playing side of professional clubs with lads living in each others' pocket everyday. He was never short of a word and his dry wit and mirth endeared him to fast become the players' unofficial spokesman in some issues with Bill Ridding.

Tommy sought out Bill, who denied all knowledge of an approach from Wolves, saying if any came he would be held to his contract. If he kicked up a fuss and asked for a transfer he'd fester in the "A" team until his contract expired.

Whilst the scenario of the football league's wage structure had always stuck in Tommy's throat it was the "Retain and transfer" system that bugged him the most. At the time clubs operated a system "Retain and transfer" which meant that clubs could keep a player's registration(thus preventing them from moving) whilst refusing to pay them after their contract had expired.

Restrictions were in place which basically said;

Once a player was registered with a football league club he could not register with any other club, even in subsequent seasons, without the permission of the club he was registered with. It applied even if the player's annual contract with the club holding his registration was not renewed after it expired. The club were not obliged to play him and, without a contract, the player was not entitled to receive a salary. Nevertheless, if the club refused to release his registration, the player could not play for any other Football League club.

If faced with such a situation the player had the following stark choice;

Quit playing football professionally and try to find employment outside the game.

"It only just stopp'd short o'tellin thee when un wheer thi cawd blow thee nose, purrit this way ah thout Hitler wer deed" said Tommy.

(The restrictions only just stopped short of telling you when, where and what you could and couldn't do, and I thought dictators like Hitler were dead.)

It was not just Tommy feeling embittered, numerous players all other the country were victims of the current contract standing that promoted newspaper scribes to label it a "Slavery Contract".

One such professional was Tommy G. Jones a well respected distinguished elegant centre half who had plied his trade successfully with Everton over the pre and post war years. Roma put a £15000 transfer bid in for him in 1948 to potentially make the Welsh international one of the first foreigners to play in Italy. The transfer fell through at the 11th hour due to alleged differences over currency details between the two clubs with Jones not allowed any say in the bargaining apart from his wish to join Roma. No deal was struck leaving Jones totally frustrated at the events and utterly powerless having no control over his own livelihood and thus a transfer that would have set him up for life and given Everton a handsome profit.

The player/club relationship was never the same thereafter, events then rumbled on for a couple of years. A club director even accused him at one stage of feigning injury although it proved the injury was bad enough to put him in hospital for four months.

The manager Cliff Britain wouldn't even pick him for the reserves and Jones told the Everton board that he was considering quitting the game. Everton refused to budge so in 1950 Jones walked away from the club and sought a living outside the game where he knew destiny was in his hands.

(A decade later T.G Jones the then manager of Bangor City persuaded Tommy Banks in 1963 to play part time for the North Wales outfit.)

Although picked in the "A" team fate played a hand for Tommy Banks on Saturday 22rnd August the 1953-54 season's opening fixture. George Higgins who played left back for the first team and the lad who had occupied the spot in the reserve fixture that same day had both received injuries in their respective games. Bill Ridding appeared to have little option but to recall Tommy Banks to the No.3 shirt.

Tommy soon showed his worth embedding himself into the team playing 46 league and cup games over the season although the thought that at 23 years of age he could have been put out to pasture like an old horse still rankles today.

Still struggling every so often with hamstring problems he played 25 games in 1954-55 ensuring that his name was now inked into the team sheet rather than the previous pencil markings of his early professional life.

Although the team only managed to finish in eighteenth position in the league in 54-55 good signs were afoot via the reserves who had won the Central League title.

The Central League contained all the top northern clubs as far as Newcastle down to midlands teams like Aston Villa and Wolves. Back then the reserve team was much more important than today with established stars finding their feet after injuries. Young players also often had to pit their wits in front of good sized crowds against 32-34 year old veterans whose careers were on the wane and looking to impress for possibly one last transfer move.

John Higgins, Derek Hennin, Dennis Stevens, Eddie Hopkinson, Ralph Gubbins Graham Cunliffe, and Brian Birch were eager young Bolton players learning their trade, adapting to professional life and building a team spirit that would carry Bolton a long way.

Roy Hartle had not been selected for a first team game in the whole of the 1954-55 season but he started to make his mark with the launch of the 55-56 campaign. He then like Tommy became an ever present whenever fit and the formation of the legendary "they shall not pass" full back partnership swung into action.

Roy was giving Chelsea winger Frank Blunstone a bit of a 'shoeing' one afternoon at Burnden Park so Frank in his wisdom thought he'd change flanks and was greeted by Tommy,

"Eigh up theer Blunny wor thi dooin oer 'ere ah thinks thi's jump'd owter fryin' pan inter fire"
(Well hello there Frank what are you doing over here, I think you'll find the going tough over this side too)

These young players were starting to burst through onto the first team stage to join Ray Parry who at 15 years and 267 days on the 13th October 1951 and after only six reserves games, became the youngest player ever to play in the first division making his debut against Wolves. The youngsters could see the huge strides that Ray still a very young man, Tommy and Roy had made and desire drove them to make the leap into the big time.

Tommy and Bill Ridding rarely saw events or incidents through the same eyes with words often exchanged in private or in the team environment. After a defeat in an away game in the midlands Bill leased his fury in the dressing room on Bolton's beleaguered team with Tommy taking exception to personal comments directed at him. Tommy would accept any justified criticism of his actions on the field but Bryan (Slim) Edwards had lost his man and he'd tried to cover for him in a last gasp effort to stop the inside forward from scoring.

Bill was not accepting Tommy's words even though Slim spoke up acknowledging his mistake with 'Hoppy' also chiming in to agree.

Tommy being the intelligent guy he is thought Bill possibly had a hidden agenda?

Was he trying to show the dressing room the strength of his position by verbally attacking Tommy due to irrelevant past issues between the two?

"Reet Bill,when wi mekkit bakk t'Bowton mi un thee wilt geet in thi car un visit Belmont, only one mon's cummin wom un it wonnt bi thee" snorted Tommy.

(Ok Bill once we return to Bolton me and you need to sort our differences out man to man in a physical way out on the moors)

In the midst of this explosion of youth infiltration Tommy was sad to hear of the departure of 1953 stalwart Malcolm Barrass Bolton's elegant centre half to Sheffield United. The player had signed amateur forms in 1944 and served the club very well winning three England caps before being sold in Sept 1956 in acrimonious circumstance due to what appeared personal differences with the manager. A scholar of the game Barrass often chatted about on and off the field events with Tommy who learned that his relationship with Bill Ridding was not good and the club did not welcome Barrass's sometime verbal directness over issues. Although he'd intimated a transfer would possibly be for the best for both parties it was tinged with deep sadness on leaving behind an emerging great dressing room spirit. The players knew that Malcolm had strong opinions of his own, he was always there to stand up for the team and individuals off the field, a really good man, and a cool cultured footballer.

Arthur Barnard who deputised in goal for Stan Hanson a couple of times in the first team in 1955 and 1956 also speaks in glowing terms of Barrass's willingness to assist.

"I had signed professional in 1950 and Bill Ridding had agreed to pay me £2.50 a month travel expenses to compensate me for my daily journeys to training. I never had a problem receiving my funds the office clerk would pay me out regular as clockwork come the end of the month. A year ticked by and I was just about to receive my usual monthly expenses payout standing alongside a few other waiting pros. when Bill Ridding stuck his head around the clerk's door. On viewing a queue of players waiting for money to exchange hands he didn't ask why we were there just roared for all of us to get out of the room. Apparently the first team had lost against Arsenal the previous day and it appears he wasn't in a good mood."

"Now at eighteen years I was pretty "frecken" of him, he was a daunting figure for any young lad. I never said a word, and neither did any of the handful of experienced professionals, we all left with our tail between our legs."

Malcolm Barrass soon heard on the grapevine what had happened and told me to bide my time. A few days later he approached me in training saying to go and collect my exes after dinner. The situation had been addressed and it was now sorted, Malcolm had "discussed" the situation with the boss.

Arthur says he had little other personal experience of Bill Ridding imposing his position on him apart from the time he felt he was back at "scoo." We'd finished training and I was just tying my shoelaces, I looked up on feeling a tap on my shoulder,

"Don't come with that long hair tomorrow or you'll be sent home" said Bill.

"Now my hair was maybe a tad longer than the regulation styles of the time but ponytail it was not. I was really unsure just how real the threat was so I decided to venture on the side of caution coming in the next morning with a crew cut," Arthur recalls.

Bill spotted me and murmured;

"That's better lad, make sure the barber stays your best friend"

Barrass's departure left the door ajar for burly John Higgins and 'Higgy' pushed it wide open to complete the jigsaw of the regular Bolton defence for the next few years of Hopkinson, Hartle, Banks, Hennin, Higgins and Edwards.

Eddie Hopkinson enjoyed a meteoric rise to claim the goalkeeping position in season 1956-57 although he'd originally signed as an amateur for the club back in 1952. National Service in the RAF once again possibly hindered his initial development but come the end of season "55-56" on his return he was looking at a raft of goalkeepers in front of him.

Football fate can deal out all sorts of blows, including kind or cruel, for Hoppy it was the former, for Joe Dean the latter.

Long standing No.1 Stan Hanson retired, Arthur Barnard had joined Stockport County and Ken Grieves an Australian who was also a first class cricketer with Lancashire C.C. had an agreement allowing him to finish the County cricket season which ran into mid September.

Grieves a gifted cricketer who became a good mate of Tommy's although neither could understand what the other was saying had come from "down under" at the start of the summer of 1947. He initially played for

Rawtenstall C.C. near Burnley as the hired Professional in the Lancashire League and stayed in the north west after his sporting days ended.

Over the cricket seasons, even today, test and top class cricketers would arrive from Australia, the West Indies, India, Pakistan and South Africa to become the paid player in the ranks of local clubs throughout the cricket leagues of Lancashire.

Rawtenstall C.C. were due to "employ" the legendary Australian Keith Miller but a last minute hiccup found him unavailable and he recommended up and coming leg spinning all rounder Grieves to deputise. Grieves suitably impressed at Rawstenstall C.C. and he was then asked to join Lancashire C.C. playing over 400 county cricket games into the mid 1960's many as the captain.

Multi talented he was also a goal keeper and decided to attend a trial for Bury which was successful, before Bolton recognised his ability and snapped him up in 1951.

Ken enjoyed a laugh and a bit of fun of the field so he soon bonded with Tommy.

In the summers whenever possible a group of players would visit the Old Trafford cricket ground to watch Ken in action for Lancashire.

"Ken would leave the best tickets in the ground for us at the door" said Arthur,

"This wasn't a good idea because after a few drinks, much laughter and Tommy "whispering" about events on the field it appears a number of older Lancashire C.C. members in the Main pavilion had been awoken from their slumbers one time too many."

Three day County cricket matches have always been for the palate of the committed connoisseur of the game often being played in virtually empty grounds. It can produce long days out in the field for one team, play is sometimes almost stationary and thus progress slow. Steady and cultured cricket rather than the spectacular "up and at 'em" approach that became the norm with the birth of limited overs one day cricket in the 60's. This instant cricket with a result ensured by close of play enticed a new breed of spectator and possibly saved the game bringing with it more of a football atmosphere.

In 1956 Arthur Barnard was transferred to Stockport but quite ironically had just moved house to be closer to Burnden Park. His new residence was in Phetian Street the next street to Tommy hereupon they became good mates still to this day.

Dunkerley's Moses Gate petrol station two minutes away always seemed to be on the look out for part time staff to man the pumps to provide a service for customers requiring a fill up, these were pre self service days.

"I'd got to know Lou Dunkerley the owner" said Arthur "So he agreed for Tommy and me to staff a couple of afternoons a week which put a few bob in our pockets"

This was a pretty cushy number no physical exertion just manners required,

"Nethen squire, worts thi pleasure?" Tommy would ask customers.
(Hello sir, what can I do for you)

Later before they left for home Arthur used to hose down the forecourt to wash away all evidence of Tommy's "baccy" chewing presence!

Joe Dean only 17 was given the nod for the first game of the 56-57 campaign in August against Wolves in the midlands at the time becoming the youngest goalkeeper to play in the first division. It was an unfortunate start for Joe who required stitches in a 4-2 reversal with Lofty donning the green goalkeeper's shirt on the keeper's premature departure from the field.

Hoppy, extremely agile and particularly brave in 1v1 although diminutive at 5' 9" by today's standards was installed between the sticks for the next fixture, Bolton's first home game where they triumphed 4-1 over Blackpool. He then went onto become the team's regular guardian and six weeks later represented England's Under 23's. A full cap in a 4-0 victory over Wales at Ninian Park in Oct 1957 soon followed and in an outstanding career he made a record 578 appearances for Bolton before retiring in 1970.

Joe Dean thus found the way to first team football blocked playing only 17 games before moving to Carlisle in 1960 and then Barrow, retiring in 1972.

Tommy enjoyed the presence of his younger team mates making their way in the game around 1956-57.......lads who mixed well together and possessed ambition and steely determination to stamp their presence on the football world.

Behind the Burnden Stand there was some spare land that had been turned into a very basic shale pitch where small sided matches took place. Occasionally a challenge was issued and the "heavies" in the squad took on the "lightweights" in these six and seven a side games. The "heavies" team comprised of most of the members of the team that was starting to take shape to become the regular 1958 F.A. Cup defence, Hartle, Banks, Higgins and Edwards plus goalkeeper Hopkinson. "Hoppy" never went between the 'sticks' in these games preferring to 'goal hang' a yard or two outside the opponents goal nicking many a last minute winner with a toe poke.

At times the "heavies" would enter the pitch marching behind big John Higgins who would be carrying a rotting old half flag pole with a torn and tattered Bolton Wanderers flag flying at full mast. The pitch was known as 'The Gravels' by the lads and 'Higgy's crew 'The Gravel Hangers' due to their uncompromising approach.

Higgins would ram the pole into the pitch around the halfway line and his men would then stand and gesture at the opposition consisting of 'ball players' Holden, Stevens and Parry. Tommy with his passion and desire on one hand and technical ability on the other could have slotted into either team.

It was the nearest challenge they could muster to an "All Black haka" without the dance, the only moving parts were a threatening finger and a lashing tongue warning not to 'take the mickey' or else!

'The Gravels' was a tight area so for players participating with the like of Hartle, Banks and Higgins around it was a potential troublesome location. The teams played these small sided games like they were battling opponents on a Saturday. Weekday training encounters were tough and passionate with the rare handbag scuffle occurring between lads. Disagreements were soon smoothed over.... these games helped to forge an undying team spirit that was to see them triumph at Wembley in May 1958.

Now an experienced professional Tommy took over the mantle of cultivating the best interests of his team mates on and off the field with his unique kind of dressing room presence and playing "for the lads" by his inimitable imposing presence during matches.

Lofty, Holden, a livewire named Dennis Stevens and a very young Brian Birch made up the eleven who would bring F.A. Cup glory back to the townsfolk of Bolton.

Chapter 10

Bolton in Europe

Bolton Wanderers qualified to play in Europe due to finishing 7th in the Premier League in Season 2006-2007 under manager Sam Allardyce. However Sam left Bolton three games before the end of the season, moving onto pastures new at Newcastle United that summer. Sam had originally achieved what many fans thought the impossible dream for Bolton by initially playing in the UEFA Cup in season 2005-06 when the Whites reached the last 32 of this competition.

Sammy Lee was installed as the manager and he presided over the qualifying games of the UEFA Cup against the Macedonian side F K Rabotnicki in September 2007 which Bolton won over the two legs. Lee's reign was brief and he was dismissed on the 15th October after Bolton had made a poor start in the Premier league.

By the time the opening salvo in the Group stages of the UEFA campaign was being fired on the 25th Oct 2007 against Braga at the Reebok Gary Megson had all but been officially appointed the new manager of Bolton Wanderers. A day or so later he took over the position occupying the hot seat to direct the fate of the club through their second voyage into UEFA Cup waters.

Bolton had originally played in Europe some 50 years plus previously but in very different circumstances to those of today's modern day players and management.

Tommy and the rest of his team mates found themselves on end of season trips into Europe over various playing years from around 1953 onwards. The players were never quite sure what to expect in the early days because of this generation, few if any, had any previous opportunity even to venture out of Britain on a personal holiday. Therefore travels abroad to play matches against foreigners in their own backyard were often the first overseas sorties most had experienced in life.

Whilst the chance to broaden their horizons was not to be missed the four, five sometime six match itinerary over around 10-14 days was generally found to be punishing on legs and minds. Players had just completed 42 matches, league fixtures in league one (now Premiership) plus cup games in all kinds of weather on surfaces that referees wouldn't cross the white line for today.

At the end of the 1954-55 playing season Bolton flew to Cologne to play quick fire fixtures around the Ruhr valley a vast industrial and coalmining district in the north west of Germany.

First opponents up were Rot-Weiss Essen who back in 1955 were a major club in the German top division prior to the formation of the Bundeslige in 1962 although today they have lost almost all their identity and play in the 5th division. Rot-Weiss ran out 3-1 winners before Bolton swiftly moved onto meet the challenge of Schalke 04.

Bolton had been invited to play against Schalke 04. This was due to the German club arranging a number of fixtures through their 1954-55 seasons with clubs to celebrate the 50th anniversary of the founding of their team in 1904 by a group of high school students. Around 1923 Schalke had picked up the nickname "Die Knappen" from an old German name for 'Miners' because so many of the players and supporters came from the coalmine workers of the local district of Gelsenkirchen.

How fitting that a former miner took the left back position that day for Bolton Wanderers, with both sides happy with the 2-2 result.

Travel most days for Bolton once in Europe was via coach over endless miles throughout the different countries. It was tough and largely uncomfortable but the money men insisted Bolton had to make a profit from the trip.

Travelling through France without a game helped the players out financially. They were only given £2 per day expenses, and Paris even back then, was an expensive place to visit.

"Tha' cuddent bey a coffee wi tha kinda munny" said Tommy.
(Paris was a very expensive place even in the fifties)

Directors and their wives received £5 each, Tommy did not understand the reasoning behind the variance in fees he felt it was not right. Tommy used to comment about the situation whilst they were all on the coach, jesting about the circumstances which the directors did not appreciate. The players were being paid the minimum rate for their endeavours on the pitch, whilst the directors were on a holiday and paying themselves the best money.

Thirteen players, plus manager Bill Ridding, coach George Taylor and physiotherapist Bert Sproston made up the playing squad with a dozen in the directors party.

If anyone received an injury they had to play strapped up unless it was really serious!

Tommy said that the trip through France to play Athletic Bilbao in Northern Spain was the one fixture on the itinerary that really excited the players. In 1955 few working class British individuals had been to Spain for a holiday.... ...Bilbao sounded an excellent place to obtain a tan. The players took their swimwear and it appears they were hoping to enjoy a bit of sun and relaxation. Apparently they did not need to have bothered packing their trunks. The environment was disappointing, not scenic, ultra industrial with only about three bucketfuls of sand to cover the "so called beach" according to Tommy.

Bolton Wanderers' status in football had preceded them and they had been invited to play Bilbao to raise money for the family of one of their players who had died from gangrene.

Athletic Bilbao originated in 1898 with much of their early influence coming from the miners and shipyard workers of Sunderland who had emigrated to gain work in the region's industrial iron mines and shipyards.

In 1909 a young Bilbao student Juan Eloray studying in the city of London had been entrusted during his stay in England to buy a new set of playing shirts which was proving difficult. Salvation came at almost the "eleventh hour" whilst he was on his way to Southampton docks at Christmas awaiting a voyage home. He realised due to walking around the neighbourhood, that the local team's colours matched the colours of the city of Bilbao. He bought 50 red and white striped shirts and from the 1910 season onwards these have been their home colours.

Athletic Bilbao to this day will only select players from the Basque country which is about the size of Wales.

On Bolton's match day against Bilbao alternate striped runs of red and white geranium flowers were decked out around the San Mames Stadium. Although 2-1 losers apparently the 25000 crowd stood up in appreciation of the Wanderers. It appears Bolton were possibly the first English team to play in this stadium nicknamed "The Football Cathedral" due to its closeness to the place of worship the St. James' Cathedral.

Four days later that May the Wanderers visited Belgium where the team experienced a totally different way to earn a living on strolling the streets of Antwerp. They watched in wonder through various shop windows men sitting cutting diamonds without a care. This was the mid 1950's, in forever changing decades since which have produced a more sinister world are those windows now protected by iron grills and multiple door locks?

The next football campaign 1955-56 end of season trip took in Norway which involved hours of travelling attending the chosen matches. Upon fulfilling the Oslo fixture the party travelled onto Bergen acknowledged as one of the most beautiful cities in Europe. A couple of days later sea legs were required as the journey to Stavanger was via a five hour boat trip through picturesque fjords. Later the party emerged from their rooms in their new hotel to an outstanding evening feast. It featured fish dishes galore and a sublime food design similar to an upside down chandelier filled with masses of prawns.... but none of it tempted John Higgins by now a naturalised "Bowtonian".

Tommy remembers the big lad, who just broke into the first team, breezing into the kitchens asking the chef to rustle him up double egg bacon sausage and beans unfortunately tomato ketchup had not quite made the shores of Norway back then.

You can take the lad out of "Bowton" but you can't take "Bowton" out of the lad!

Tommy recalls the trip to Seville in 1960 to mark the 50th anniversary of the Real Betis club, a kind of knock out tournament played over a few days.

Prior to the game Graham Cunliffe and Tommy had ventured into Seville Cathedral and ultimately marvelled at its sheer size and grandeur. The cathedral the third largest church in the world is the burial site of the great explorer Christopher Columbus.

Bolton had beat Borussia Dortmund in a friendly a few days earlier in Germany 1-0 followed on the next step of their tour by a rare hat trick from left winger Dougie Holden in a 3-2 victory over Stuttgart. Again they played Dortmund this time losing by the odd goal in 5 with both teams acknowledging the warm applause of their efforts by 20,000 spectators on leaving the field.

Next up were the host Real Betis who were used to the very humid conditions which caused games in May to start at the bedtime hour of 10 pm. Real Betis known as "the team of the night" due to their late kick offs in Spring sneaked home by 2 goals to 1. It was a game Tommy recalls well remembering that even at ten o'clock at night the Bolton team were sweating profusely before the kick off.

Tommy jumped to head a ball close to the touchline when the opponent's centre forward caught him with a late challenge sending him spilling into the crowd.

Thankfully no damage was done but Tommy smiled at this chap as he got to his feet and greeted him in his usual style,

"Nethen owd luv,wossupwithee,welcum t' mi world"
(Now then my friend, what's your problem, I can play like that if you want)

Bolton then let the Betis players know who was the boss, having big lads like Hartle Higgins and Hennin helped in making it a physical tussle. Betis did not want to physically compete when the challenges became rougher and never stopped complaining to the referee but somehow Bolton couldn't score again and Betis hung on grimly to achieve their win.

Due to their defeats Bolton unfortunately did not play the world renowned stars of Real Madrid however they did get to see them at close quarters by sharing the same hotel.

Real Madrid had just beat Eintracht Frankfurt 7-3 at Hampden Park, Glasgow in front of 127,000 spectators to win the European Cup. Hungarian talisman Ferenc Puskas scored four whilst Alfredo Di Stefano helped himself to the other three.

Real Madrid appeared to have wine with every meal of the day, even breakfast.

"Ah sweer one mons cornflakkes wer swimmin in claret" Tommy was heard to comment.

(It looked like he'd poured wine on his cornflakes)

In the pursuit of friendliness the two groups of players gathered one evening around the hotel bar for a chat. The Real Madrid team featured mixed nationalities and with the "Bowton" lads only knowing their own native language communications were somewhat 'stone age.' Much hand gesturing ensued and guessing on the interpretation of words plus Tommy's best Farnworthian lingo was a further challenge and brought blank looks and numerous "excuses" from their football counterparts.

One of the true Spanish players who spoke good English whispered to Tommy,

"My team mates think you're from Mars, they can't understand you"

"Art owd fettlers growin praytus in theer ears or shudah tawk proper" replied Tommy.

(Are they growing potatoes in their ears that's making them hard of hearing or should I talk the Queen's English)

Real Madrid right winger the Brazilian international Cannario was a fine player but he also revelled in his own importance. He seemed to spend an eternity that evening gloating to Tommy giving him chapter and verse about just how quick he was off the mark.

"Ee sez a lot but sez nowt" quipped Bolton's unimpressed left back letting him ramble on in his pigeon English.

(He loved to talk about himself)

Tommy's mind drifted, he thought it will never happen but.... Cannario should come and play against Bolton in the midst of winter on Burnden Park. When the birds appeared to be almost stationary flying into the teeth of the horizontal driving chilling rain and the mud's deep we'll soon see how quick he is and if he fancies it?

At the end of the 1958/59 season Bolton embarked on a six weeks tour of South Africa involving ten matches all over the country, apartheid was obviously present but did not disrupt the football matches, Wolves had been previous path finders.

Winning eight with two losses it was the sight from the coach of the desperately poor shanty towns on the outskirts of Johannesburg that stuck in the memories of the players that made up the travel party. The players thought they were not very well off in monetary terms but on seeing the horrendous conditions people endured in these Shanty towns put everything into perspective.

Dougie Holden had by now won a few England caps, and early this summer was representing the country on a tour of South America.

Bolton were running out of players due to injuries, once Holden had completed his last game in Rio against Brazil he flew to London then straight out to join the team for the last couple of weeks. It was some journey for Holden but these Bolton lads enjoyed each others' company so much he was reported to have commented,

"It was never a chore the company was brilliant."

The Bolton lads each received a £25 bonus paid over the course of the trip.

Tommy had bought Maggie a gold bracelet which lightened his pocket but he could not understand why only he returned home virtually penniless. He stepped down from the bus at Burnden Park counting his lose change whilst the rest of his mates were counting their notes.

It was not hard to fathom out who had been buying all the drinks!

Chapter 11

George Taylor

Much was made of the role Bill Ridding played in Bolton winning the 1958 F.A. Cup and rightly so. Any man who could basically take two different sets of players within a short span of time, 1953 and 1958 to Wembley finals, with the financial restrictions that a small town club sometime brings, deserves all the given accolades.

Where did the idea come from to produce their own players rather than delve into the transfer market is difficult to pin down?

Was it that Bolton just fell lucky that so many young lads came through at one time to make the grade plus they gelled as a team on and off the field?

Whatever the answer the 1958 £110 Cup winning team had character and fight plus individual attributes that ensured their "general" dragged every ounce of ability out of them.

The "general" or to give him his official title "chief coach" was none other than George Taylor a man who made it known in late 1950 that he had no wish to be considered for the vacant managerial position at Bolton due to his desire to continue coaching.

His coaching was solid rather than sophisticated, with much emphasis put on squeezing every last ounce of passion, drive and desire from the players.

The game did not possess the tactics and playing systems of today, plus the pace of the game with goalkeepers allowed to pick up back passes was slower. The leather footballs held water and heading a ball at times, with a slightly protruding lace, could and did cut foreheads. Footwear was like wearing heavy army boots in comparison to today weightless dancing shoes which are ideal for today's magnificent fast pitches for the alert technical players who have mastered one and two touch play.

Bolton and most teams lined up 2-3-5, two full backs, three half backs, five forwards.

The first and foremost job of the full backs and centre half was to defend, a role that the uncompromising Hartle and Banks revelled in with Tommy also possessing deft left footed distribution. The full backs swivelled off and covered the centre half depending on the position of the ball, big burly John Higgins was the rock to pivot off.

Half backs Hennin and Edwards prime aim was defensive ensuring the opposition inside forwards were contained and once in possession using the ball efficiently then pushing forward to add support.

With Hennin lively and strong, these half backs helped the inside forwards who were the main men in fetching, carrying and creating scoring opportunities, and also getting amongst the goals themselves.

Stevens a tireless goal scoring worker with ability to burn, pulled the levers alongside the effervescent Parry who always wanted the ball and possessed a wand of a left foot. These two lads kept the engine stoked and they were key figures in the side's success or failure.

Wingers were also vital to the team's cause in making or scoring goals.

Their role was to reach the bye line and pull the ball back or provide teasing crosses. Birch's directness also contained an eye for an opportunity of a goal which complimented Holden who possessed magical feet that bought him a yard where none existed to provide ammunition.

The major goal threat fell to the team's number nine.

Powerful and quick, add a fearsome shot in both feet, an awesome leap way betraying his moderate height to a fearless approach and Bolton had the full package in the name of Nathaniel Lofthouse.

George Taylor knew every attribute each player possessed to a tee, he did not ask them to try to perform duties that they were not comfortable with; no square pegs in round holes. George was the football brain of the club, Tommy remembers him as a wonderful man who was very knowledgeable about the game in the 1950's.

"Eewer a visionary,alluv lads luvv'd im 'ee nar swore or lows'd 'ees temper un leet thee play t' thee strengths"
(He expressed his ideas well and in a calm manner, all the lads respected him, George never swore or lost his temper to make a point and allowed us to use our individual ability)

George a wing half of some standing made 244 appearances for Bolton from 1931-1939 before serving as a Sergeant instructor in the Army PT Corps during the war, playing whenever available in the wartime friendlies for the Wanderers.

Coaching was his true calling, a strict disciplinarian yet his kind disposition endeared him to understand players' problems. George was a modest man possessing a keen sense of humour which made him so affectionately respected by the club's youngest junior to the oldest senior professional. Although more of a defensive coach he was at his happiest organising and cajoling the players with his great enthusiasm for the game.

George retired from coaching the senior players in the mid sixties and commenced scouting for Bolton, covering schoolboy games the length and breadth of the country at weekends. Many of these lads became the club's apprentice professionals and during the working day you'd find him once again coaching them out on the field the place he loved until the early 1970's.

George was awarded a testimonial by the club with an All Star X1 playing a Bolton X1 on Burnden Park in April 1967.

Superstars Tom Finney, Stanley Matthews and Nat Lofthouse all paid their respect to George in the best way they knew by taking to the field for the All Stars X1 against a Bolton X1.

George Taylor was without question one of Bolton's unsung heroes of the period.

Chapter 12

1958 FA Cup Winners

Bolton Wanderers 1958 F.A. Cup winning team are part of football's golden period in England, certainly every man who played became heroes within the town, especially the local lads.

Football came alive in the 50's, the 1939-45 Second World War was long passed and the green roots of change towards a more modern day society were beginning to emerge late in this decade. This was the start of one of the most eventful periods in the history of English football and Bolton Wanderers played more than their part in the action, the fortunes of the team mattered strongly to the townsfolk.

It was a time of modest wages earned by Bolton players loyal to their club, an age when they found football to be fun generated by an unquenchable team spirit which became the 12th man on the field of play.

1958 was Tommy Banks's year, the pinnacle of his football career, when all he had striven for since putting on his first pair of boots in his childhood came to meaningful fruition. He was a F.A. Cup winner for his beloved hometown of Bolton and he had also represented his country in the World Cup Finals tournament in Sweden.

To Bolton supporters the players who wore the famous white shirt back on the 3rd May 1958 have become a massive part of Bolton folklore;

This was the £110 team, every player cost the club no more than the mandatory £10 signing on fee, a close knit all English team who had come through the reserves, each player had showed their hunger and learnt their trade.

No-one knew each and everyone of those players, both as a player and an individual, better than Tommy Banks.

Tommy had become a regular item in the Bolton team from the 1953-54 season.

The "53" Cup Final losing team was generally being disbanded and he was passionate to help mould the evolving new kids on the block into an all for one unit. Brothers in arms, the players possessed a great team spirit and deep camaraderie. The bond is still there today when they hold their own informal reunions although as the years pass numbers have and are unfortunately dwindling.

"Uz wer a teem,ifthee kick'd one o'uz thee kick'd alluz"
(We was a team with an excellent spirit to fight for each other)

Any team that wins the cup these days may need interpreters because of all the foreign players now plying their trade in British football, it's very different than the 'owden times.' Tommy doubts if there will be any reunions in years to come of the successful teams of these current times....

1958 FACup Run;

Preston North End v Bolton Wanderers; 4th January 1958

Bolton Wanderers were drawn to play Preston at Deepdale in the 3rd round and knew that there were easier teams that could have come out of the bag in their favour. It was a short trip up the road to play their near Lancashire neighbours with the mighty Tom Finney amongst the Preston's ranks. Preston with home advantage appeared to be deemed the favourites by all the newspaper pundits amongst the 40,000 crowd who saw Bolton play in an unfamiliar red kit to avoid a colour clash. Bolton's eleven names on the team sheet that 4th day of January were by now the club's regular recognised first team, the same eleven lads who on the 3rd May 1958 would clinch F.A. Cup glory.

Bolton Wanderers;
Hopkinson; Hartle; Banks; Hennin; Higgins; Edwards; Birch; Stevens; Lofthouse; Parry; Holden

What a lacing, what a shock for Proud Preston!

They held out for an hour against tough rugged Bolton before three well deserved goals, midway through the second half, from Parry, Stevens and Parry again left Preston shell shocked. This win owed nothing to luck; Bolton had won at a canter with some methodical football allied with constructive efficiency via Holden. Stevens and Parry ran the midfield denying Preston the opportunity to feed Tom Finney who was being starved out of the game.

Finney's well known threat was blunted when he was served some ball by big Roy Hartle's decisive robust tackling so he thought he'd try his luck on the right wing. However the equally determined and composed Tommy Banks repelled any ideas his good 'off the field' mate had to forge a late rally relaying a few words to Preston's finest;

"Ah'd bi thinkin twice abeawt cummin oer 'ere Tom owd lad"
(Tom, don't think you're in for an easy ride over this side my friend.)

York City v Bolton Wanderers; 25th January 1958

Bolton Wanderers;
Hopkinson; Hartle; Banks; Stanley; Higgins; Cunliffe; Birch; Stevens;
Lofthouse; Parry; Holden

"This is York, this is York, welcome to York" boomed out over the station tannoy as the Bolton spectators, who had travelled by rail alighted onto the platform before the 4th round tie at Bootham Crescent.

The week prior to the game snow had frozen on the pitch making the game extremely doubtful, although a decision was to be made as late as Saturday dinnertime.

A thaw had set in on Friday night but the pitch was still hard underneath and both teams expressed disbelief that the referee had deemed it fit around 12.30pm. With rain falling later by 3pm large pools were starting to form on various parts of the playing surface, although the 23,000 capacity crowd may have deterred the referee from a last minute cancellation.

Creative football was virtually impossible on this morass with Bolton's higher level of fitness showing against their 3rd Division part time opponents. Bolton dominated the game with young 19 years old stand in half backs Graham Stanley and Graham Cunliffe prominent in the testing conditions.

In the dying minutes with the game looking set for a replay, a long hopefully punt downfield skidded off centre half John Higgin's head landing in a big pool leaving the York centre forward a clear opportunity in front of goal. Try as he might the striker hardly moved his shot 10 yards out of the water giving Bolton keeper Hopkinson time to race from between the posts and nullify the danger.

"Bi crikey uz wuz lucky,gud job tha pool favvor'd Farn'urth baths" said a relieved Tommy Banks.
(We was lucky the pool was very deep)

Any team that wins a Cup that involves a number of rounds needs lady luck to be on their side at some point throughout that run and this was Bolton's first slice. Was that late incident away at York City's ground going to prove to be the lucky omen that made Tommy alert to think that it could be the Trotters' year?

A side destined to make Wembley and become part of Bolton folklore? Maybe, just maybe....

Bolton Wanderers v York City (replay); 29th January 1958

Bolton Wanderers;
Hopkinson; Hartle; Banks; Stanley; Higgins; Cunliffe; Birch; Stevens; Alcock; Parry; Holden

The replay at Burnden Park on the following Wednesday enticed an enormous crowd of 34,000 considering it was for a midweek afternoon kick off.

Bolton fans had a late scare when the announcer gave the teams out over the tannoy thirty minutes before kick off with Lofthouse being replaced by Terry Allcock. Apparently an overnight virus had struck Bolton's kingpin but winger Brian Birch soon put a smile on the faces of the home spectators with a second minute goal. Stand in Allcock more than played his part, adding a second before half time, and doubling up with time running out. Once again young half backs Stanley and Cunliffe had performed well helping the team tick over effectively in the 3-0 victory.

Graham Cunliffe fully acknowledged the vocal help that Tommy Banks playing behind him not only gave him in these cup ties but every time he made the first team.

"Tommy was not only great in the tackle he was very good with the ball at his feet, he had a deft touch and could caress the ball into feet or dink it into space plus always verbally tremendously supportive" commented Graham.

"Cum bakk 10 yards Cunny thees in no mons land thi con then watch owt fer thi runner cummin across thee"
(Graham adjust your position slightly so you'll be able to see your opponent if he makes a run)

On winning the ball and playing it simple Tommy would encourage,

"Well dun Cunny neaw push up t'gi Ray sum support"
(Well done Graham now push up behind Ray Parry to offer support if he needs it)

Two days later, when the players arrived for training, the teams for the weekend were already pinned on the dressing room notice board. Following their successful cup appearances both Stanley and Cunliffe were extremely disappointed to see themselves back in the "stiffs" with fit again Hennin and Edwards picked in the 4 and 6 shirts.

Graham (nicknamed Cannon) Stanley coerced Graham Cunliffe into seeking an immediate showdown with manager Bill Ridding over their non first team selection.

Tommy Banks recalls the way the two youngsters later described to him their brief meeting.

"What do you two want" said Bill Ridding rather gruffly when they walked through the manager's door after being told to enter.

"Why aren't we picked?" asked Cannon.

"Because the regular half backs are fit again" replied the manager.

"We want a transfer" said Cannon with Cunny's mouth dropping open in amazement.

"A transfer, who the hell will want to sign you two, you're like a rotten box of apples in a corner...not wanted"

"Now get out of here and start running around that track, think yourself lucky to be here" bellowed the main man.

The following weekend, when the team sheets went up in the dressing room, Stanley and Cunliffe found they had not only slipped out of first team reckoning but also the reserves and "A" team.

"We were down to play with the 16 and 17 years old likely lads in the "B" team in some far flung wild location east of Blackburn"

"Eleven days previous 34,000 had watched us against York on Burnden Park now there were only a flock of nosey sheep peering over the fence from the farmer's field next door sussing us out." said Cunliffe.

"We were pros. and took it on the chin we had no option, Bill Ridding was flexing his muscles imposing his authority and showing who was boss" added Cunliffe.

Bolton Wanderers v Stoke City; 15th February 1958

Bolton Wanderers;
Hopkinson; Hartle; Banks; Hennin; Higgins; Edwards; Birch; Stevens; Lofthouse; Parry; Holden

The draw for the last sixteen of the cup favoured Bolton with a home tie against Stoke City although on match day the terrible weather really made the game a lottery. Continuous heavy rain fell for a couple of hours before the kick off.

With over 56,000 spectators packed into the ground a second pitch inspection by the referee 15 minutes before 3pm was most probably the deciding "yes" factor to save a lynching. Realistically with the pitch deteriorating rapidly within minutes of the kick off it was doubtful if the game would be completed.

It turned out to be a black day as well as a rainy one for the visitors from the potteries. In the ankle deep mud Bolton's stamina and heart plus adapting far better to the testing conditions saw them three goals to the good through Lofthouse, Stevens and Parry.

Late in the second half when Tommy Banks slipped and fell on the ball the referee quite bizarrely awarded Stoke a penalty. This was converted but it was too late to have any real impact and with the majestic Dennis Stevens patrolling every inch of the heavy field Bolton coasted home 3-1 winners.

Bolton Wanderers v Wolverhampton Wanderers; 1ˢᵗ March 1958

Bolton Wanderers;
Hopkinson; Hartle; Banks; Hennin; Higgins; Edwards; Birch; Stevens; Lofthouse; Parry; Holden

The sixth round tie home to the team of the 50's Wolverhampton Wanderers still lives strong in the memory of all Trotters supporters fortunate to be part of a near 60,000 Burnden Park crowd, it epitomises exactly what this Bolton team was all about from positions 1-11.

Good, but never the best collectively ability wise to be classed a great 'footballing' team this was a determined band of brothers displaying deep reserves of steel, strength, endeavour, passion and endurance. Sweat pouring from every sinew in their bodies surfaced in a will to win that day that could never have been surpassed.

Wolves the aristocrats of English football throughout the decade, destined for the league title, brought their best game to the table enjoying good possession only to be thwarted time and again by the massive hearts of the Bolton players.

A seesaw first half saw Bolton draw blood through the dynamic Stevens just before the half hour mark only for Mason to equalise a minute later for Wolves. Right half Derek Hennin sustained a hamstring injury around the interval mark severely restricting his movement in the second half with Stevens then being employed more in a defensive wing half role. On the hour mark Bolton won a free kick around the edge of the Wolves penalty area.

"Trey a chip ah whisper'd t'Ray as Wolves wer leenin upth'wall" said Banky (I said to Ray try a chip as the Wolves players were making a defensive wall)

Ray Parry took on board Tommy's words and totally bemused Wolves goalie Finlayson with his deft touch directing the ball into the net to the ecstatic delight of the bulk of the enthralled spectators. For the last 30 minutes Wolves pounded on Bolton's door but could not break it down, the mighty last defensive barrier of Hopkinson, Hartle, Higgins and Banks shored up the fort repelling all efforts. Twice the woodwork was peppered and Hartle and Banks appeared from nowhere to block shots on the goal line that were too good for Hoppy.

Parry was stretchered off with 10 minutes remaining, suffering concussion, following a clash of heads.

This resulting in the final act of a truly memorable game being played in the Bolton goal area which represented a scene from a traffic jam. There were no policemen to assist monitor the one way flow that constantly poured towards the Bolton goal with the home side down to nine men and a brave limping Hennin.

Buckets of courage, team spirit and the smile of lady luck saw Bolton emerge 2-1 victors in possibly the greatest ever game witnessed on Burnden Park.

Fourteen years old Dave Hatton soon to be a "Wanderer" and play over 570 league games for Bolton, Blackpool and Bury was a near neighbour of Tommy's back in Thorne Street, Moses Gate, Farnworth, Dave was listening to the game on the radio whilst sat on his front doorstep.

"It felt like I was at the match from my Moses Gate home at least a mile and half away I could hear every roar of the crowd in relationship to radio commentary from events on the field." commented Dave.

If the football authorities could have bottled, for preservation all that is good in the game, this competitive highly exciting match, played in an excellent respectful spirit would have been the one, bubbling passionately with the cork forever popping.

Tommy Banks's eyes proudly sparkled with delight on being interviewed after a refreshing bath,

"Worragam, itwer a smookker, ah feel wonderful, ah cawnt describe it, ah noes tha' cawnt bey it"

(That was a marvellous game, I feel great, I can't quite describe it but I know money can't buy it)

"Ah'll enjoy misell t'neet ahmet geet a sweigh on"
(I enjoy myself tonight I might have a few beers and be rather tipsy)

Bolton Wanderers v Blackburn Rovers; 22rnd March 1958

Bolton Wanderers;
Hopkinson; Hartle; Banks; Hennin; Higgins; Edwards; Birch; Stevens; Gubbins; Parry; Holden

Three weeks had elapsed since the epic Wolves game before Bolton met Lancashire rivals Blackburn Rovers on the 1st March in the semi final of the F.A. Cup at Maine Road in front of over 74,000.

Ten days prior to this showdown, "Leader of the Bolton pack" Nat Lofthouse had sustained a dislocated shoulder at Tottenham. It took a lot to keep Nat off the field but he required immediate surgery in an attempt to be fit for the May final, should the Trotters overcome their then second division opponents. Terry Allcock who had scored two goals in the replay against York City had been transferred to Norwich City days before Nat's injury leaving the team without a recognised goalscorer.

Bolton turned to utility player Ralph Gubbins to spearhead the attack.

Ralph had now worn every forwards' shirt this season standing in on a dozen league occasions for colleagues who were sidelined with injuries.

With Bolton now the bookie's favourites to walk down Wembley way it was a serious blow to their hopes when the Rovers took a 18th minute lead through a Peter Dobing header.

Bolton were spluttering, stalling and misfiring with no rhythm to their play so it came as a big surprise in the 38th minute to the watching throng when Gubbins rounded keeper Leyland to equalise with the Blackburn defence routed to the spot claiming offside. It was only Bolton's rugged determination that had kept them in the game up to this moment. When a Banks free kick was expertly controlled and dispatched by Gubbins beyond the keeper 60 seconds later an amazing pendulum swing in the game had occurred.

Bolton emerged for the second half a more vibrant outfit with inside forwards Stevens and Parry more to the fore offensively but the team never quite got out of second gear. However it was the hustle, bustle and tough tackling of the Bolton defenders thwarting any potential Blackburn threats that enabled the pride of Bolton to hold their 2-1 lead until the final whistle.

Every Bolton player knew they had stolen through by the seat of their pants.

The team were thoroughly delighted to now know they would be visiting the twin towers although they also acknowledged that a much improved performance would be required at Wembley.

Modest match winner Ralph Gubbins declared he was so glad he had been able to help the boys through although he knew that come the final, if fit.... "Lofty" would lead the line.

Ralph, never a first team regular is always fondly remembered by the Bolton fans for his 90 minutes of fame that propelled the team over the last hurdle leading to the final showdown.

After changing big John Higgins hid his face in mock disgrace, and Roy Hartle conceded to the waiting press that they had not been very good but Wembley beckoned.

Tommy Banks ever the realist declared,

"If uz con geet throu semi wi tha'display,ah'm certin Bowtons name's onth'cup"

(If we can play so badly yet still win the semi final I'm sure we will now win the cup)

The tragic Munich Air Disaster earlier in February 1958 had made Manchester United the team everyone else, apart from the people of Bolton, wanted to win that final. If not Bolton, no matter who the other cup finalists would have been that season practically the whole country and abroad would have been rooting for the Reds.

Bolton players did not take the feelings personally they empathised with the situation having known many of the victims off as well as on the field.

The Bolton players conceded they would be the "make weights" in the publicity stakes in all bar the local papers leading up to the final and this caused them to jokingly refer to themselves as "The other team"

Many of the Bolton lads used to associate off the field with the United and Manchester City players usually on a Saturday night particularly in the Cromford Club in Manchester.

A good mate of Tommy's, Les Berry owned a big van with large sliding doors on either side which they used to travel in after rendezvousing at The Railway Public house at Moses Gate. Tommy was amazed how they all got into that van there were so many of them, it was like the animals entering the ark he thinks some lads went right through and out the other side.

All sorts of individuals from various walks of life infiltrated the late evening scenes of Manchester's city centre. John Higgins seemed to know most by name, the lovable centre half introduced one or two dubious gangster style characters to Tommy. One such stranger told Tommy he was going to place a large bet on Bolton losing a forthcoming game and offered him a small fortune to see it happen.

"Ah ses sling thee hook tha's tawkin t' wrong mon 'ere"
(I told him to forget it he was talking to the wrong man I was not interested in any bribery)

Much fuss was made over the disposal and distribution of the wad of Wembley tickets each player was allocated, each man did his own thing!

Big John thought he was on a winner giving his bulk to a Manchester gangster to bring home a pot of gold that's still today somewhere over the rainbow...the money never transpired.

Tommy made sure all his family were looked after then him and "Slim" left their remainder with a "good sort" who rewarded them with a nice little earner. This fellow they trusted to move them on sensibly rather than sell them to any touts because they could possibly have been traced back to the players. They did not wish for any unwanted publicity that may have ensued in the national newspapers.

Bolton's No. 8 at Wembley, Dennis Stevens, was the cousin of the colossus Duncan Edwards who died later from injuries sustained in the Munich Air Disaster.

Tommy was never in any doubt that Bolton would win the final they had rarely lost in the local derby encounters over the previous four seasons and had beaten the "Busby Babes" 4-0 at Burnden Park in the September of 1957.

Bolton usually stayed at the Great Western Hotel near Paddington Station when playing in the capital. However because it was the one off of "Wembley" it seemed for once, money was no object to Bolton, and they lodged at Hendon Hall the recognised England team head quarters.

Relaxing in the hotel foyer on the Friday night Tommy was chatting to a group of wealthy American business men who basically knew nothing about football or the history of the F.A. Cup at Wembley. Tommy had no doubts whatsoever that Bolton would win the cup even though they had won only one of their ten league games leading up to the final since the semis. He knew that the vital ingredient of luck had played a small part at important times in the York and Wolves games and he was 100% convinced it was Bolton's year letting all and sundry know his feelings.

"If tha' wannts t' mek sum big munny geet thee houses un alluv thee yachts un Bowton t'win cup wi bookies cum morn" Tommy said to the Americans.

(Tommy told the businessmen to invest heavily with the bookmakers on Saturday for Bolton to win the Cup)

Although he did not show it Tommy said he found it to be an emotional day, Wembley generates pride and passion. All professional footballers dream of playing in the F.A. Cup Final, he had carried his dream since being a very young child.

Bolton Wanderers v Manchester United; 3rd May 1958

Bolton Wanderers;
Hopkinson; Hartle; Banks; Hennin; Higgins; Edwards; Birch; Stevens; Lofthouse; Parry; Holden

Manchester United;
Gregg; Foulkes; Greaves; Goodwin; Cope; Crowther; Dawson; Taylor; Charlton; Violet; Webster

100,000 fans greeted the players as they made their way down the tunnel, Bolton were at Wembley for the fifth time in their history.

Bolton were the winners of the historical first every cup final at Wembley known as the "White horse" final of 1923.

This was owing to policeman's horse "Billy's" ability to gently manoeuvre some of the reported crowd of over 200,000 back behind the playing arena. Bolton also proved successful in 1926 and 1929 before defeat in the final minutes of a seven goal thriller in the "Matthews final" of "53" against Blackpool.

The noise of the crowd could barely be heard in the dressing rooms but leaving the tunnel it hit like an oncoming hurricane, the atmosphere was great and Tommy knew Bolton were in good shape and well prepared for the match. Nat Lofthouse and Dougie Holden picked up losers medals against Blackpool in 1953, there was to be no repeat if ambitions were to be achieved. Public sympathy had to be put to one side as this time Bolton were determined to lift the trophy.

Tommy thought the game flew by, half time arrived and the Bolton goal did not seem to have really been threatened. Lofty had converted a pass from "Slim" inside the first three minutes into a goal to settle any unwanted nerves and the team was ticking over comfortably.

The tireless and talented Stevens and Parry plus the boundless energy of Hennin ensured Bolton had a firm grip in the middle of the park on the course of the match. Bolton were doing all the pressing and moving the ball around well on Wembley's maximum size playing arena.

United came out displaying more urgency after the half time break.

Within ten minutes Bobby Charlton unleashed one of his specials that hit a post but with 'Hoppy' frozen to the spot the ball fortuitously rebounded into the keeper's arms. Bolton immediately went down the other end and scored again to go 2-0 up. When it came it was a goal that would be extremely controversial if given today. Harry Gregg had just caught a Stevens's shot he had initially palmed into the air and he was nudged by a 'Lofty' shoulder charge that took him over the goal line to put Bolton two in front.

Tommy concedes that the second goal may have been disallowed today,

"Futbawls neaw leek a non contek sport"

(Football's now nearly a non contact sport)

The game lacked the intensity of the Wolves match petering out with an alleged head butt on Dennis Stevens by Webster the only really other incident of the second half. On the final whistle, the jubilant Bolton players realised that a possible once in a lifetime ambition had been achieved. Very few players in their careers, even many so called stars through the decades had played, never mind won an F.A. Cup medal at Wembley. After Nat received the Cup, the players collected their medals and descended the steps from the Royal box.

Roy Hartle turned to Tommy Banks asking his fellow full back what were his plans for the rest of this momentous day?

"Cum on Roy, uz'll mek fer dressin'rooms weer dun un dust'd" replied Tommy

(I thought that's it, the summits been achieved let's get changed)

Seeing the pair of warrior like defenders heading south wily old Bert Sproston chimed up,

"Where are you two going, get yourselves around that track enjoy your lap of honour you deserve it, it will live with you forever"

Tommy soon discovered that Bert was correct the atmosphere generated by the Bolton fans on greeting the players on their victory walk was electric. The outpouring of joy from the fans made him feel so immensely proud, the occasion so very special.

Once back in the Bolton changing room the frivolity stopped for a brief period when United's manager Matt Busby, who had been badly injured in the Munich disaster, slowing strode in walking with the aid of a stick. He generously congratulated the winning team shaking the hand of every player and member of the Bolton staff. After Matt had gingerly limped out through the door Tommy respectfully remarked to his hushed team-mates,

"Matt's feenest sportsmon allus wilta ever sin"
(Matt's the finest sportsman we will ever see)

On Matt's departure, champagne corks began popping and Bill Ridding delves into his pocket and comes up with an illegal payment to Lofty. It is the pound the centre forward won when he bet a few weeks ago from his hospital bed that he would recover from his shoulder operation in time to lead the team. It is a pound that will never be spent, Nat intends to frame it and keep it with his England caps and medals that would hold the memories of his career.

How fitting that the man known in the football world as "Mr. Bolton Wanderers" should score the two goals that secured victory for the "Trotters."

The Wanderers achievement that day in May now rests serenely in the annals of football history.

As often seems to happen on Cup Final day at Wembley the game never quite lived up to the pre-match hype. Bolton had many good performers that afternoon with the Manchester United lads below par; the newspaper scribes gave top billing to Tommy Banks.

There was still little to no football shown on television in "58" players were just names that the man in the street/across the nation read about in the daily papers or heard about on the radio.

Outside of Bolton Tommy was viewed as a combative, reliable defender who read the game well. The Wembley showcase highlighted his intelligent intervention and constructive inventive passing allied to his close control to the watching millions. Whilst always enjoying a tackle, without question he possessed a range of strengths within his own game that made up his fine all round ability.

The watching England manager Walter Winterbottom must also have been suitable impressed by this steely competitor.

Tommy was thus called up to join the England party two days later in quite bizarre circumstances via his journey home from London.

Wanderers..."The other team" in a final drenched in public tears had triumphed.

Wanderers, a side built on an insistence that they could take on the world and survive driven by a spirit that would not be quashed were the victors.

Tommy's own........Team Mate pen pictures
Tommy's pen picture assessment of his 1958 Cup Final team mates

EDDIE HOPKINSON; 1956-70; 578 games; 14 England caps
"This mon useter gee 'ees teeth sum hommer"
(Eddie used to have more than plenty to say)

By heck Hoppy could talk and shout when he was playing, he never made a mistake in his own eyes. The ball could roll through his legs into the goal and he would "chunner" blaming anyone within his sight, we all used to just turn away to avoid an ear bashing.

He was also a buoyant friendly guy with a roller coaster personality that helped feed the dressing room banter and he took and gave his fair share of stick in good part.

Quite an amazing keeper, he was elastic with what appeared extra long arms to assist his 5 feet 9 inch frame, brave and tenacious he radiated confidence.

Eddie excelled at every facet of the keeper's art but his speciality was dealing with one on one situations. As a forward bore down on him he would stand up until the very last possible moment then spread himself as the opponent attempted to jink past him ..... only a few were successful.

Hoppy was a good mate who would simmer down at half time with a couple of draws on a cigarette!

ROY HARTLE; 1952-66; 499 games 13 goals
"Meyt Dr. Jeykll un Mr. Hyde, Roy wer a mean mon onth'fee"
(Roy's a lovely man but he was a changed character once he was on a football field, very aggressive)

Off the pitch you could not meet a pleasanter nicer chap, well dressed, extremely polite and he "tawk'd proper" a Bromsgrove lad from the Midlands he came north in 1952 and stayed.

Known to the fans as "Chopper"(the original) although Dennis Stevens

117

always referred to him by his Sunday name of Royston. Once he crossed the touchline with his Bolton strip on Roy was a ruthless, uncompromising and ultra determined character.

A big strong lad for a fullback he would thunder into wingers with his massive legs, pick them up then let them know who was boss next time they received the ball.

A good friend throughout the past and present, we often share a laugh today.

TOMMY BANKS 1946-1961; 255 games 2 goals; 6 England caps

I loved to be constructive and pass the ball, in all of my career at Bolton I was only booked once in a game for dissent, I was never sent off.

Referees were much more lenient, it was a man's game the art of tackling played a big part in gaining supremacy. I was partial to a sliding tackle plus clattering an opponent put a bit of fear and intimidation into them, it put doubts in their mind.

I used to speak to the winger on kick off,

"Owdust thee wannit rough or smooth"
(Give me no trouble and you're in for a nice peaceful game)

Occasionally I realised I had overstepped the legal mark with my tackles but you could speak to refs and most warmed to a bit of off the cuff humour. I had connected with one opponent, slightly mistiming my slide tackle and his momentum took him off the pitch onto the track around Burnden Park although he did kiss the gravel on his way down cushioning his fall, saving his knees! I could see the ref was racing over to confront me so raising my arms as though I was surrendering I said,

"Sorry ref that's worse takkel ah've 'er made,"

The ref was by now almost nose to nose with Tommy so his features were blatantly obvious,
"Owdonabit that's worse 'aircut ah've 'er sin ah ses" pointing to his head,
(Just one moment please I said, I am not impressed with your haircut)

"Werrit dun bi ceawncil wi edgecutters, thi's a big chunk missin o'er thee reet ear"
(Did you really go to a barber's shop because it looks more like the council

workmen have used hedging shears, you have a big piece of hair missing over your right ear)

Thankfully he (and most refs) had a sense of humour and let me off with a stern warning although I could not look him in the eye when he was telling me off for fear of laughing at his haircut.

DEREK HENNIN; 1952-61; 183 games 9 goals

Derek looked physical slightly awkward and ungainly due to his knock knees but he was very fit.

He could train and run all day endlessly, he was an excellent trainer, great team man and the side's unsung hero. Derek was not the most gifted of players however he possessed magnificent athleticism, a fearsome tackle, plus great grit and he was very popular.

One of a few quiet lads in the team, still with Higgins, 'Hoppy' and me forever 'tawkin' it balanced out otherwise no bugger would have been heard.

He was a good professional, Derek turned out at centre forward in emergences scoring a hat-trick against Aston Villa on one such occasion.

I organised a double skipping rope jump contest between the lads and thought I would walk it. I managed over 60 with no-one else close then up steps Henny and we had to stop him once he reached 85 otherwise he might still be jumping now.

"Ah ses,wheers thi geet alluv thum fro,ah'd thee deawn fer abeawt six"
(I said to Derek, how have you managed all those jumps you have really surprised me I did not expect more than six from you.)

JOHN HIGGINS; 1952-61; 202 games

Big Higgy was a warm lovable guy always with a cheery smile on his face until he stepped onto a field of play where his strength and commitment were first class.

John lived life to the full, he would have a go at any other sport; low golf handicap, good crown green bowler, snooker player, cricketer and darter, he could play poker all night and still train ok the next morning. He also thought he could sing like Frank Sinatra, regularly bending our ear holes although I enjoyed a few duo's with him to entertain the lads.

John was always ready for a jape and his outgoing spirit endeared him to everyone who met him. A colossus he was a better footballer than often given credit for... his first priority was to be our rock and solid he was, it took forwards an age to circumnavigate his bulky frame.

I used to say to him,

"Higgy thee shudave bi inth' Olympics thi con do 100 yards in 10 minutes" (Quickness wasn't one of John's best attributes)

BRYAN EDWARDS; 1950-65; 518 games 9 goals

My best pal in the team, "Slim" also a tad quiet was a typical George Taylor player.

He loved defending he had more cuts and stitches than boxer Henry Cooper from heading the back of an opponents "yed"

At 6 feet plus he was decent in the air few got the better of him and decisive in the tackle, erring on the side of caution with the ball I was always cajoling him,

"Let mi 'ave bawl Slim ah'll passit fer thee"

(Slim give the ball to me I'll use it to construct)

Slim played over 500 games and gave the club 15 years service without receiving a testimonial. He was a solid steady player not good enough for England, however Tommy reckons Slim would have got into any team that England selected for eating.

He obtained the nicknamed 'Slim' because he never put on any weight even though he was a profound eater, whilst 'Higgy' only had to look at food and the pounds would pile on.

BRIAN BIRCH; 1954-64; 191 games 28 goals

Brian was still a part time pro and the youngest in the team at 19, he was something of an elusive character because once he had made the first team we hardly saw him due to his two years of National Service. He would train all week at his airbase in Yorkshire and appear on match days but his natural ability helped him quickly settle into the team pattern.

Brian was still a baby in football terms and relatively quiet amongst the players, on the field he was direct, sharp enough without being rapid possessing a good shot in both feet and grabbed a few goals.

For a short spell Birch appeared lethargic and very under the weather and he was sent by the club to have blood tests conducted and to see a specialist. On his return to Bolton he told the half a dozen players left in the dressing room after training that he had to have more malt.

"Ah towd im geet sum more vinegar on thee chips"
(I said Brian if you need to take malt put more vinegar on your chips)

DENNIS STEVENS; 1953-1962; 310 games 101 goals; England U23's

Dennis was the youngest of 12 children brought up in Dudley, Wolverhampton

"Stevie wer fust Duracell bunny"
(Dennis never stopped running)

Dennis would run forever, all and every game and could he play, he was a bundle of dynamite a player who never stopped working for the team. He was full of desire and grit never being short of encouraging words. He could look after himself on the field he was teak tough and possessed bags of ability.

Even in a beach football kick about on holiday in Newquay Dennis couldn't resist a challenge and his winning mentality resulted in a few waiters limping in carrying the main course that evening.

1966 World Cup winner and Farnworth's other favourite son Alan Ball said he based his own non stop style on Dennis his favourite footballer from his junior days when watching from the Burnden Park terraces.

Dennis was the "pin up boy" of the team you couldn't get past him for wenches flocking around him after the games,

"Lucky boy," thought Tommy

NAT LOFTHOUSE OBE; 1946-60; 503 games 285 goals; 33 England caps 30 goals

"Nat wer one o'uz a top mon wi a wick'd sense o'humour 'ee fully deserv'd 'ees Lion of Vienna tag 'ee shirk'd nowt"

(Nat was one of the lads he possessed a great sense of humour and he fully deserved his Lion of Vienna title he was so brave and fearless)

He was hewn from oak and although only just over 5 feet 9 inches he was built and ran like a steam train, it was like hitting a brick wall when challenging him.

Nat led from the front he was the team's talismanic leader, goals were his cause, his name sent shivers through opposing centre halves when the teams were announced. Nat an old fashioned centre forward was an archetypal human battering ram who created havoc and plundered goals. He had a magical average of a goal in less than every 2 games for Bolton and 30 in 33 for England which were tremendous feats.

If he was playing against me on "The Gravels" he would say

"Banky I'm going to wear my shinguards on of my calves today."

His body took an awesome pounding, he had outstanding aerial ability propelled by a prodigious leap and complemented his pace and power with explosion in both boots, only injuries and operations prevented him from adding to his goal tally.

George Taylor used to say to Nat,

"Lofty you can run, head and shoot, the rest of the lads will provide the ammo you fire it."

RAY PARRY; 1951-61; 299 games 79 goals; 2 England caps

Ray was a very stylist dresser, always looked like he came straight out of Burton's window, he became a trendsetter back in the late 1950's; he was also a perfectionist when he played football.

I could always find Ray with a pass if I was in trouble,

"Gi it 'ere Tommy ah'll 'ave it"
(Ray always wanted the ball he always seemed in space available to receive)

He would always have a twinkle in his eye, he loved a bit of fun and he was much cherished by the lads. Ray had a brilliant left foot, he would caress the ball around the park with great accuracy and like Dennis Stevens put a full shift in every game and what a hammer of a shot he had scoring many goals.

He could have signed autographs with his left foot!

DOUGIE HOLDEN; 1950-62; 463 games 44 goals; 5 England caps

A true gentleman, a lovely man, extremely quiet a bit like a church mouse, you would not have known he was in the dressing room.

"Another mon thi cud gi bawl to anyweer un 'ee'd keppit,"
(Dougie was another player you could always pass to with confidence)

I used to shout "Owdit Owden" and he would instantly control the ball and be off teasing the full back with his dribbling ability.

He was a classic winger, not the quickest but a ball playing tricky player who could beat a man either way and manufactured a yard of space out of thin air to cross out for Lofty. He played for England five times in 1959 and but for the presence of Finney and Matthews would have won many more caps.

RALPH GUBBINS; 1952-59; 101 games 18 goals

"Ralph was a real gent, impeccable manners, always smart."

"If thee 'ad a teenage dowter thi wannt 'er t'meyt this mon"
(Ralph was the kind of guy you would like your teenage daughter to meet)

He was an intelligent footballer, lacked a yard of pace but could find and use space.

With his extreme versatility it allowed him to play in every one of the forwards positions during his Bolton days.

Ralph's goals saw us home in the semi final but he did not fuss or make an issue of being 12th man at Wembley even though he never received a Cup Final winner's medal.

....

Tommy's descriptions acknowledge what a tightly knit bunch that Bolton team was, no superstars apart from Nat and he did not act like one. They revelled in each other's company and the mix of personalities blended into a one for all fighting outfit, team spirit was everything; it won them games.

Here was a bunch of lads possessing tremendous solidarity and fierce determination.

No-one was going to become rich on their pay but self esteem mattered deeply. Just knowing they had given their all for the team after every ninety minutes meant they could look themselves in the mirror with pride.

Loyal ... Every one of these lads gave the best years of their career to Bolton Wanderers!

Chapter 13

Stop the Train

After the euphoria of the F.A. Cup win at Wembley, Tommy was sat back enjoying the return train journey home with his Bolton team mates, when he heard his name being called.

"Thomas Banks, Thomas Banks, where is Thomas Banks" shouted a seemingly irate railway official.

The Station Master had just entered the train at the Rugby station and was making his way through the train carriages he had boarded. Monday's London to Manchester midday train had just been flagged down to the bemusement of all aboard to make an unscheduled stop in the Midlands.

"Az oer 'ere what dust thi wannt wi mi, thee's geein t' teeth sum hommer" Tommy retorted.

(I'm over here what do you want with me, you are doing a lot of talking.)

Tommy was extremely concerned, only his mother and wife called him Thomas, Manchester should have been the next stop.

"You have got to return to London on the orders of the Football Association", came the sheepish reply from the stationmaster somewhat taken aback by Tommy's robust words.

"Artshoorothat owd fettler,ah wer cawed gooin wom wi mi mates" said the surprised footballer.

(Are you sure of that my friend, I was supposed to be going home with my mates.)

"Yes, here is a telegram that came through to the station within the last half an hour we have had to force the train to make an emergency stop to get you re-routed."

Tommy asked to look at the paper fearing that one of his team mates had set him up to enjoy a laugh. Initially he was questioning if the stationmaster was for real, but sure enough the telegram words appeared genuine.

The Football Association had summoned him back to London for training with the England World Cup squad and to attend a friendly against Portugal at Wembley on the 7th May prior to the 1958 tournament in Sweden later in June.

The Bolton players had enjoyed long hours rejoicing over the weekend in London after winning the Cup Final and were now on route back to a town hall reception in Bolton via the inter city express.

After the Wembley game, there was a pre arranged club dinner on the Saturday evening at the Café Royal to be attended by the players and wives and all employees of the club plus other dignitaries invited at the behest of the directors. Tommy was surprised to see so many people at the dinner, people who were not employed by the club, people he had never previously seen at Bolton games.

Later that night after the official reception, the players went out en-bloc to a pre-arranged venue in London to celebrate their victory at a club they had organised during a trip to the capital a few weeks earlier to play a league fixture.

However when they arrived at London's Celebrity Club it was overflowing with Bolton fans who must have heard of the arrangements and attended in their droves. Therefore although the fans inside were waiting to greet the team the nightclub manager said it was full to the door and graciously and respectfully spoke of safety issues.

Nat Lofthouse suggested that returning to enjoy a good drink in the hotel bar would therefore be the best option to finish the day in style for the team.

Bill Ridding had given them just fifty pounds to take out all their wives and girlfriends. The money was soon spent and the next thing Tommy knew champagne had been ordered and a tab created under the club's name.

The atmosphere was bubbling so to give the lads a laugh he drank it out of his wife Maggie's shoe. Good champagne is not cheap anywhere and it was London prices so Bill Ridding was not impressed the next morning when the hotel manager thrust a considerable bar bill into his hand.

Tommy thought a bit of humour was called for so he took a fiver from his top pocket and waved it at Bill,

"Ow much werrit Bill, ah wannt mi change bakk"
(How much is it Bill, I want my change back.)

The club had made a handsome profit because of the Wembley success yet in Tommy's opinion the lads who played the game were being chastised over a few pounds.

When the players had arrived back late in the evening at the hotel for their drink to complete their Wembley day, chief coach George Taylor was just going to bed, so was George Hunt the assistant coach, or so they thought.

George Taylor was a good singer, the team choirmaster, he knew every song going.

"Worraneet, areet purler,ahm not coddin, ah'm tellin thee itwer beltin" enthused Tommy.
(We had a great night it really was one to savour, etched in my memory)

A few of the team had their breakfast around 5 o'clock in the morning, Nat, John Higgins and Tommy never went to bed, too late then the next day was dawning.

As Tommy trundled off the train at Rugby, he was pleased in a back handed way to be called up by England, but also deeply gutted to miss what turned out to be never to be forgotten homecoming scenes. He now realised that he would not be able to be with his team mates due to be welcomed home by the Bolton fans drunk on success later that day on the Bolton Town Hall steps.

Only eight of the players who performed so heroically at Wembley alighted at the London Road station in Manchester. Tommy had been high jacked, 'Hoppy' never left London having been selected for the forthcoming England v Portugal game and young part timer Brian Birch was back with his RAF unit in Yorkshire having been granted extended absence for special training leading up to the big match.

It was a wonderful homecoming, although travelling from the station in Manchester through Salford the open top coach was pelted by tomatoes, flour, eggs and sods of earth. Once the winners had safely passed through "cheyenne" territory smiling faces were awaiting at the Kearsley border. Fans lined the streets all the way through Farnworth down the famous Manny (Manchester) Road passed Burnden Park into Bolton's town centre.

It did not matter to the players whether the flour and eggs had hit home or not they were happy, they had won and would soon be greeted by a massive throng on the Town Hall steps, plus they were due a win bonus.

"Abeawt ten grand each mon," laughed Tommy,
(About ten thousand pounds each)
"Hundred quid inth' trowser pokkit wer awe'l uz geet,"
(A hundred pound was the winning bonus)

Money was not important that day.
It came a long way third to the team spirit that the lads had generated over time and the achievement of winning the F.A. Cup for the people of Bolton.

126

The slow moving coach was saluted by thousands of ecstatic folk witnessing the nearest thing to the passing of Halley's comet it seemed that long since the club had last won anything of note, in fact the same F.A. Cup back in 1929.

"Trotters" supporters sought every vantage point they could find to salute their heroes. The mass of folk jammed so tightly that they filled the Town Hall square and way beyond as the Bolton cup winning team, minus Tommy, Hoppy and Birchy were welcomed home by the Mayor to unforgettable and memorable scenes.

Tommy might not have made the Bolton Town Hall steps but his mother was there to be greeted by the Mayor. After learning of the reason why her son was missing Mrs. Banks said,

"Never mind if he gets into the England team it will make up for tonight's disappointment"

With the World Cup on the horizon, the world was at his feet, not bad for a clog wearer from Farnworth.

The year of 1958 was indeed set to be the highlight of Tommy's football career...

Burnden Park queues were a familiar sight in the 1950's.

Cycling back to fitness after injury!

Pounding the track in inclement weather: Stevens, Lofthouse, Banks & Parry.

1958 Celebrated victory over Wolves: Lofthouse, Higgins, Hennin.

1958 The epic Wolves quarter final.

The gruesome twosome; Banks & Hartle (insert).

*1958 Wembley bound: l–r frogs; Holden, Gubbins, Banks.
l–r obstacles; Hennin, Edwards, Hartle.*

*Frontrunners; The Magnificent 7: l–r; Edwards, Banks, Hartle,
Stevens, Higgins, Hennin, Lofthouse.*

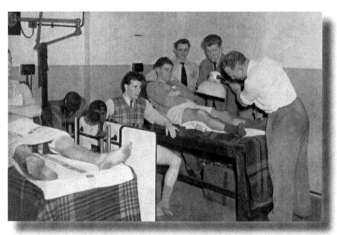

*Treatment room:
Stevens, Banks,
Bannister,
Barnard,
Sproston.*

BWFC Caricatures 1958.

1958 F.A. Cup Final, Bolton v Manchester United. Banks, Hopkinson, Higgins & Edwards look on anxiously.

Post match celebration dinner at the Cafe Royal, London.

1958 F.A. Cup Winners.
  Back row l–r: Hartle, Higgins, Edwards, Hopkinson, Hennin, Banks, Sproston.
  Front row l–r: Birch, Stevens, Lofthouse, Ridding, Parry, Holden, Gubbins.

BWFC Staff: Ridding, Sproston, Taylor, Hunt.

Disgruntled Manchester United fans bombard the Bolton team with eggs, flour and sods whilst transporting the F.A. Cup on route to Bolton.

Tommy Banks slides in to thwart Bobby Charlton at Wembley.

Tommy alongside Bill Ridding at Wembley.

The jubilant Wanderers team arrive at Bolton's town hall square.

Bolton fans welcome the F.A. Cup winners home.

First caps; Lenin Stadium, Moscow 1958; l-r McDonald, Shepherdson (coach), Banks, Clamp.

England 1958 World Cup squad.
Back row l-r: Hopkinson, Howe, Clayton, Clamp, Finney, Robson, Douglas, McDonald, Kevan, Brabrook, Smith, Haynes.
Front row l-r: A'Court, Norman, Slater, Wright, Charlton, Sillett, Broadbent, Banks.

1960 George Taylor expressing a point with a young Francis Lee peeping over Roy Hartle's shoulder.

Burnden Park 1984; This is similar to the view that would have faced 16 years old Francis Lee back in 1960 when he attempted to throw a golf ball over the far Burnden Stand from out of the players tunnel to win a bet for Tommy Banks.

Braziers defrosting the pitch, typical method in the 1950's.

1958 Civvy street: l-r Edwards, Parry, Holden, Banks, Higgins, Stevens, Hennin, Gubbins, Lofthouse, Hartle.

Posing in Zuiderzee, Holland.
Back row l-r: Codd, Pilling, Higgins, Banks, Hennin, Edwards, sportswriter
Hayden Berry.
Front row l-r: Stevens, Neill, Sproston.

BWFC 1959 South Africa tour; Lofthouse, Higgins, Banks at forefront.

Chapter 14

World Cup Build Up

Arriving back in London to meet up with the England 1958 World Cup squad, Tommy soon realised he was back at the same hotel that he had left earlier on Monday morning May 5th, before boarding the train to return to the north with his Bolton colleagues.

Walter Winterbottom the England team manager was waiting in the hotel's reception to greet him has he arrived that evening, but Tommy spoke first.

"Thees a bonny bugger Walter"
(What's going on Walter?)

"Sorry Tommy for your travel inconvenience, I decided late this morning to bring you down to join the squad, different to my original plans. I was very impressed with your display at the Cup Final on Saturday and I wanted you here with all the other players for Tuesday morning's session." was the reply from the England manager.

England had a friendly with Portugal at Wembley on Wednesday May 7th. Tommy had been told prior to the Cup Final on the 3rd May, that he would not be considered for this match. However he was now to be part of the England party in attendance. Bolton's Eddie Hopkinson had remained in London after enjoying the F.A. Cup celebrations he did not leave the capital, unlike Tommy!

'Hoppy' had been informed the week previous that he would be keeping goal in the Portugal game barring injury in the Cup Final and at that moment in time looked the firm favourite for the No.1 position in the World Cup.

Tommy now knew he definitely featured in Walter's World Cup plans. He also realised that if he been told earlier in the morning he could have stayed in bed and not have had to travel backwards and forwards like a fiddler playing a violin.

Walter Winterbottom had informed Tommy a couple of months prior to the Munich air disaster on the 6th February 1958 that he was in his thoughts for the World Cup squad in Sweden. He was told if selected he would be going as likely cover for Roger Byrne the Manchester United and current England left back, although other players were also under consideration.

Sadly Roger Byrne was one of eight Manchester United players and twenty three travellers in total to lose their lives due to the plane crash that fateful day.

Tommy aged 28 had no England caps to his name, but was that to change with the England team scheduled to play a few international games in quick succession?

England won their international against Portugal 2-1 at Wembley on the 7th May although it was an all round disappointing display.... Jimmy Langley of Fulham occupied the left back position.

England had trained at the Bank of England sports ground on the Tuesday before the Portugal game. Players were informed this day if they would be part of the England party departing for international games in Belgrade and Moscow in the build up to the World Cup in June. On Friday 9th May twenty players including Tommy Banks plus England staff flew out of London bound for Belgrade.

When Walter Winterbottom announced the team to play against Yugoslavia on the 11th May Tommy found out, that much to his dismay, Jimmy Langley had kept the left back shirt.

The Munich disaster had cost Winterbottom the services of a number of Manchester United players notably, Duncan Edwards, Roger Byrne and Tommy Taylor causing the England team to be in somewhat of a transitional stage. These three players already had 70 caps between them with many more football years in front of them, Byrne at 27 years old being the oldest.

Tommy felt the England manager was searching for a settled team that with the benefit of games under their belt would quickly gel together. His hopes of making the World Cup starting eleven had suffered a jolt with this team selection. Time was quickly running out for him to show his worth by making an international appearance.

His chances looked very dicey, after Yugoslavia there was only one more fixture pending against Russia in Moscow, prior to Sweden, to convince the selectors that he was the man for the job.

Would he be given the opportunity?

A good display against Yugoslavia from Jimmy Langley, Tommy knew that the Fulham man would most likely play again in Moscow, and possibly his fate would be sealed! Langley was a decent player but in Tommy's eyes not good enough to be picked in front of him for England.

"Ow dust thee geet pick'd 'fore mi, ah'm tellin thee ah'm afther thi shop" he bluntly told Langley.

(Tommy thought he should have been the choice to play left back and duly informed Jimmy Langley)

From the very start of the Yugoslavia game things went badly wrong for England.

In the radio box at the top of the Army Stadium, one of the few spots where there was any shade, the thermometer soared to 96 degrees. These conditions were a million miles away from those found in the usual English playing arenas and for once Tommy was grateful to be a spectator. On the field the heat must have been oven-like and England soon found out they were the turkeys bound for it.

Eddie Hopkinson, Bolton's goalkeeper was beaten early doors and three more goals were chalked off for offside. The weary England team despite being over run had somehow managed to make the sanctuary of the dressing rooms at half time only a goal to the worse. One nil soon became two early in the second half before finally the defence completely collapsed. Three more goals followed in quick succession and England sank with hardly a gun fired in return.

The recriminations of this 5-0 drumming were considerable!

Winterbottom spoke angrily about a team that did not fight, whilst Mr. J.H. Mears Chelsea chairman and chairman of the English selectors promised several changes before the team played Russia. In the outcome Hopkinson, Langley, Ronnie Clayton and Bobby Charlton shouldered the blame for the result. It seemed to appear that Winterbottom was starting to mould the team again at the 11th hour!!

When Tommy Banks was picked to play for England against Russia in Moscow he also knew that the elements had been very kind to him by playing a big part in his selection. The intense heat so very uncommon to English playing conditions had been a major factor in Belgrade. He thought the English management had not totally given full credence in the post game assessment to just how sapping of energy this was without being given adequate pre match days to acclimatise.

Also Langley's personal cause was not helped when Aleksander Petakovic the flying Yugoslavia right winger scored three of the goals.

So after one more day in Belgrade the party flew off to Moscow, via Budapest, in the Soviets' relatively new Giant Jet of the Skies the TU 104A. When this jet had landed in London in 1956 Western observers where shocked by its advanced technology which they did not think secretive Russia was capable of building. Inside it was extremely plush; luxury decorating a plane was quite unknown in this day and age, with lavish "Victorian" trimmings of mahogany, copper and lace.

"Ah thout ut time ah'd board'd t'Orient Express itwer reet posh" recalls Tommy.

(I thought at the time I had boarded the Orient Express train the plane was so luxurious.)

The Lenin Stadium was situated in a superb sports complex including a ski jump, indoor ice rink, and a number of football training pitches. The Russians had constructed this multi functional supreme sporting arena endeavouring to win the vote to stage the 1960 Olympics, unfortunately for them this did not come to fruition until 1980.

Tommy could sense that the eleven English lads chosen to play had already captured a positive outlook to wipe out in Moscow the memories of Belgrade. When an emphatic defeat is suffered, the next game for any professional is extremely important in terms of morale and confidence. Steeliness and determination were going to be vitally needed to be shown in Moscow to demonstrate that England had the necessary bulldog spirit in their quest to win the 1958 World Cup.

There were two other new caps alongside Tommy on the 11th May in the huge and magnificent Lenin stadium with seating for all of the 104,000 spectators. Colin McDonald of Burnley was in goal and Eddie Clamp of Wolves at right half. Bobby Robson later to become the England manager in the early playing days of Paul "Gazza" Gascoigne was restored to the inside right position to hopefully help blend the attacking play more fluently.

Russia in 1958 was virtually unknown to Westerners and Khrushchev had been installed as recently as March of that year as the new Premier of the Soviet Union. Few travellers were allowed into the country and most realistically did not feel the need by choice to visit this powerful Communist state. Only a couple of years previously the Russians had put down an Hungarian uprising that attempted to overturn its communist enforcers, thirty thousand people were never seen again !

As soon as the England party stepped off the plane they were followed everywhere by the inquisitive KGB, Russia's secret police, guns and all!

It was the equivalent of "man for man" marking all the time until they departed for British shores.

One of the KGB guys kept pestering Tommy asking to buy the suit he was wearing. The Russian would have looked good, Tommy's 5' 7" tall the Russian must have been 6' 4".

"Britches wudave favvor'd heawf mast leek sum mons deed" laughed Tommy
(My trousers would have finished high up his legs way above his shoes like a flag at half mast when someone's died)

"Ah ses thee munny's nar gud,ah cawnt bey a bag o'chips in Farn'urth wi tha"
(I told him that the Russian currency wasn't very strong)

Big Derek Kevan, a robust strong striker, was preferred to Brian Clough "the people's choice" to lead the attack. It was a Kevan header just before half time past the legendary Lev Yashin nicknamed "the black spider" owing to the all black outfit that he always wore, that gave England a well deserved one goal lead.

Tommy thought the Hungarian referee who had possibly been appointed for political reasons was beginning to lean far too easy in favour of the Russians on 50-50 challenges and blurted out a mouthful.

"Art thee frikken o'em ah ax'd"
(Are you frightened of the Russians, I asked the referee)

The referee might have heard his comment, however most of the England team could not understand their team mate from Bolton so he imagined the referee had no chance. This game was a rehearsal for the forthcoming group encounter in Sweden. Preston's Tom Finney was a constant thorn in the Russian side and they remembered him well, much too well sadly to his misfortune in the June 8th World Cup match. Russia equalised in the second half but keeper McDonald was rarely threatened thanks to the sterling work of Tommy Banks and his fellow defenders repelling spasmodic breaks.

"Tha noes when tha's play'd weel, tha downt need sum scribe t'tel thee inth' pappers"
(You know when you have had a good game you do not need a reporter to write about your performance in the papers)

The result and moreover the display had galvanised the team, spirits were high as the England party left Moscow's skyscrapers behind and headed back to London.

The team changes had worked and it appeared England's World Cup structure was now standing on reasonably sure foundations.

Chapter 15

World Cup 1958

Fifty three countries had originally entered the qualifying stages of the 1958 World Cup to be staged in June in Sweden. By the time the draw was made on the 9ᵗʰ February in Stockholm by FIFA organising committee, this number was down to sixteen to be made up of four groups of four.

Somehow this FIFA committee had managed, by a strange form of seeding, to put three of the "big guns" Russia, Brazil and England in the same group alongside Austria. It therefore seemed an even stranger decision by the English FA to agree to a friendly in Russia three weeks before the start of the tournament in Sweden.

Did England want to see what Russia had got to offer on the field?

Whatever the reasons the 1-1 draw in Moscow on the 18ᵗʰ May had given a very proud Tommy Banks his first England cap.

Tommy was 28 years and 188 days old that day in May.

Arriving back home in Farnworth, a few days after the Moscow sortie, Tommy found he had time on his hands once again owing to what seemed another strange decision.

He came home with well over a week to kill before going to Sweden and trained by myself on the spare land at Doe Hey near to his home.....surely that would never happen today for the current England players.

It was the English close season and Burnden Park was virtually closed, the staff of Bolton Wanderers missing, enjoying a summer break after their Wembley victory. However, it is hard to imagine today that with the ultimate prestigious competition in the world of football brewing, an England player appeared to have been left by the Football Association to his own devices to maintain peak fitness.

England's opening game was on the 8ᵗʰ June in the pleasant old seaport of Gotesborg on Sweden's west coast where they prepared to face the Russians. The Swedish city proudly called itself "Little London" and the game had captured the imagination of the locals hoping for an English victory.

Walter Winterbottom had no hesitation in naming the same side that had outplayed Russia in Moscow. The Soviets however played cat and mouse, not issuing their line-up until thirty minutes before the kick off. Expecting a last minute "bugle call" speech outlining the battle ahead from Winterbottom just prior to leaving the dressing room the players were surprised when it seemed kit issues were the main concern.

"Remember lads whatever the result do not exchange your shirts at the end of the game with the Russians" said Winterbottom.

Apparently England had only brought one set of white shirts to cover the whole tournament, with red as the alternative, if required, owing to any potential colour clashes.

What a contrast to the modern day player of today who gives them away like confetti.

A sign of one of the changes that time has brought to football.

The watching world regularly sees bare-chested lads leaving the field after the final whistle with a Premiership opponent's shirt slung over their shoulder.

England v Russia; June 8th 1958 at Gotesborg

England Team;

C.McDonald (Burnley); D. Howe (West Bromwich); T. Banks (Bolton); E. Clamp (Wolves); W.Wright (Wolves); W. Slater (Wolves); B. Douglas (Blackburn); R.Robson (West Brom); D.Kevan (West Brom); J. Haynes (Fulham); T.Finney (Preston)
Score; 0-0

Tommy found his immediate opponent was not Apoukhlin the flying winger, who he had contained so well in Moscow, but a full back Andre Ivanov who it seemed had been instructed to assist his own fullback stop the threat of Tom Finney. Tommy was very content because during the game this player never tried to take him on he was more concerned with doubling up in a defensive role to nullify Preston's best.

England made a dismal start and for long periods the 50,000 spectators watched the red shirted Russians dominate the play. A goal down within fourteen minutes and a second, just before the hour mark, seemed to seal the game in Russia's favour.

However the supremely gifted Tom Finney shook off his double marking shackles to be at the forefront of an English revival that saw a Derek Kevan goal give hope to the people of "Little London."

Russia resorted to dubious means to restrain the magnificent Finney who was consistently picking himself up off the floor. It came as no surprise with five minutes to go that Finney converted a penalty after Johnny Haynes was brought down in the penalty area.

The result gave England an essential point towards qualifying from this tough group for the quarter finals stage, but it had been achieved at a severe cost.

The ongoing brutal treatment dished out in this game to Finney, the man Russia feared the most after the friendly in Moscow, resulted in him being forced out of the rest of the tournament through injury.

Tom Finney England's talented floating left winger had sustained a torn muscle behind a knee which would require time to recover. The extent of his loss could not be over estimated, he was one of the few players in the world even at 36 years old who was able to change the course of a game.

"Banky" always expresses his great feeling, fondness and respect for his good friend Tom Finney. Alongside Di Stefano, Tom was his favourite player in the world, a real gentleman and very modest off the field.

Finney's ability was well known, he was mainly left footed but very comfortable with his right, and also a very direct player. He could dance past defenders either way outside or inside, he was quick and strong with a fierce shot in both feet and always put the needs of the team first.

Later in life Tom Finney fittingly became Sir Tom Finney OBE.

Sir Tom played all his 433 league games for Preston North End scoring 187 goals and could, and would play, in any of the five forward positions with effortless success.

Nicknamed the "Preston Plumber" due to learning the family's trade at 14 he also found the net 30 times for England in 76 games.

Tom being comfortable in any of the forward positions was the perfect professional, a maestro who never got booked at any time in his playing career.

Tom Finney drove a tank in the Second World War fighting in Montgomery's 8th army and later covered the vast miles on one command directive from El Alamein in Egypt to Berlin.

He was one of the few players who returned to football in 1946 as though he had never lost a big chunk of his career.

England had to soldier on without their "main man" for the next fixture once again in Gotesborg. They faced the samba skills of Brazil who many pre-tournament pundits had made the favourites to win the World Cup.

England v Brazil; June 11th 1958 at Gotesborg

England Team;

C.McDonald (Burnley); D.Howe (West Brom); T.Banks (Bolton); E.Clamp (Wolves);
W.Wright (Wolves); W.Slater (Wolves); B.Douglas (Blackburn); R.Robson (West Brom)
D.Kevan (West Brom) J.Haynes (Fulham); A.A'Court (Liverpool)
Score; 0-0

On 11th May England ground out a 0-0 draw, with a disciplined defensive display restricting the usual free flowing Brazilians to only a handful of real chances, yet few who witnessed the game could deny it was something of a beauty v beast contest.

It was a game that Tommy had thoroughly enjoyed.... the papers gave Don Howe (right back) and him high credit for their astute covering of centre half Billy Wright and their tactical nous.

In Tommy's case his subtle ability to caress the ball with accuracy, weight and disguise of pass was fully recognised by the watching press.

Prior to the game, Walter Winterbottom was outlining to the English players what he thought would be their opponents' line up. The Brazil team would be selected from a squad possessing numerous quality footballers.

Walter a northerner by birth, but very eloquently spoken relayed his thoughts to Tommy on his immediate opponent the legendary Garrincha.

"Thomas, he is skilful, tricky and very elusive you may have to take appropriate action to prevent him causing us trouble".

Tommy replied, "Yon mon meight pass mi once but next takkel ah'll 'ave 'im off pitch onter cinder trakk, it'll gi 'ees ass a reet gud grittin"

(Garrincha may pass me once but my next tackle will be strong and forceful, he might find himself with a gravel rash on his behind from the surrounding cinder track)

Walter was somewhat taken aback by Tommy's passionately spoken words delivered in his strong Farnworth accent suggesting the course of action he would take if required.

"Er, er, um, yes, yes Thomas something like that" said the stunned England manager.

"Ah'd geer'd misell up t' face Garrincha, cum kick owf owd lad azunt med teem" said Tommy

(I was all set to play against Garrincha, however come the kick off the lad had not made the team.)

Critics had described Garrincha also known as the "little bird" as the Stanley Matthews of South American football. Somewhat knock-kneed in one leg and bow-legged in the other Tommy knew he would have had to have all his wits about him to restrain this elusive wizardry flyer.

Brazil for their own reasons, possibly thinking he was a bit of a maverick, did not release Garrincha into the World Cup battle until their next game against Russia where he created havoc on the right flank in a 2-0 victory. Tommy's immediate opponent was Joel, who although a talented player, did not possess Garrincha's 'off the cuff' ability.

Two points from their major group opponents filled the squad with optimism as they travelled to Boras, a tiny town 40 miles from Gotesborg, to face the Austrians on the 15th June. Seeding wise the Austrians had been classed as the weakest link in their group.

An English victory and passage into the last eight of the tournament would be guaranteed at the expense of Brazil or Russia. Both these sides had beaten Austria and drawn with England, in those days it was only 2 points for a win.

England v Austria; June 15th 1958 at Boras

England Team;

C.McDonald (Burnley); D.Howe (West Brom); T.Banks (Bolton); E.Clamp;
W.Wright; W.Slater ;(All Wolves) B.Douglas (Blackburn; R.Robson (West Brom);
D.Kevan (West Brom); J.Haynes (Fulham); A.A'Court (Liverpool)
Score; 2-2 (Haynes) (Kevan)

Weakest link or not Austria's Karl Koller smashed a 25-yarder through a crowded penalty area to put England under real pressure inside the first 15 minutes.

Just after half time the same individual increased the Austrian lead and England were more or less on the plane home.

Once again this second goal brought a positive change around the hour mark in another Jekyll and Hyde England performance. A serial onslaught on the Austrian defence finally resulted in a tap in for Johnny Haynes, and within a couple of minutes, Derek Kevan had equalised with little time remaining on the clock.

England had got out of jail.... this was the game they were expected to win so they were grateful to grasp a draw from the abyss thus leading to a play off against Russia.

Brazil (5 points) topped the group having beaten Russia in Gotesborg, England and Russia had finished with identical points (3) and both sides also scored and conceded four goals each with Austria finishing bottom. (1 point)

The night before the play off against Russia in Gotesborg Tommy was in his room snuggling down for some well earned sleep when a scuffling noise outside intrigued him.

On popping his head around the door he saw the familiar figure of Tom Finney in his "jarmers" attempting to sprint up and down the corridor.

Tommy thought to himself, what a brave man, he wants to play so badly he is testing his knee out.

"Fer once ah ses nowt, clows'd mi doower un wiped tears fro mieens"

(For once I said nothing, closed my door and wiped the tears from my eyes.)

"Sir Tom" did not pass his own fitness test so England started the game without their key forward, the man who had toyed and tantalised the Russians in the two previous encounters.

Herman Apoukhtin the Russian "pigeon catcher" was restored to the right wing after (according to reports) catching flu soon after the team had arrived in Sweden. One wonders about the Banks factor in the "flu" saga, Apoukhtin had hardly had a kick of the ball in Moscow directly against Tommy. Also in another encounter for the Russian Army team at Burnden Park in a "friendly" in November 1957 he was withdrawn at half time!

England made a number of changes in the hope of being a more potent force in front of goal; Clayton, Brabrook and Broadbent had replaced Clamp, Douglas and Robson.... the nation held its breath.

England v Russia; 17ᵗʰ June 1958

England Team;

C.McDonald (Burnley); D.Howe (West Brom); T.Banks (Bolton); R.Clayton (Blackburn)
W.Wright; W.Slater (Both Wolves); P.Brabrook (Chelsea); P.Broadbent (Wolves);
D.Kevan (West Brom); J.Haynes (Fulham); A.A'Court (Liverpool)
Score; 0-1

Once again in this "winner takes all" match decider, Apoukhtin, for all his pace rarely threatened Banks even though again England were still in first gear for most of the opening half. A spirited second half though should have brought victory but fate decreed otherwise with the Russians scoring the only goal of the game from a rare counter attack.

Tommy left Sweden with his head held high having produced the form which had originally earned him his place in an England shirt. Bolton's humorist-in-chief with his rapid fire comments, and quirky northern dialect, had helped to maintain a high state of morale within the England camp.

However, on the serious side, he also knew come 1962 his age would be against him possibly playing in the next World Cup tournament to be held in Chile.

On the 29ᵗʰ June Brazil went onto beat the host Sweden 5-2 in the final in Stockholm with a free wheeling inventive display that showed the world the emergence of 18 years old Pele who scored two goals.

Pele went on to grace the world for the next decade with his sublime skills, with Brazil winners again in 1962 and 1970. Who knows what the outcome of the 1966 World Cup would have been had he not endured brutal on the field treatment from Bulgaria in the group stage which made him a spectator for most of the time in England.

Tommy arrived back in England from the World Cup and all the players went their separate ways, some catching other flights or calling black cabs, Tommy jumped on a train bound for the north.

Personally he had enjoyed a fine world cup series and he was now known nationally throughout the length and breadth of the country. Half a dozen hours and a few train connections later he alighted at Moses Gate leaving the station for the short walk to his home.

Tommy was immaculately dressed in his England blazer with the three lions crest prominent on the pocket, grey flannels, white shirt and England tie. He was carrying his England suitcase and just has he passed the local butchers a middle aged woman who had known him since he was a child spoke to him.

"Hello Tommy you look very smart" she said

"Tar" said Tommy.

"Have you been to Blackpool for your holidays" she added without a hint of jest.

Tommy never had any edge to his character, what you see is what you get, but if he had this would surely have been a big put me down.

Tommy smiled, "Nah not this time Mrs Green, not this time"

Chapter 16

Model 'Mon'

1958 was certainly turning out to be Tommy's year;
Whatever next could be on the horizon?

He was relaxing one Saturday morning, having not been home long from England's disappointment in the World Cup, when an official looking envelope dropped through his letter box. Inside he read a letter from Jimmy Hill the then Chairman of the Professional Footballers Association. Jimmy had been approached by a company to provide a likely candidate for a couple of lucrative advertisements.

Blue Gillette razors were looking for a sportsman to advertise their product. This was to be via a TV commercial and also on billboards in prominent places around the country.

"Was he interested?"

"Wer ah interest'd, duz neet follow day, too reet ah wer interest'd" roared Tommy.

(Was I interested, it was a forgone conclusion, when do I start)

The blade company required someone well known, a household name in sport, but not a superstar so to speak. What they required was a 'bloke' the man in the street could imagine having a pint with. Tommy's success with Bolton in the F.A. Cup and impressive World Cup displays in Sweden had brought his name to the forefront of the public of the country. Also with being a down to earth character Jimmy Hill thought him the perfect choice.

A week or so later Tommy left Maggie and young son Dave at the home of his older brother Ralph in Weymouth whilst he journeyed into London to fulfil his modelling commitment. A night's sleep in the Waldorf hotel at the pleasure of the sponsors ensured an early start was possible filming at London ITV studios.

In the sketch Tommy needed to remove his shirt and saunter over to a sink to carry out an imaginary shave using a Blue Gillette blade, no words just actions. Straight away the director pulled him up commenting,

"You can't wear that" referring to brand new white vest which Maggie had bought him specifically for the shoot, the director said it would look grey on the television.

The film crew solved the problem by giving him a blue vest which allegedly portrays white under the cameras. It seemed strange to Tommy but they were in charge and must have known what they were doing.

"Ah'd dun monny takes,shavin'creem wer nar offmi face"
(I did endless action shots, the shaving cream never seemed to be off my face)

About five o'clock the director said "Tommy we aren't quite getting the shot can you come back tomorrow?"

"Tha wor ....owdonabit owdlad ah'm only onth' commercial fer sixty seccunds, yon reels full" snorted Tommy
(I beg your pardon, hold on a moment my friend I am only in the shot for a minute and you have already taken a full reel of takes)

Half an hour later, peace was restored, the cameras had captured good sequences and Tommy left the studio. Thus he became the first England sportsman to advertise Blue Gillette on ITV. The advertisement was shown around 8-30pm, prime time on Sunday nights when viewers were watching Sunday Night at the London Palladium.

Another night between silk sheets in the Waldorf was followed by a morning taxi dash across the city to a barber who had been given the contract to shave him pre stills photos. The big Greek guy took his cut throat razor ever so carefully to Tommy, very delicately removing, to his relief, the signs of overnight stubble.

The next taxi dropped him at the address of the stills photographer where he was greeted at the door by a pretty women all of six feet. He followed her through the building to be introduced to her diminutive "face for radio" cameraman husband, a married combination Tommy thought to be rather odd. Here was an elegant mid thirties lady as tall in today's terms as Penny Lancaster (Rod Stewart's latest wife) married to a much older guy who was no Omar Sharif and no taller than actor Danny Devito.

Tommy did not dwell on the marriage match, his professionalism kicked in, he quickly directed his thoughts to the photo shoot ahead. However, he soon found out the photographer could talk for England he never stopped firing questions at Tommy. He was bombarded with .... why, where, what, when, Bolton's international full back was constantly being quizzed over the outline of his life up north.

155

"Im shudavebin askin 'questions on Mastermind"
(It was like he was asking questions on the rapid fire quiz show Mastermind)

"Ah sez t' yon mon ah bet thi teeth are reet glad when tharts asleep,tha'cawnt heawf chunner"
(I said to the photographer you really ask a lot of questions, you want to know many details.)

The photographer, who Tommy recognised by his accent, to be from Yorkshire had moved to the capital apparently because that is where all the well paid work was for his chosen photographic career. It also soon became obvious that he had not taken to Londoners, particularly the men who he worked with on a daily basis. It appeared he was extremely pleased to be in the company of Lancastrian Tommy, someone he could identify with from over the Pennines.

When Tommy answered the "What's your career" question thrown at him by saying "futbawler" the photographer was not impressed, footballers were two a penny he told Tommy.

"Would you like to come to live in London, I can make you a very rich man in years to come."

"I work for all the top magazines and daily papers and they usually leave the choice of model to me and you are just the job" stressed the photographer.

"Ah thank'd this mon but nah London wernt fer mi, ah wer a true blue warkin northerner,useter a prayto pie un a pint."
(I thanked the gentleman for his offer but told him London was not a place I wanted to live I was too attached to my northern roots and way of life)

A couple of weeks later Tommy was enjoying a pint in the Egerton public house near his Thorne Street home at Moses Gate when a long distance lorry driver, a near neighbour, when home, collared him.

"Art awe reet" enquired Tommy with a firm handshake.
(How are you?)

"Last Friday I had a real scare in my wagon when I was just about to enter a tunnel near Heathrow airport, I almost crashed." said the lorry man.

"Aye, wor wer tha' deawnter" asked Tommy inquisitively
(Oh yes and what was the reason.)

"A bloody big billboard saying 'Men shave with Gillette' and thy mug grinning at me" laughed the driver.

For a while after returning to pre season training at Bolton instead of instigating the banter he became the butt of the jokes due to his "Modelling" He took it all in his stride, he did not mind giving the lads a laugh at his expense. His pockets were weighed down with £250 from the TV commercial and £100 for the still photos all plus generous expenses.

His F.A. Cup winning bonus of £100 had been much harder to earn.

Chapter 17

Maximum Wage 1961

Formed in 1907, the Professional Footballers Association is the world's longest established professional sportspersons union. Since that year it has been fighting to protect, improve and negotiate the conditions, rights and status for all professional footballers in England and Wales.

The P.F.A. efforts have achieved a number of notable successes over the decades which have resulted in benefits for the members of the day and those who followed in their footsteps.

One such momentous victory, the abolition of the Maximum Wage, was achieved in 1961.

Its 50th anniversary almost slipped by without recognising the huge part it played in the fiscal structure of the game today.

In 1957 Fulham player Jimmy Hill became Chairman of the P.F.A. and he initiated the campaign for the abolition of the maximum wage payable to professional footballers.

After the Second World War players had pushed hard for pay increases which did gain them a small increase in 1947 and possibly averted a pending strike. However, Middlesbrough's England international Wilf Mannion was far from happy.

Mannion, a talented ball playing inside forward with an eye for goal had started with Middlesbrough in 1936. He became the team's star player before leaving to serve on the front line for his country in France and Italy during the war. Although the war took the best years of his career this marvellous instinctive player was soon established in an England shirt on his return. In 1948 aged 30, on hearing from England colleagues that some top clubs were keeping their key players "sweet" by under the counter payments he sought a transfer hoping to financially benefit before his legs "went."

Confrontational dialogue began;

Middlesbrough refused his request stating,

"Even if a club came with a cheque for £50,000 we would not transfer Mannion."

"Why should we let the best player in England go?"

Mannion went on a one man strike, refusing to turn out for the Wearsiders, who refused to pay him, but retained his registration.

"If Mannion will not play for us he will never play in the Football League again" the club reported.

Mannion replied,

"The club can put me right out of the game if it wants to but why in the name of fairness must I or any of my colleagues be treated like cattle with no respect"

"I do not hold Middlesbrough entirely responsible; I blame the system which allows such treatment."

The dispute was costing Mannion money, and just before he caved in and returned to Middlesbrough, Jimmy Guthrie, the then chairman of the P.F.A. added his support to the player.

"The transfer system as it is today was evolved around the turn of the century."

"It just will not do today, the P.F.A. want a free market and none of this current retention system."

Tommy Banks failed to understand why other senior players throughout the country did not back Wilf Mannion at that time; he felt the push for a better deal should have happened then.

Wages were as follows by 1951 £14 max; 1953 £15 max; 1957 £17 max; and 1958 a £20 maximum had slowly been achieved.

Players transferred between clubs only received the mandatory £10 signing on fee.

Only a few players were paid the maximum wages!

Most players, particular the lads in the low leagues, were just about grinding out a living way down on the figures quoted.

In the 1920's Bolton players received £2 for a win and a £1 for a draw. Here we are now some thirty years on and this bonus had not changed. The 1920's Bolton's footballers always looked well dressed pictured in the sharp suits and crombies of the time. They were relatively well paid back then, pound for pound over the years time had not seen the same progress continue for the lads of the 1940/50's.

In 1946-47 professional football had recommenced properly again after the war. These proved to be ongoing seasons of booming numbers of spectators, boosting attendances throughout the country. Grounds were full on Saturday afternoons and the game was advancing on and off the field.

Poorly paid players were asking questions of their employers,

"Where was all the money going?"

Stadiums were full yet the players were not receiving decent wages, only a fraction of the revenue that was being generated through the turnstiles. The players felt aggrieved that they were putting on the "show" but they were not being rewarded well enough for their efforts whilst the clubs were in clover.

Players were still having their summer wages slashed with many taking part time employment to make ends meet.

Tommy Docherty, Preston North End wing half in the 1950's and later to become the manager at Chelsea, Aston Villa and Manchester United is alleged to have confronted the club's chairman after hearing a playing colleague was on £20 per week all year round.

"He's a better player than you!" was the response.

"Not in the summer he ain't" quipped Docherty.

It took Jimmy Hill the then P.F.A. Chairman and Cliff Lloyd, the pipe smoking P.F.A. Secretary, four long years starting in 1957 to bring the battle to the boil. Cliff was a tenacious fiery extremely likeable Welshman who would fight his corner for any player, if he deemed the cause worthy.

In these protracted years Tommy Banks knew that the abolition of the maximum wage would arrive too late in his own career for him to benefit financially to any noticeable degree, if at all. This did not prevent him from thinking of younger colleagues by offering his opinion and generally relaying information back to Bolton's rank and file of the ins and outs of progress and voicing his concern to be strong together.

Initially all players were not fully behind the P.F.A. stance of proposing strike action. There was much rumour, and counter rumour, that some clubs were making under the counter payments to some players to boost their wages, thus keeping them happy.

Regional meetings were held throughout the country and in early January 1961 a mass P.F.A. meeting at The Grand Hotel in Manchester was attended by northern players to give all players an opportunity to air their views. Many opinions were sought and given.

A Bury player stood up saying his father was a miner and that his dad did not quite earn as much as he did for playing football, and he was against a strike.

An emotionally charged Tommy Banks then rose to his feet and chimed;

"Ah think its neaw time ah spokk Mr. Chairmon"
(Mr. Chairman, I think its now time that I spoke)

"Ah'm tellin thee t'tell thee far'her ah'm on 'ees side, ah noes pits nar fun ah 'avebin theer misell but theer wonnt be thirty thousand watchin im dig owt coal cum Munday morn, theer wilbe thirty thousand peyin gud munny on Setdi ut Burnden Park t'si mi tryter stop Brother Matthews 'ere", pointing at Stanley Matthews with superb timing that could have been straight from a knife edge theatrical drama.

(I'd like you to tell your father I know the pits a tough life having worked below ground myself. However there will not be thirty thousand people watching him extract coal on Monday morning, but there will be thirty thousand paying spectators on Saturday at Burnden Park watching my battle with Stanley Matthews.)

There was a slight pause, as Tommy's words were digested by the audience, so that you could have heard a pin drop, then a great roar. Graham Cunliffe who was a young Bolton professional was hanging onto Tommy's every word. He still remembers with affection just how passionately Tommy's speech hit home to all the young and old professionals present.

Jimmy Armfield was sat alongside his Blackpool team mate and former England colleague Stanley Matthews, and remembers vividly to this day the impact Tommy's words had on the members in attendance.

"Tommy was not looking for laughs but his words spoken so strongly basically changed the mood of the meeting and the way of thinking of many of the members who were up to this point undecided"

"Stanley Matthews did have a bit of a giggle though when he referred to him as 'Brother' Matthews."

"Stanley knew from personal experience just how competitive Tommy was on the field, they had a mutual respect for each other!"

Manchester United and England's Bobby Charlton was sat in the midst of many of his club team mates and remembers Tommy standing to address the room;

"Tommy's 'Brother Matthews' speech, although decisively serious, was tinged with the touch of humour that turned the corner and helped relay the union's wishes in trying to obtain a fair wage deal for the members."

"He brought a smile to players' faces; it was Tommy's speech as much as anything that lifted the tension and uncertainty, lads bought into the aims of the P.F.A. committee"

"Every player present that day will never forget Tommy's words and charismatic presence, it will always be an abiding memory" added Bobby.

Tommy fully realised due to speaking his mind that the clubs and the game administrators would not be happy, but facts had to be faced. Once a player's best years were behind him the club soon dismissed him and he was out in the wilderness, often struggling seeking another way to earn a living. It's important to remember that the original dispute was over a matter of principle, the right to negotiate a contract, not figures.

An unanimous vote by players from forty three Northern clubs decided to back the union officials in rejecting the league clubs' "final offer."

After the players had talked for over two and a half hours Cliff Lloyd came out of the meeting and invited the waiting pressmen to be witnesses to the unanimity of the players. The press filed into the hall and stood to hear the players roar their backing for the committee, it went like this;

Hill; "Lads, you are being asked to vote on whether you accept this offer from the Football League?"

General Chorus; "No"

Hill; "Are there any who want to accept?"

General Chorus; "No"

Hill; "Do you give your P.F.A. committee full power to carry on their negotiations?"

General Chorus; "Yes"

Hill; "Is there anybody in this room who if the League refuses to negotiate with us will not strike on Saturday week?"

General Chorus; "No"

Hill said the press had been called in, because at times, up and down the country things had appeared in newspapers that the players did not feel was correct. Manchester United's Wilf McGuiness asked him to make it clear that the request to call in the press had come from the players not the committee. The press witnessed a startling display of solid support from the P.F.A.'s northern members. What they had not witnessed was how many anti-strike players had changed their minds.

Brian Clough the Middlesbrough centre forward, had said the previous day, that if his delegation had to vote it would be in favour of no strike action. After his hand had gone up with the others pledging to back the committee he was asked by the press.

"What happened to all the lads who were against striking?"

"They must have got lost on the way here" replied Clough.

Liverpool players had decided beforehand that they were opposed to the strike so too had the lads from Grimsby Town, Huddersfield Town, Chester and Lincoln.

However when they were asked that vital question;

"Is there anybody here who will not strike?" there was not one "Yes".

Various bodies were involved with the P.F.A. in the negotiations; The Football League, The Football Association, Ministry of Labour.

Pressure mounted on the Football League for an agreement which came to a head in mid January 1961 soon after the players meeting in Manchester.

The Football League had offered a gradual increase up to a maximum of £30 per week taking over five years, which the players had flatly refused. With the Players Union now receiving almost unanimous support for strike action from its membership from around the whole country something had to give. On the 18th January 1961 the Football League agreed to the immediate abolition of the Maximum Wage.

Fulham's Johnny Haynes was rumoured to become almost overnight the first £100 per week player.

Whether this figure and the speed it was introduced was true for Haynes, only few knew the facts. Tommy Trinder, Fulham's chairman, had previously been relatively vocal in the media about looking after his best player.

It must be stressed that most players, including the main men at the elite clubs, only received modest increases next time their terms came up for review. Bryan Edwards who was with Bolton until 1965 told Tommy that the highest weekly wage he ever received was £25, and Tommy knowing his good friend "Slim" as he did, had no reason to doubt him.

Clubs still had a major hold over players at the end of their contracts, which were heavily weighted on the side of the employer. A lightening of this grasp occurred in 1963 when the P.F.A. backed and won George Eastham's high court case contesting the current retain and transfer system (Restraint of trade).

This had always been Tommy's biggest grievance; Football League contracts ensured clubs had an iron grip over the players.

George Eastham 1963; Retain and Transfer system.

The High Court ruled it to be contrary to the law of the land and subsequent negotiations with the Football League established a procedure to permit a player to join another club at the end of his contract. Clubs were only able to hold the registration of a player providing the terms offered were not less favourable than those in the previous contract. The "Retain" element of "Retain and Transfer" was greatly reduced providing fairer terms for players looking to resign from their clubs, plus setting up a transfer tribunal for disputes. At the end of a player's contract, clubs could no longer keep a player's registration (thus preventing them from moving) while refusing to pay them if they requested a transfer.

The player's status in society was slowly changing from that of a blue collar image to one more in keeping with the new wave of working class actors and entertainers.

Most players came from working class backgrounds and they still do so today.

Later in 1978 a player's right to move at the end of his contract was fully recognised with a more efficient procedure being established. An Appeals Committee with an independent chairman was set up to consider disputes arising from the question of compensation (transfer) fee and the P.F.A. was represented on this committee.

The launch of the Premier League in season 1992-93 potentially brought about the sharpest increases in wages owing to Sky TV's involvement. The ruling bodies of football, including the clubs, profited very handsomely from the millions Sky invested to bring the game regularly to the armchair pundit. Players once again quite naturally sought their slice of the action.

Belgian footballer Jean Marc Bosman's long drawn out Restraint of Trade saga prior to coming before the European Court of Justice was the ultimate source of player power today.

In 1990 he wished at the end of his contract to move to a French team which his parent club rejected because the transfer fee offered was deemed too low. Bosman then became an exile within his team and he was in limbo for five years until winning the 1995 decree.

Players were now free at the end of their contracts, and thus able to seek out the best deal anywhere in Europe that they could. With no transfer fees to pay clubs were upping their bids to players in order to secure their services usually on excellent long term deals.

Dutch international Edgar Davids, who moved from Ajax to AC Milan in 1996, was one of the earliest, most notable individuals to take advantage of the ruling, the full realisation in English football not really coming until 1999.

Steve McManaman enjoyed the most lucrative move of the time in British football and became Britain's first high profile departure when he left Liverpool for Real Madrid. This resulted for a period in McManaman becoming the highest ever paid British player in history from 1999-2001, his contract running until 2003 upon his move to Manchester City.

Cliff Lloyd died in January 2000 aged 83, Tommy Banks' full time professional career ended in May 1961.

Could they ever have visualised or envisaged players of 2012 reported to be on £200,000 per week when the disbandment of the Maximum Wage agreement was struck in January 1961?

Every well paid Premier League player of the past two decades, many now millionaires should be eternally grateful to the likes of Jimmy Hill, Cliff Lloyd, Tommy Banks and the rank and file past P.F.A. members who over 50 years ago fought so hard to end the £20 per week maximum wage.

In a quest to pave the way for better wages and the transfer rights (George Eastham case of 1963) that are taken for granted by the players of today, the professionals in 1961 put their careers on the line being prepared to strike to obtain better working rights.

Tommy fully appreciates you are born when you're born and thus play when you play in the professional game. He also recognises the status and immense power modern day players now hold which seems a fairy tale story to 50 years ago.

Without doubt the catalyst that generated the player power of today came via the Bosman ruling.

Changes were initially due to the disbandment of the 1961 maximum wage followed by George Eastham's 1963 restraint of trade case and finally the Bosman ruling, a ruling never envisaged five decades ago. The Bosman logic appears to have been quite unforeseen by the world football's administrators, right up to the court verdict going in favour of Jean Marc Bosman.

Tommy is proud that he played a part in lads getting better rewarded for their skills through the years since 1961. However it is Bosman and the introduction of Sky TV that have given the top players untold wealth.

Sadly he doubts if the highly paid young men of 2012 really comprehend, or are bothered one tad, for the history of the struggle that past players fought for. Players' rights were the aim in 1961 and once achieved the growth of the game and vast money entering particularly the Premier League since 1992 have given modern day players great opportunities of wealth.

The game has progressed for the better in most quarters, with magnificent new grounds, pristine surfaces and vast improvements in equipment and training methods. The emergence of Sky TV and the money that has been poured into clubs has subsequently seen the players naturally seeking bigger and better deals. The Bosman ruling tipped the boat fully over in the players favour regarding bargaining rights and they now appear to hold all the aces in negotiations.

Tommy thinks that if a club is prepared to offer a player x, y, z then it is not the player's fault if he accepts. Whilst some wages are reported to be astronomical the clubs should only agree to pay wages they can afford. Let players walk out through the door, players do not earn money that has not been offered to them.

When he made his speech in Manchester, Tommy knew he was towards the twilight of his career, but also knew he was right in seeking a better deal for players. What he does find particularly galling with today's players is the utter lack of respect some appear to show in their actions and dealings on and off the field. Their ways blacken the image of professional footballers in the eyes of the public. Too many think only of a "what's in it for me" mentality, greed is rife off the field. On it, diving and play acting antics are sickening setting extremely poor examples for young impressionable boys, the players of the future.

Chapter 18

1958-1961

Tommy had not long to wait after returning from the World Cup before he re-commenced training with Bolton for the 1958-59 season.

By now Bolton had earned a fearsome reputation for their wholehearted approach and had become a well respected team, particularly on their own patch of Burnden Park. Few teams returned from away games at Bolton with anything recognisable to their credit apart from bruised and battered legs plus the odd black eye.

The regular defence of Hartle, Banks, Hennin, Higgins and Bryan "Slim" Edwards made up the usual full back and half back team sheet names. Tommy was upbeat, he enjoyed playing alongside these lads, each individual would battle hard and they could look after themselves in challenges. No-one liked to play against them, Hartle and Hennin were big robust lads and Higgins was even bigger whilst pencil thin "Slim" was just as determined and combative.

Bobby Charlton recalls Manchester United had huge respect for Tommy and all the Bolton team.

"This set of Bolton lads were always difficult to play against particularly at Burnden Park they had engendered a tremendous team spirit between themselves."

"If Tommy could see you were a tad soft he would certainly test your desire with a weighty challenge, but he was also quick, and a good footballer, who rarely gave the ball away."

"Football today is much maligned and rightly so in certain cases."

"Back then that Bolton team, over a number of seasons, epitomised how a potent mix of honest endeavour and passion, sprinkled with a fair degree of skill generating great camaraderie, could take a team a long way."

"It was a man's game and tackling was a major part of the game to upset the opposing team's rhythm, referees tended to keep their whistle in their pockets."

Bobby Charlton also remembered well a game at Burnden Park,

"A meaty Roy Hartle challenge on Mark Pearson brought a scream from my colleague and a few minutes on the sidelines to recover."

"Moments later Pearson screamed again at the audacity of yet another Hartle tackle which found him again withering on the ground."

"Roy picked Mark up and I could hear Tommy's voice sympathising."

"Roy, dust thee wanna chip im oer 'ere un let mi si if ah con 'meyt un greet' 'im" said Tommy.

(Roy would you like to send him over, I'll introduced myself and look after him)

The great goal scoring genius Jimmy Greaves remembered his first few seasons with Chelsea before going to play abroad with Milan and later at Tottenham.

"Bolton was a place where men were truly men we feared their sheer brute force."

"For those of us who they regarded as Southern Softies there was no more daunting place to visit."

Tommy was soon to gain his 6th England cap being called up for the international in Belfast against Northern Ireland on the 4th October. The game at Windsor Park finished 3-3 and was the last time Tommy appeared in the white shirt of England.

Bobby Charlton, scorer of two of the England goals that day, had also travelled with the World Cup party to Sweden but at only 20 years old he'd just missed out on a place in the team, Bobby recalled Tommy's England games.

"Tommy from his very first England game had no fear of reputation. If he thought well established internationals like Johnny Haynes, or any of the other players, were not pulling their weight they would receive a sharp blast of words across their bows." said Bobby.

Tommy was troubled throughout his career with pulled hamstrings, and in this game the injury stuck again. No substitutes back then so he soldiered on playing most of the game on one leg at centre forward, but he was then sidelined for many weeks.

He also knew how difficult it was to retain a position and become an established player in the England side, and two weeks later, when England played and beat a poor Russia team at Wembley, he knew the writing was on the wall.

He was 28 years and 327 days old his international career had covered 139 days of his life.

Of his six games, five were draws with the only loss being the crucial world cup qualifier play off against Russia in Sweden in June. Tommy should have received six caps but was told that he had already played against Russia twice before the World Cup play off, so the Football Association would not be sending another against the same nation!

He therefore received only five caps, but in another quirk, two of the caps which arrived in the post were for the same match against Brazil and no cap against Austria. Poor administration on behalf of the Football Association, but Tommy did not complain he let sleeping dogs lie. Years later he found out, via Johnny Haynes, that he had received two Austrian caps and no Brazilian cap, they laughed it off and kept what they had. How different is today's scenario which highlights a player popping onto a field as a substitute for five minutes or so in an international game, and sees his cap count mount up swiftly.

Two days later on the 6th October Bolton faced Wolves in the F.A. Charity Shield played at Burnden Park. Nowadays the match between the league champions and the F.A. Cup winners is always played at Wembley as the pipe opener to the new season.

Tommy missed the game due to his injury, sustained in Belfast, but for once these usual trench warfare clashes between two of the country's top teams was a milder encounter. Only just under 16,000 fans turned out to watch Bolton triumph 4-1 with two goals from Nat Lofthouse and one each for youngsters Neville Bannister and Freddie Hill.

Freddie was an extravagantly gifted naturally talented ball player, a schemer with the ability to thread dagger like passes through the heart of the opponents defence. Freddie also had another quality that appears so rare today ....the ability to dribble. His stooping gait hid deceptive speed which, allied to innate self confidence, enabled him to shuffle past would be tacklers with a shrug and twist of his shoulders that sent them into row z of the stands.

"What if ?"...... is often said in football circles and applies to Freddie. He failed a medical due to high blood pressure, probably down to the excitement of an impending move to Liverpool. Would playing in a fashionable team have further enhanced his reputation and England chances due to his tremendous ability on the ball?

Freddie similar in talent, though not temperament, to Paul Gasgoigne should have added to the handful of England caps he received. Freddie was a cultured one off of the period, an inside forward whose jinks through the middle of the field or along the touchline enthralled the Burnden faithful.

England missed a trick, the nation's team should have been built around him for a decade with the only instruction given to him to simply be;

"Play Fred, just play."

This was the message Tommy used to give to Freddie!

Tommy fully realised Fred was gifted and told him not to worry about other players or opponents. He had to play his own game on the field because he had ability given to so few, fantastic natural skills that could not be taught.

169

Nat showed his versatility in the Charity Shield against Wolves by going in goal when young Joe Dean who was standing in for Eddie Hopkinson dislocated a shoulder.

Later that season Bolton looked like they were set for Wembley again beating old foes Wolves 2-1 at Molineux in another epic encounter. It took a replay at Burnden Park to dispose of Preston as they progressed into the quarter finals, before the agony of losing away to Nottingham Forest the eventual winners.

Historical evidence from within the Bolton camp that season showed that the team had struck a rich vein of form in virtually all the campaign. Whilst they were realistic enough to concede winning the championship would possible be a step too far to achieve, the quest to retain the F.A. Cup was distinctly on the cards, so losing at Forest was a massive disappointment.

Bolton finished the season in a remarkable 4th position behind runaway champions Wolves, five points behind Manchester United and level with Arsenal who had the slightly better goal average. This season the team had virtually picked itself, the 1958 cup winning eleven were almost ever presents barring the odd injuries.

Tommy had played in 37 of the possible 42 league games.

His hamstring injury sustained in Ireland costing him his England place, a month on the sidelines and most likely a full house of outings for Bolton.

Still fresh from their cup loss Blackburn Rovers invited their semi final conquerors Bolton to celebrate the opening of the floodlights at their Ewood Park ground. Bryan Douglas had waltzed around Tommy a couple of times early in this exhibition game and as he jogged back Tommy gave him a verbal broadside.

"Aye Dougie ah thout this wer a friendly"
(Bryan I thought this was a friendly)

"It is replied the Blackburn winger"

"Ok, lets kepp it friendly, or else" warned Banky.
(That ok, just as long as you remember)

In the pre-season of 1959-60, 15 years old Francis Lee a future England international was taken onto the Bolton Wanderers ground staff. Francis a local lad from Westhoughton ('Howfenner') had all the top clubs seeking his signature but opted for the team he had supported from being a toddler, partly due to his family's wishes for him to live at home.

170

As a new starter walking into a testosterone filled professional football dressing room environment to be greeted by thirty plus individuals is not for the faint hearted, the banter can be cutting and a rhino skin is the basic requirement.

The first emotional punch to hit Francis was the "effing and jeffing" that players who he had hero worshipped from being a nipper seemed constantly to use in their vocal interaction. In those early days he recognised that Tommy Banks stood out in this respect, he never swore apart from the very odd "bloody" only used to emphasise his point of view.

"I did not have a sheltered upbringing no-one does coming from 'Howfen' but my parents never swore and I was into my early twenties before they heard me so it was something of an early shock" said Francis.

"Straight away I was drawn to Tommy like a magnet, his presence was awesome."

"Here was this loud England full back with a booming voice who found time for everyone."

"Tommy is a bright intelligent guy who soon picked up back then that I was shy and easily blushed. He would include me in his conversation whenever he could to build my confidence and help me feel comfortable until I acclimatized" said Francis.

"Leeey wort thi dooin ut wick'end, iz thi turnin owt fer "Howfen" ut cricket?"

(Francis have you anything planned for weekend, are you cricketing for Westhoughton)

Lee soon found himself inducted into life on "The Gravels"

A surly Higgins tackle left him after training queuing behind the senior pros awaiting his turn seeking medical attention for his badly cut knees from Bert Sproston. A slap on his backside found him turning to face his aggressor who it appears was looking out for the welfare of the young star,

"What's that for Mr. Banks?" asked Francis.

"Tha's geet nast under thee toe nails, gi thee toes areet gud scrub with yon brush dipp'd in iodine" suggested Tommy

(You have a potential problem with infection under your toes give them a good scrub with that brush dipped in iodine)

"Yes Mr. Banks, thank you" replied the youngster.

171

The early league games saw Tommy start the season on fire, scoring his first of only two goals for Bolton in 233 league appearances. It came against West Ham at Burnden Park on Sept 12th 1959, whilst a young Neville Bannister achieved a hat trick in a 5-1 victory.

Tommy reminisced, with a grin on his face, at being happy that Bill Ridding had finally allowed him to cross the half way line after all these games he had played for the club. So with his new born freedom he tried a long range hopeful shot from about 40 yards, the ball hit a divot and bounced over the keeper's head.

In mid October once again Tommy's hamstring hoodoo struck, and this time lingered much longer than he wanted with a number of false dawns forcing the Bolton management to seek a reliable left full back replacement.

Teenager Syd Farrimond, a local lad from Hindley on the outskirts of Wigan, was given the vote of confidence and a chance to stake a claim, he had made his debut the previous season deputising for Tommy at Preston.

Of the full time players only the seasoned pros changed for training in the first team dressing room at Burnden. All the rest... reserves and wannabes were directed to utilise the away team changing room. The first team squad of some 15-16 players then trained with George Taylor so many "ships in the night" passed each other without any proper introductions.

Soon after signing professional forms Syd and Tommy virtually introduced themselves by bumping into each other emerging from their respective changing rooms.

"Nethen dust thee no mi" said Tommy without any hint of arrogance,
(Hello there, do you know who I am)

With Syd being struck dumb on meeting his idol he replied by nodding like a Blackpool donkey in acknowledgement,
Tommy added,
"Let mi gi thee sum gud advice wi thee bein a young lad"
(I feel you may benefit from a little bit of advice because you are young)

Syd thought with Tommy's vast football experience, being an international left back, he is going to tell me how to "jockey" a winger or cover a centre half so he was taken aback a tad when Tommy advised,

"Ah'm tellin thee wor thee wannts t'do is geet thisell a gud insurance policy"
(My advice is that you need to buy yourself a good insurance policy that will stand you in good stead in the future)

Syd acted on Tommy's words and realised some 20 years later, when the endowment policy he had purchased had handsomely multiplied, that monetarily speaking, they were without doubt the best words of advice he has ever received. When Syd thanked him many years later Tommy revealed he should have followed his own advice. Apart from the cheap insurance policy he had been press-ganged into by manager Walter Rowley back in 1946 when he signed as a part time professional, Tommy had always put off until tomorrow any form of proper insurance investment.

During the 1959-60 season Tommy made 20 league starts, one in the no. 6 shirt alongside Syd who managed 23 appearances. Syd realised a career in the game beckoned when physio Bert Sproston told him he had found him a peg in the home team dressing room for daily changing.

Syd eventually played many seasons at Bolton and although being slight of build and frame at times found himself in goal. These were the occasions in the pre substitute days when injury to Bolton's keeper during games saw the team looking for a stand in to complete the match.

The 1960-61 campaign dawned with Tommy notching his other league goal against the old enemy Wolves on the 31st August 1960 in a 3-1 reversal down at Molineux.

Syd was now the regular deputy for Tommy and when the first choice left back's major injury problem flared again, the former England youth international was now pushing hard to be included on his own merits.

Tommy was forever the voice of encouragement and reason to all his team mates, his vast experience coming to the fore in a game at Everton where he wore 2 and Syd the no 3 shirt.

"Very early in the first half Billy McAdams scored Bolton's opener at Goodison Park and as I was setting off to run to congratulate him I heard Tommy's familiar voice bellowing," recalled Syd.

"Aye thee, wheer dust thee think thi's gooin, geet theesell bakk'ere ah expect thi'll need tha puff soon" roared the experienced full back.

(Syd, use your head, save your energy, Everton will be pushing for the equaliser)

Francis Lee had made a scoring debut in 1960 at 16 years old alongside Nat Lofthouse who also notched a goal against Manchester City on coming out of retirement after injury.

A visit to Highbury in front of 55,000 saw Francis Lee named in the team as Mr. F.H. Lee because he was still an amateur, being paid by the club, only for his official groundstaff duties. Francis was paid for concreting, painting, sweeping up etc. after training in the morning, not a penny for his football. Prior to the game Francis was strolling onto the pitch alongside Tommy when Arsenal's right winger Danny Clapton, who knew Tommy from the England call ups, with a solitary cap to his name greeted Tommy.

"Nice day today Tommy" quipped Danny,

"Theer wilbi nowt neece abeawt t'day Danny boy if thee gi's mi any trouble" Tommy replied through gritted teeth.

(It might not be a nice day for you Danny, if you give me any trouble prepare yourself for some physical treatment)

40,000 watched a Birmingham fixture with ground staff lad Francis Lee being paid £5 less national insurance and tax, pocketing £4 12 shillings and 6d come pay day. Rich or poor it did not matter to Tommy all eleven white shirts were in the same boat pulling for "Bowton" and he hollered across to Lee during the game.

"Leeey deawnt thi gi tha' bawl away agen tha' easy treat it leek thee girlfriend"

(Francis do not you give the ball away so easily again treasure it like it was your girlfriend)

Around this time much was being made in the Bolton Evening News of a man from the district of Darcy Lever a real character known as "Woody." Here was a guy who could throw a potato over the local high train viaduct near the Lever Bridge pub, quite a considerable feat with no run up. Numerous other individuals took up the 'spud' challenge with Ken Grieves bringing some of his Lancashire C.C. team mates to the location to attempt, without success. A couple of the Wanderers sought to conquer with Tommy's spud landing on the train tracks.

"Slim" was talking in the dressing room to Tommy about the spud throwing when Francis Lee told them he reckoned he could throw a golf ball from under one set of goals over the far crossbar at the opposite end of Burnden Park. "Slim" a cricketer himself with Heaton C.C. in the Bolton League knew young Francis was a budding quick bowler "with a yard" of pace to burn by his displays for his home team Westhoughton C.C.

'Banky' thought the word of a "Howfenner" could usually be relied on to fulfil what they intimated although he was aware that the townsfolk are also known as "cowyeds".

This humorous pseudonym came about due to the mythical tale of a "Howfen" farmer on discovering one of his cow's stuck head first through some railings decided the best solution was to cut the cow's head off rather than trim the railings.

The pair of F.A. Cup winning chums thought there is money to be made here. They backed the youngster with Slim running a "book" offering good odds on it not being achievable, which the majority of the playing staff gambled on. Tommy and Slim stood to lose their next couple of month's mortgage money if Lee failed, so Tommy thought he would just check the confidence of the fair haired young lad.

"Thi con dooit connt" Tommy sternly asked.
(You can do it can't you?)

"Yes Mr. Banks I reckon I can, no worries" said the confident teenager.

On the day it was no problem to the stripling his aim was true and long with yards to spare.

The out of pocket troops immediately requested a double or straights bet to hopefully retrieve their money. The task put forward was for young Lee to throw the golf ball from out of the tunnel leading onto the pitch across the ground and over the far Burnden Stand onto "The Gravels." training area. Now this was a real tester because the projectile's trajectory needed to clear the high stand roof very late on its journey. Tommy need not to have worried, young Francis's self propelled surface to air missile was well directed and all three amigos enjoyed a good day at the races with the winning proceeds.

At this stage, Bolton housed in its dressing room ranks, some useful cricketers; alongside Lee, "Slim" Hoppy, Parry, Higgins, teenagers Farrimond and Dave Hatton all distinguished themselves in local charity matches.

Tommy's legs were ageing in football terms not helped by re-occurring troubles with his hamstrings. The everyday training in heavy conditions did not seem to do him any favours.

No-one trained harder than Tommy when fit and he would try any remedy to overcome the problem.

He started to jog to the ground in the mornings to help his warm up, and indulge in lots of skipping, returning in the afternoons to strengthen his already fine physique. Much as he fought to beat his jinx he had only made eleven appearances this season with the last one way back in February.

Tommy was always committed no matter the team he was picked in or the circumstances involved, he was forever a true professional. He played in a few reserve fixtures in an attempt to regain proper fitness but kept experiencing the same problems with his disruptive hamstrings.

In one second team game, Bolton's winger playing in front of him was Reg Hender who possessed ability but was known to be lazy. After half time Tommy was about to leave the dressing room and whispered in Reg's ear,

"Thee 'ave a rest fer ten moor minutes onth' treatment table with yon blanket and si if thi con geet thisell warm"

(Reg you need to stay in the dressing room for a tad longer to warm up because you must be freezing)

Tommy had a young family with the birth of his second son Lee in 1960 following Dave in 1955. He fully realised he had to sort out his future with his growing responsibilities. Continually plagued by hamstring trouble Tommy knew that his time earning a living, as a full time professional in the top division, was coming to a crossroads. He also realised that the directors were not happy with his ongoing words to the rest of the Bolton players regarding fighting for their contractual rights. The administrators of football in England knew his speech to other P.F.A. members at a mass meeting in Manchester had played a large part in convincing players to be strong and stand together in their quest to end the maximum wage barrier.

The maximum wage was abolished in January 1961, giving the players more clout in negotiating their contracts that coming summer and a fillip to all players every year thereafter. Ironically Tommy was not to profit by one penny.

Towards the end of the season, Jack Rowley the manager of 4th Division Oldham Athletic had made his interest in Tommy's future known to him by the stealth of a newspaper contact.

"If you are allowed to leave Bolton on a free transfer I would like you to join me at Oldham" the script related Rowley's words to Tommy.

Now this appealed to Tommy, he did not want to move from his Farnworth home. Jack would allow him to play and train on a basis that suited Tommy on almost the same wages that Bolton paid him, whilst he built up his building business. It was almost the last kick of the season and Bolton had still not yet declared their retain list of players for 1961-62 so Jack spoke with Bolton over Tommy. Next day Tommy was shocked to hear from Jack that Bolton wanted £10,000 for his release.

"Sorry Tommy ten grand's way out of our league a free transfer was our only hope" Jack said.

"Here was a proud Tommy Banks with fifteen years of commitment to Bolton behind him approaching the twilight of his career looking for a gesture of goodwill in the form of a free transfer to Oldham only to be denied a dignified exit."

Tommy pulled Bill Ridding to one side the following day;
"Wor's gooin on Bill, ah've gi club 15 years loyal service"
(Bill, why are you asking a transfer fee for me, I have given 15 years of loyal service to this football club)

"Directors want money for you, it's not down to me this time but you will not be first choice left back next season" replied Bill.

"Artshoorothat thi mustave a say in geetin mi a free if thi's bent on tossin mi aside next season." asked Tommy
(Are you positive, surely you can influence obtaining me a free transfer if you are not going to play me next season)

The eventual famous George Eastham 1963 case regarding the overturning of the Restraint of Trade for players in professional football was still two years away. He knew he was not a free man under the current football league registration. Bolton could hold his registration indefinitely and offer him virtually nothing, payment wise, if they wished for the next season.

Tommy had sweated blood and tears for his beloved Bolton and thought the directors were being awkward to say the least. In short, Tommy like many times in his life contemplated and made his own mind up. He was adamant that Bolton were not going to hold him to ransom. Tommy made the surprise decision to leave the first division and go and play as a part time professional, in non league football, and to start working for a living outside the game. Upon delivering this news Bill Ridding asked Tommy where he intended to play in non league....the reply was straightforward.

"Bill, ah'll tell thee who ah'm signin' fer thee mek sure thee forrerts alluv papper wark on!"
(Bill, once I have decided I will let you know make sure you forward all the release papers onto the relevant football administrators.)

177

Tommy took one last trip down the tunnel leading onto the Burnden Park pitch.

He crossed the track that had felt his fleeting feet pound a million laps over his career and had possibly taken him "around the world in fifteen years" and up the banking that fell steeply some three feet plus from pitch to track. This well pounded and well renowned track had seen the occasional visiting winger obtain a painful gravel rash after disappearing down the slope following one of Tommy's meaty sliding tackles.

Stepping onto the end of season barren rutted playing surface he gazed towards the corner of the Embankment End remembering the disaster of the 9th March 1946 when 33 fans lost their lives in a bottleneck crush. From his view that afternoon, from the opposite Lever End, he knew nothing of the sad details until his tearful mother flung her arms around her teenage son on seeing him returning home safely.

His eyes followed round higher up the Embankment to take in the scorebox uniquely linked to the back of the train signal box. The scorebox overlooked the ground displaying the Saturday half time scores from around the league by the means of letters and numbers corresponding to the fixtures in the programmes. The smell of smoke from a slow moving shunting engine brought back visions of smog that drifted on match days from countless local factory chimneys across the pitch, or the mist that hung low on wet December days....those were happy times even accounting for ankle deep mud.

The Burnden Stand stood tall and proud, on the roof in front of the black and white clock was an early form of advertising.

No-one could miss "Dine at the Pack Horse Restaurant, Nelson Square, Bolton" emblazoned across the length of its frontage.

The steps inside this stand he had trod numerous times on "Hunty's" command for "four" of this or "four" of that, all activities to build stamina. Behind the stand was "The Gravels" the infamous small game arena that had witnessed countless aggressive challenges in mini football games amongst his team mates.

He turned and headed for the dressing rooms casting an eye up at the Press box, the best place in the ground to watch a match from within the Manchester Road stand. This brought a wry smile to his face as he recalled where he always hid his bucket of eggs until training had finished.

Once inside the dressing room he let his thoughts drift back to the laughter and good times plus the great football days he had experienced. He had one last look around the deserted home team dressing room seeing a friendly face with every different peg he viewed. Proper pegs had in time replaced the nails since he started fifteen years ago although it appeared the finances gained from the 1958 F.A. Cup success had not run to any new training kit. He soon shut the door on smelling the steaming well worn kit drying on the industrial size pipes in the laundry room.

Tommy had a quick peek into Bert Sproston's "territory" and a bench he had spent too much time on in recent seasons having treatment for his dodgy hamstrings. He collected his boots tucking them under his arm and headed for the dressing room exit. He pulled the door behind him, heard it click, and turned towards the Burnden Park entrance/exit for the last time as a Bolton Wanderers player. Tommy a man of decency, honesty and integrity who had given his all for the Wanderers was to stand by his decision.......new horizons beckoned.

As the Motown group the Four Tops sang later in the decade he had to, "Do what you gotta do."

Chapter 19

After Professional Career

Walking away from Bolton Wanderers for the last time in the late spring of 1961 after being associated with the club for over 15 years was not easy for Tommy Banks.

He left behind in the dressing room the bulk of the 1958 team.

Lads who were friends, not just team mates on the field, lads he enjoyed everyday banter with during training. Lads he journeyed with up and down the country and abroad, lads he would share a couple of beers with after matches. Lads he would have stood shoulder to shoulder with if war had broken out again.

He also left behind in the dressing room, the thick roll neck sweat-stained jumper he had been handed back in 1946 to train in containing his TB initials. This was the only piece of Bolton kit that was truly itemised to belong to him apart from his boots and pumps.

For any player who has ever been a full time professional, leaving the game can be and does sometimes turns out to be a trying time. Particularly without any notable savings to fall back on in the days pre Premier league even stretching back to the very early 80's prior to when wages substantially improved. For many of the lads who had played in the previous eras after the war, late 40's 50/60/70's without a wealth cushion to take the impact that becoming an ex player can and did take a degree of adjustment.

People are different.....some lads shrug off the change like water off a duck's back and glide through life without a problem. Others never quite get the buzz and match day adrenalin rush out of their systems, but survive. Some players felt the game, the only thing they had known since leaving school owed them a living. These lads never realistically harmonised or adapted to a change in work direction and could be quite bitter.

Circumstances and timing can and often dictate an acceptance of one's fate.

A player coming to the end of a long career, with his personal agenda mapped out stating his own chosen retirement year is in a prime position. Plans for a future outside the game can be put in place well in advance. This was not always the case for lads usually classed as 'journeymen' on short one or two year contracts... with clubs often leaving decisions on a further offer until the eleventh hour.... they were often wondering where their future lay?

Had they to uplift their families to another part of the country should they be fortunate to receive an offer; e.g. Ralph Banks (Bolton to Aldershot).

Players always have deep in the back of their mind that an injury at any time even during training can end their career depending on its severity. Cruciate knee ligament damage for one example was a "killer" back before improvements in medical science and operations rendered it possible to now return almost like new.

Tommy, a strong independent character, fully realised that one day you are a player involved with the team, the next day you are out of the door, another name that's now part of the club's history and got on with it asking "nowt" from anybody.

It had felt strange leaving Bolton and Tommy initially found it perplexing to comprehend.... Bolton had always been his team. He had left behind good team mates but it was his decision and had happened ultra quick, it was time to move forward in a new direction.

However Tommy did muse over facts, reckoning that with using good common sense he had a couple of years left in his legs at first team first division level. If he had been treated back then with the individual respect players who are suspect to known injuries tend to receive today, maybe the answer would have been to ease back a tad on the punishing daily routine. He was always one of the best trainers and retained his cardiovascular fitness very well slotting back into the team after his lengthy spells on the treatment table, without any undue breathing issues. After these spells on the sidelines it was like he had never been away. Possibly lessening his daily workload would potentially have been the solution to combat his dodgy hamstrings but he would never know now.

What he did question though was whether his outgoing personality, with being somewhat outspoken, had played a part. He had spoken on occasions within the club for the benefit of the Bolton players plus speaking up for professional footballers in general against the maximum wage structure.... had his words done him any favours within the hierarchy at Bolton?

Tommy did not really want to move house away from the area for the sake of staying in the professional game. Oldham Athletic would have been ideal but he was almost thirty two and now increasingly troubled with his hamstring problems. He knew, hand on heart, his best days in the top league would have been well and truly behind him should he have stayed at Bolton.

During some of the summers since 1953 apart from the World Cup year, he had worked on the building sites. He had gained labouring experience carrying the hod stacked with bricks, blocks or mortar to keep the brickies in materials.

He had tried to look over the horizon, to his future outside the game.

Tommy was somewhat prepared for the day that his name would not be shouted (good or bad) from the Burden Park terraces and his face not staring out from the back page of the local or national newspapers.

Building houses appealed to Tommy, therefore very early in 1961 he had applied for and was granted by Bridgewater Estates (now Peel) of Worsley a parcel of derelict land in Elsie Street, Farnworth to build 16 semi detached bungalows. Back in the 50's /early 60's this landowner was prepared to give land for houses on the understanding that ground rent would be payable forever and a day in such circumstances.

Today such land is like gold and would command a pretty penny.

"Ah wer chompin ut bit t' start when mi mam sez worrabeawt 'ur Ralph" recalls Tommy.
(I was raring to start when my mother said "what about our Ralph")

"Ah sez worrabeawt 'ur Ralph, eez in Weymouth"
(I said what do you mean, he's living in Weymouth)

Tommy was always close to his mother and she persuaded him to set up in the building business with Ralph who she would like to see living back in the northwest.

Ralph upped sticks and soon the brothers were ready to commence the build of the bungalows in Elsie Street.

In hindsight Tommy knows he should have set up in business by himself.

He was too loyal to his brother taking him on board owing to the wishes of their mother.

They were now a partnership both making decisions regarding business which did not work out in the end.

With his typical wholeheartedness Tommy threw himself into the building trade and requests for the services of the brothers soon snowballed. Tommy bought the best quality clogs with laces to race around the sites where they were building. The work was stacking up because other developers were asking the former footballers to build for them.

Banks and Banks were employing gangs of bricklayers and various tradesmen to subcontract for them with their site workload beginning to spread wider and wider.

Tommy found himself chasing around the sites, organising men, weighing up potential new jobs and also buying some land at Charnock Richard out towards Chorley to build more houses for themselves.

Tommy also took over the reins of ordering materials when he realised various problems were occurring regarding issues with deliveries on their behalf. It was a catalogue of errors....lorries were arrived on the wrong day or not at all with too many of one item or not enough of another, a complete shambles.

"Ah tuk bull bi t'thorns" said a forlorn Tommy,
(I realised I had to sort out this mess)

It came to a head when Tommy heard a guy who was a site agent for them ordering concrete on the phone he knew then he would have to do all the ordering of materials himself along with running around the sites. The concrete supplier was seeking directions to the site,
"Where are you" asked the delivery driver.
"I'm in the cabin on the phone to you" Tommy's man replied!
In the midst of growing his business with Ralph, good mate Alan Longworth (bricklayer) and Tommy started a different company with another couple of fellows, but this soon went pear shaped. Alan was just happy with a trowel in his hand he preferred to work with no management responsibilities. He never wanted to be a boss and Tommy was all over the place trying to keep all the wheels running smoothly but it was all uphill.

Arthur Patterson, a labourer who worked alongside them chewed tobacco spitting it out anywhere and everywhere without realising the consequences of his actions.

On a site one day sitting around on some old planks after having a brew Ralph came to put his boots on only to find a form of glue had nestled in his inner soles due to Arthur turning his head to empty his mouth. Definitely uncouth, manners nil, and fortunate to not receive five fingers in a fist, men like Arthur were solid working men no thrills and certainly no graces.

These were the days of the 'lump' method of payment.

Companies who employed sub contractors (subbies) had little responsibilities. Site men were self employed no cards into employers, paying their own tax on earnings and buying their own National Insurance stamps. Gangs preferred cash for the materials they laid on a no questions asked basis, either bricks per thousand, blocks per square metre. There were no guaranteed wages if it was raining or freezing... tough luck. Today's health and safety inspectors would shudder at some of the scams pulled to earn a wage.

Companies would order for sites, the bare minimum of scaffolding, sometimes resulting in a guy on another's shoulder to finish laying a chimney stack. No safety rails, boarding out walkways that could hold hidden traps due to saving on planks, no hard hats etc. Thankfully over time through the directive and implementation of rules regarding Health and Safety the supervision of sites has now vastly improved.

Men who were employed as bricklayers would just up and leave a build for slightly better pay elsewhere without warning. Some bricklayers never seemed to stay long anywhere, they lived their life like gypsies.

Tommy turned up at one such site to find the brickie's labourer, usually two bricklayers to one labourer had "walked" due to a disagreement so Tommy's jacket was straight off to get stuck in carrying the hod. Tommy had also promised to show some 'chippies' (joiners) on this site his 1958 cup final shirt, so in a lull between shouts from the scaffold for materials, Tommy put his No.3 shirt on.

"More mortar Tommy" a brickie requested from high above.

Without thinking, acting instinctively Tommy loaded his hod and scampered up the ladders a couple of times dumping the mix.

"Ah then cudave shrik'd, mi Wembley shirt wer fullur mortar"
(I could have cried I realised my Wembley shirt was full of mortar)

The mortar was thick and now ingrained, particularly on the shoulder, and he knew it would not wash out of a white shirt. Tommy finished the shift in his Cup Winners shirt then threw it in the skip, if it was not going to look pristine for ever after he could not face seeing it.

Altrincham one of the top non league teams in the Cheshire League had agreed to take him on a two year deal as a part time professional. Tommy had to make his way around tea time twice a week to Walkden, a couple of miles away. Once there he was collected and driven to training by either vice chairman Noel White or the club's chairman Peter Swales who at this stage were both striving to improve the fortunes of Altrincham. Both individuals eventually moved on years down the line to more salubrious surroundings, Noel White to Liverpool F.C. and Peter Swales to become the chairman of Manchester City F.C.

Paddy Fagan, the former Manchester City winger, had been installed as the new player manager in the summer of 1961 and he ensured Altrincham snaffled up Tommy's services once they knew he was looking to play somewhere part time. Tommy remembers Peter Swales visiting him at his

Moses Gate home to talk about a part time contract, second son Lee was still a baby so Tommy was looking to make every penny count. Swales did not ask Tommy what he wanted he just sat down and spurted out he would give him £200 cash for signing on plus £15 week and bonuses with transport provided. Tommy looked at Maggie and she nodded, they both realised this was too good a deal to refuse, so he signed without hesitation on the dotted line.

All the paper work for the land at Elsie Street had still not been completed so Tommy took a job hod carrying near home during the day for a local contractor. He had to work a Saturday morning on site but his first week's wage was ten shillings more than he had ever received at Bolton as a full time professional for a win in the first division.

Fagan's training was good and Tommy was pleasantly surprised by the standard of the football through the league with the likes of Ernie Taylor an old adversary of Blackpool and Manchester United fame patrolling the Altrincham midfield.

Amongst their ranks, Altrincham had ex league professionals and some good semi professional players from a range of backgrounds. The teachers and solicitors were well paid in their full time professions which resulted in no pressure when they collected a few pounds for turning out on a Saturday afternoon.

The flow of the football in the games was a tad more disjointed than football league matches with more rough and tumble and the ball often came off exhausted after being pummelled rather than caressed throughout the ninety minutes. In one match a bit more than the usual argy bargy occurred and Tommy found the referee pushing him away with a finger in his chest in an attempt to calm the situation,

"Ref if thee prods mi agen wi thi finger ah'll bite it off upter knuckle" threatened Tommy.
(Referee I am getting rather annoyed at you accosting me, don't)

When Swales was Tommy's taxi home he always used to have the car engine running out on the car park. Tommy reckons he must have wondered why he was always the last to leave the dressing rooms after training. So keen was Tommy to maintain his peak fitness he always did a few extra laps thus helping him stay trim and also relieved the dressing room congestion. The communal bath was very small so he could have the bath to himself after the lads had finished.

When Fagan relinquished the manager's job Tommy turned Swales's offer down to take over the hot seat. It was not for him he had enough problems in 1962 growing his building business to find the time to take on more potential anguish.

Charlie Mitten the former Manchester United goal scoring winger took the reins for Tommy's second season with The Robins. Mitten possibly the greatest left winger never to play for England was a gifted extravagant player who had been something of a rebel in his day.

He was a trailblazer in the player's contract revolution.

In 1950, a Colombian millionaire baron promised him a fortune to play for Independienta Santa Fe in Bogota if he left Manchester United.

The Dimayor league, formed in Colombia in 1948, had broken away from FIFA control with the wealthiest clubs enticing prominent players with wads of money. Many Argentina players including Di Stefano joined due to the non payment of transfer fees to clubs holding players' registrations.

It is doubtful if the Manchester club was ever officially notified of any transfer request because Charlie had fled the country before United, it appears, fully realised.

This Colombian league was then unaffiliated to the world game and he became known as the "Bogota Bandit" receiving a hefty signing on fee and playing for very handsome rewards only returning to England when the money dried up. Manchester United still owned his rights and both they and the England football authorities were not impressed by his actions. On his return he was suspended and cold shouldered for six months before Manchester United eventually sold him to Fulham.... the England selectors blackballed him, never to be considered for the national team.

Tommy and Mitten should have gelled well together both being known for their extremely colourful characters although a bit of "previous" from their pro days seemed to prevent any real bond. Banks and Mitten was a workable professional football relationship to get the job done, off the field they spoke but were never close friends.

Mitten during his Fulham days had once allegedly ordered England star Johnny Haynes off the team's medical table so he could administer ultra sound treatment to his wounded greyhound.

"I've got to get this dog fit for the prestigious Greyhound Derby in a couple of weeks at the White City" demanded Charlie.

London's "White City" staged this race which was the climax of the UK greyhound calendar until 1984 when the loss of the facility resulted in Wimbledon's Greyhound track benefiting.

At the end of the 1962-63 season Swales called Tommy over for a quiet word;

Tommy could see by the dour look on Swales's face as he approached that something ominous was afoot,

"Ast getten sum muck stuck onthi'top lip" Tommy asked.
(Have you got something to say to me?)

The chairman wanted to talk wages with Tommy asking him to play in the reserves in the Manchester League and bring the young kids on with his experience.

"Nethen Peter, let mi stop thee theer, ah'm dun ah wannt nowt fro thee"
(Before Swales could speak Tommy said he had finished)

Tommy, who had played in the World Cup less than five years before, reckoned this was a downwards step too far and "hung his boots up" on the spot. Tommy was all set to fulfil his self made retirement promise but Tommy G. Jones the former Everton centre half had other ideas. A week later standing on Tommy's front doorstep was the former Everton player and Welsh international centre half. T.G. Jones had been denied the opportunity of a lucrative move to Roma back in the late 1940's owing to the procrastinating of the Everton board over currency issues.

T.G. who Tommy held in high esteem was now the manager of Bangor City also in the Cheshire league, but elegible to compete for the Welsh Cup.

T.G. had guided Bangor to beat Wrexham in the 1961-62 season to win the Welsh Cup which then saw Bangor thrilled to play Italian giants Napoli in the following season's European Cup Winners Cup. Bangor's semi-pros unexpectedly triumphed 2-0 over the Italians on home turf at Farrar Road before succumbing to a 3-1 reversal in the away leg in Naples with 80,000 in attendance. The competition rules back then decreed a replay otherwise Bangor would have gone through on the away goals rule. Unfortunately in the decider a late Napoli winner resulted in a 2-1 defeat at Arsenal's Highbury stadium prevented Bangor from holding an unforgettable place in UEFA history.

Four times T.G. ventured from his home in Wales to try to persuade Tommy to join him in his vision of more glory nights for little Bangor at home and abroad.

Tommy had a lot of time for T.G. Jones but he did not think, with all the travelling plus running his business, he could justify his request.

Tommy finally agreed to sign on the understanding that he would only attend to play in matches.

If he felt the endless travelling was too much he would be allowed to dissolve his contract.

He played for Bangor for two seasons the pay was good £18 per week with bonuses and travelling expenses, he was only drawing £25 from his business. He felt privileged to know T.G. Jones, who was a real gentleman and treated all the team with respect. Tommy also felt it was good to concentrate on football rather than the worries of his building business for a Saturday afternoon.

Forever the professional, Tommy trained by himself at night twice a week running in the dark out on Farnworth's Doe Hey wasteland which was dimly lit by a solitary nearby street light. Doe Hey had, Tommy recalled, been his host some 5 years previously when he had been left by England to his own keep fit devices prior to departing for the 1958 World Cup in Sweden.

Bangor City's intensive pre season training was during the working day so Tommy took a week off work, to show his commitment to the club, and use the opportunity to bond with his new team mates. Regular night sessions were impossible it was a 109 mile trip from the front doorstep of house to the ground. On his first day of training Tommy could see a few of the Welsh speaking lads would talk amongst themselves in their own language and spoke to rectify the situation,

"Reet, alluz speyk English, alluz wilt speyk English nah clikks, one teem" (Right, we all can speak English, we will all speak English, no cliques, one team)

Tommy was often on the last minute for games due to visiting building sites on Saturday mornings, then trekking pre motorway days, to North Wales in his old works van which was very temperamental. One Saturday Tommy left Padiham near Burnley with time to spare, but his van's engine blew up outside the Granite Church in Rhyl... he was forever on the go he had never checked the oil level.

Tommy found a phone box and rang the club!

A mate of T.G.'s picked him up in his Jaguar car, and with this guy knowing every inch of the road, he just made the dressing room with minutes to spare. Although the rest of the Bangor team were on their way out onto the field the No.3 shirt was still on a peg. T.G. told Tommy after the game that they would have played with ten until he arrived, a sign of the mutual respect between the two men.

Bangor made the Welsh Cup final again in Tommy's first season 1963-64 this time their opponents were the full time professionals of Cardiff City. This was a side that numbered amongst their midst the mighty John Charles of Leeds and Juventus fame playing alongside his brother Mel and wispy winger Ivor Allchurch. All three had been major contributors in Wales's run to the last eight of the 1958 World Cup in Sweden before dipping out to eventual winners Brazil.

However, this was Bangor's Farrar Road ground a long way from the trimmings of Stockholm. The ground was a tad ramshackle and run down, the pitch dropping away some six feet into a corner. Dressing rooms that were unwelcoming to say the least but nothing compared to the reception reserved for the visiting team on the 22nd April 1964 by 8,500 partisan Bangorians.

The one eyed crowd played their part in a two goal giant slaying ensuring the Welsh legends trailed home with their tails between their legs mulling over how they were going to pull back the deficit at Ninian Park in the second leg. Cardiff did win 3-1 a few days later and with the away goal rule not counting, a replay at Wrexham's ground would decide the placement of that season's Welsh Cup.

Tommy had blossomed late in his career into something of a "goal scoring machine" his only two previous football league goals against West Ham and Wolves whetting his appetite…. manager T.G. Jones trusted him with dead ball kicks. Tommy took the free kicks around the penalty area and the penalties scoring over a dozen via a combination of both routes, he was always confident of beating the keeper from 12 yards.

Bangor were awarded a penalty early in the play off game so up stepped Tommy;

"Ah thout bawls gooin reet deawn middul inter onion bag"
(I decided to aim right down the middle of the goal)

Tommy fully expected the goalkeeper to guess and to dive to his left or right.

He struck the ball sweetly, too sweetly…. he connected with power but as the goalkeeper anticipated and dived to his right, the ball hit the crossbar and rebounded passed him back into play. Unfortunately for the vast numbers of travelling Bangor supporters Cardiff City went on to win 2-0 dashing Tommy's hopes of adding a Welsh Cup winners medal to his 1958 F.A. Cup Wembley triumph and a thus a dabble into European football.

For Tommy, Bangor although in the Cheshire League, a home game was distance wise an away day, some one hundred miles from doorstep to ground. Besides Altrincham most fixtures were closer to his Farnworth home, with the league containing teams such as Northwich Victoria, Runcorn, Macclesfield Town, and Hyde United. After a couple of seasons and many miles of journeying to Bangor in pursuit of football, Tommy decided to hang up his professional boots in the summer of 1965 with his 36th birthday around the corner.

He might have finished playing professionally, but Tommy's love of the game and wish to help others less fortunate than himself, brought about him forming a mixed team of ex Bolton players and showbiz personnel to raise money for charity. Local celebrity Stuart Francis later of "I could crush a grape fame" was a young budding comedian and Norman Vernon a well established member of the comedy circuit was often the 'spongeman' whenever a game for charity was arranged. Alan Ball then at Everton also unbeknown to the club put his boots on once when the team were short, thankfully he survived intact. Tommy ran the team for over ten years with his last game around 48 years of age being on the old Walkers Institute Ground in Great Lever, Bolton against a Manchester City XI. That mad keen Blues fan Eddie Large (Little and Large) a spectator on the day took to the stage to do a turn after the match in the clubhouse.

Tommy recalls starting to struggle to walk for a couple of days after games,

"Ah adter caw it quits mi hip wer onth' wey owt"
(I had to retire my hip needed replacing)

Business lurched on in the mid 60's, the semi detached bungalows were built and sold in Elsie Street with Tommy snaffling one and Ralph another of the early ones built moving their families from the terrace properties a mile away in Thorne Street, Moses Gate.

Nigel Howard a lifelong friend of Tommy's son Lee remembers their carefree young days growing up in the 60's and early 70's playing on the large field behind the Banks's bungalow. Nigel, Lee and a gang of friends would spend hours playing football and cricket on their winter "Wembley" and summer "Lords" outside in the fresh air, no computers back then. However the final whistle on many a game was called by one man and one man only.... Tommy....he had a rousing whistle. He was not, by the way, refereeing the game.....no.... Tommy would march up to the back fence and then blast out such a strong shrill whistle that half of Farnworth's town folk would freeze on the spot, followed by "nethen bi dooin" and that was it.

"No extra time or penalties the game was over and we all trudged off home, never once did Lee ever disrespect his dad" said Nigel.

The land they bought for houses at Charnock Richard though cost them big time, it was out on a limb and did not attract the punters the brothers thought it would, it was dead money when cash flow was tight. Some developers they had sub-contracted for went bust owing money to Banks and Banks whilst others were dragging their heels on paying for work done. It was a bleak situation with wages to find for workmen and materials to pay for, it was a disaster waiting to happen.

Banks and Banks had grown too quickly too soon and spread so thinly without the cash flow to sustain the up and downs of business, the partnership went under.

Tommy realised he was not a businessman!

"Mi office wer clumps of papper inmi bakk trowser pokket un alluv rest wer swimmin areawd in mi yed"

(I was not organised carrying bits of papers around in my trouser pocket and not writing down any records, the only details I had were in my head)

Try as they could, sadly the inevitable finally happened, and they went bust in 1968. Tommy was declared bankrupt and lost everything including the car apart from his house which somehow he managed to hang onto. Sons Dave then 13 and Lee 8 knew little to nothing about the demise of the business. Tommy always cushioned events never letting them know any of his problems preferring to take the issues fully on his own back.

Tommy had fought hard to keep the business afloat but now his only option was to take up the hod on a permanent basis and earn a living back on the "tools" to feed his family. He was soon up and running sub contracting for various local builders, labouring for his good friends, bricklayers Alan Longworth and Bob Walton. They seemed to work practically every daylight hour in the boom years, although they would sometimes finish Saturday lunchtime.

These were the Saturday afternoons that Tommy and Arthur Barnard would venture out on their away days if Harry Gordon had been in contact with invites to watch matches at football league grounds. Harry now a brewery representative was a former professional who had plied his trade in the lower divisions of the football league. He had become an acquaintance of the Farnworth lads during a spell at Bury. Harry through his job was given complimentary tickets to take clients to games throughout the region.

However he could at times struggle to persuade customers to attend and rather than waste the "freebies" Tommy would be contacted for first refusal. The afternoon could stretch into the late night but come a Sunday morning, no matter what time he had arrived home the night before, he would be up with the lark if the chance of overtime or a "foreigner" was in the offering on the hod.

With the passing of years Dave and Lee were turning from boys into men and Tommy would regularly inform them of his own teenage years. These were the days when he was never still, dashing everywhere delivering papers, milk, running to work, home or training always in a pair of clogs.

In Tommy's own words he would say,

"Mi clugs were allus smookkin"
(I was never still)

Both lads recognised just how hard Tommy worked forever carrying the hod, for weeks they would hardly see him.

Lee was renowned for asking questions,

"Dad, have you made this choice to work for someone else rather than risk setting up in business again without the potential perils, pitfalls, stress and worries that the building industry can bring for a small outfit?"

Tommy would question back,
"Owt wrong wi Dave"   "No" I'd reply said Lee
"Owt wrong wi thee"   "No"
"Owt wrong wi mi"   "No"

Tommy told Lee to stop worrying both Dave and himself had grown into fine respectful lads not causing him any bother or embarrassment with neighbours or the police.

Dave even in his twenties would not smoke in front of his father, and Lee never felt comfortable if by chance he was in the same pub as his dad in his late teens. Lee a bit of a very likeable rebel felt he might have been stepping on his father's toes at eighteen years old. He ensured he let his hair down in his youth outside Tommy's immediate vicinity so not to risk causing his father any potential embarrassment.

Both sons have tremendous respect for their father; they know he has always been great with them. He does not exaggerate he is totally honest whether they like it or not and does not interfere, but will advise them if asked his opinion.

Years on, eldest son Dave had served his time learning his bricklaying trade elsewhere but when he came to join "Tommy's gang" he realised just how demanding his father was to work alongside.

"He would hardly speak all day, he would be fully immersed in the job servicing two brickies is hard but three is for the elite. Constantly active he would be up and back to us fuelling the build with materials, eating on the move and taking command of the situation."

"We would be around the back working on a house extension and we could hear him telling the owner at the front door... no they do not want a cup of tea and yes pay us at end of the job instead of stage payments to our disbelief!"

"Bob had many kids to feed he was not impressed!"

Dave added, "We would always work weekdays in the summer months until around 6pm including Fridays which come lunchtime is for many bricklayers, their afternoon in the pub."

"As bricklayers for us we dreaded hearing late any day Dad's poetic words,"

"Theers a big white elephant inth' front o'yon mixer"
(There's a mound of mortar just come out of the mixer which needs using)

"He would upset a few site foremen with his strong sometimes outspoken views on how a job should be done, but 95% of all site workers took to him, as does the man in the street."

A young Quantity Surveyor had been monitoring their work for a day or so and was inquisitive about what Tommy was chewing and spitting into the mortar churning in the mixer.

"Backky it meks fer a bet'thur mix" Tommy said keeping a straight face.
"Dust thee wannter tre sum?"
(Tobacco it helps the mortar mix better, do you want to try a bite)

The young man took up his offer and was chewing away merrily for around a minute until the pure nicotine hit the back of his throat. He turned green and was sick on the spot, spending the rest of the afternoon recuperating in the site cabin.

A reporter from the Manchester "Pink" newspaper contacted him asking to write a "Where are they now" article and offered to buy him lunch,

"Nah nay time fer lunch, ah'll tawk t'thee but thi'll aveter stand bi mixer"
(Sorry, no time for lunch, I will talk to you but you will have to stand by the mixer)

When the article was printed Maggie was dismayed to see Tommy's own description of his working role.

"Ah'm a donkey fer three brickies"
(I am a labourer for three bricklayers)

Maggie said, "That's typical you under valuing yourself, why do you always put yourself down"

Dave said "Dad as usual shrugged it off he says what he wants and does what he wants. He is one on his own, no airs and graces, take him as you find him and he is fine by you, however if he does not like you, you have done !"

"There's no front to Dad, he has never bummed himself up and possesses old fashioned powerful values"

Dave and Lee have never seen him in a pub in his working clothes. He is always clean and tidy when he goes out he will refuse the offer of an after work drink rather than compromise his beliefs. Totally disciplined he will wash and change before turning out smartly dressed with clean shoes before trying a pint.

Occasional Sunday nights in Tommy's mid thirties through his early forties he would visit a few of the local old fashioned pubs of Farnworth, one well known haunt was "The Saddle." Just before last orders the familiar cry would go up in the vault (darts & dominoes room) of "Clear the floor" and all the chairs and tables were pushed to one side. Emerging from the Gents were two well lubricated local Sumo's stripped down to their underpants ready for a wrestle.

Both men were and had been good mates since their schooldays, one was a 6' 2" toothpick dressed in an Italian suit which he had cast aside for the bout, whilst his mate could just about see over the bar and was as wide as he was tall. They would roll around on the vault floor encouraged by the laughter and jeers of the regulars. Sometimes, somehow, they would burst through the doors into the best room to the disdain of the landlord where couples in their Sunday best clothes would be seated.

Rumour turns to myth: was Tommy once cast in this role?

For once the truth may reside in the depths of The Saddle!

Both sons were more than useful footballers and trialled for football league clubs. Dave was told by Dennis Violet at Preston, "You're not as good as your Dad" whilst Tony Book at Manchester City asked Lee, "How's your Dad going on" rather than enthuse over his own potential.

There is no doubt that Tommy, who is well known throughout the region, still holds tremendous respect from past players within the game. Bryan "Slim" Edward had been fortunate to be employed in football after hanging up his boots in 1965 with his only league club Bolton. Initially he was appointed assistant coach at Blackpool followed by a similar short spell at Preston before accepting a move to Plymouth Argyle in 1970 to take up the chief coach's position.

Preston manager Alan Ball senior had promised Tommy a couple of tickets when the "Lillywhites" were due to host Plymouth for a midweek fixture which was some trek for the "Pilgrims." Tommy and Arthur only had twenty miles to navigate as they headed for Deepdale, Tommy was keen to catch up with Slim again.

Delays and detours en route left the Farnworth pair with five minutes to spare when they asked the main entrance commissionaire to kindly check his envelopes for complimentary tickets under the name "Banks."

After checking on his desk the uniform attendant responded by saying that all tickets on his list had now been allocated and his name was not even registered.

"Steam was starting to come from Tommy's ears" said Arthur as Tommy spoke,

"If thi weeshes t'kepp thee job gow un geet Bally neaw, tell 'im Banky wannts 'im"
(If you wish to keep your job go and get Alan Ball this minute)

"They will be kicking off any moment he won't see anybody now" replied the concerned Preston official.

"Geet Bally reet neaw 'ee'll si mi" boomed Tommy
(Ask Alan to see me urgently, I am sure he will)

The official swiftly disappeared and returned a minute later with the agitated Preston manager beside him.....shaking Tommy's hand Alan Ball guided the Bolton pair through the main entrance.

"Tommy I was just in full flow of my pre match speech to the players, sorry tickets must have slipped my mind," he blurted as he ushered them into the boardroom,

"Sit anywhere in the directors box apart from the chairman's seat"

Tommy eventually got to meet up with "Slim" later that evening!

In the mid 70's Andrew Dean then a milkman, now the Promotions Manager at Bolton's Reebok Stadium "contracted" Tommy and his crew to erect the bricks on his self build house at The Woodlands near Beaumont Hospital off Chorley New Road in Bolton. It was a "foreigner" to the bricklaying gang involving Saturday and Sunday work on this quiet pleasant site.

Awaiting them the first day was an old fashioned cement mixer complete with iron wheels which ran on petrol and was kicked into action by a wind up handle. This relic had been on Andrew's farm for donkey's years and looked way past its working sell by day. Tommy's eyes widened with glee on viewing this old fashioned monster mixer, he had used plenty of similar devices in his 'apprentice' labouring days. He was ultra keen to whiz it into action, it brought back many memories of the early site times of his building partnership with brother Ralph...."Banks and Banks."

Other neighbours were well established in this cul de sac and soon started to complain vigorously over the ongoing grating and grinding noises that the mixer threw out. Complaints were so vociferous and many in number that the council came down to open the rule book on the whys and wherefores of environmental pollution...noise wise. The earliest the mixer was therefore only allowed to be started on a Saturday was 8am with a 9am kick off giving the surrounding residents an extra hour of rest on Sundays.

Sunday mornings were exceptionally quiet and peaceful near the Beaumont Hospital but come 9am!!

Tommy would count down the seconds before whirling the starting handle rousing the neighbours on hearing the Town Hall clock a mile away strike nine. He would clean the mixer at the end of each day with the same care and attention a parent would apply to looking after a child.

Bolton drew Manchester United away in the F.A. Cup in 1990-91 season and the "Reds" kindly invited Bolton's 1958 Cup winning side to walk the outfield alongside their former opponents prior to the match. Bobby Charlton told Tommy if he ever had his own testimonial dinner not to forget to invite him along.

"Ah ses watch eawt fer flyin pig fust" commented Tommy.

(I said I do not think that will ever happen)

A month or so later, the committee at Farnworth Social Circle Cricket Club, were looking for a celebrity to speak at their annual fund raising dinner and asked Tommy if he would see if Tom Finney would attend. Tommy knew Sir Tom did not do after dinner speaking but told them to hold on a while and he would see from within the past football brethren who may be willing to speak.

Son Dave said, "Dad rang Bobby Charlton, if it had been for Dad alone he would not have asked but he knew the cricket club were struggling financially so it was all hands to the pump."

Bobby readily agreed although he was not an after dinner speaker. Tommy then informed the committee it was to be a basic pie and peas bash, questions and answers do, with a couple of tales thrown in, ticket preference must be for all the local lads.

Bobby went down a storm but understandably made his excuses to leave before the comedian rose because he was on a dawn flight out to Hong Kong, he also refused any payment. The tributes paid to Bobby on this occasion were well deserved, he could have declined with impending business elsewhere in the world but he was eager to help his old football mate.

Barry Stansfield one of the Farnworth Social Circle club's former cricketers was an old friend of Tommy's going back to those early pioneering holidays in the sixties in Spain. It was during these holidays in Sitges that Barry developed a love for Barcelona F.C. which led to him venturing out at least once a season to attend a game at the Camp Nou.

Barcelona appointed Bobby Robson as their manager back in the eighties and Barry was also a Bobby Robson nut, writing to him at every club Bobby managed including Barcelona.

Team mates never forgot Tommy, former England manager Bobby Robson was delighted to respond to a request from Tommy regarding Barry Stansfield. Tommy kindly organised a once in a lifetime rendezvous for Barry with Bobby Robson when Newcastle United, who Bobby managed from 1999-2004, played a fixture at The Reebok stadium.

This was on an understanding with Barry that first he must obtain a new set of false teeth prior to the meeting with Bobby Robson. This special meeting for Barry came very late in his life. It was only a brief ten minute chat, but a memory that achieved an ambition for Barry, and one that Tommy was grateful he had managed to pull together in time for a sadly missed good friend.

January 1961 Professional Footballers Association (PFA) mass meeting in Manchester where Tommy Banks's speech registered with the union members.

2007 The PFA celebrate the union's centenary. Back l–r; Richards, Barton, Weaver, Eastham, Hunt, Douglas, Armfield, Reid, Rush, Robson, Sedgemore. Front l–r; Finney, Banks, Taylor, Rooney, Giggs, Neville(G), Powell, Moore, Griffiths.

Blackpool beach 1964.

1964 Aerial view of "wakes week" holiday makers packed onto Blackpool's beach prior to the boom of cheap overseas package holidays.

Tommy was an overseas holiday pioneer since 1962. Pictured with son Lee in Sitges, Barcelona in 1978.

1979 Tommy at son Dave's wedding. Dave, Tommy & Lee.

2012 Tommy meeting distant relative Bolton Mayor Noel Spencer at the Reebok Stadium.

1990 Charity Bowls day at Flixton's Sports Club
Standing (l-r 7th & 8th) John Higgins & Nat Lofthouse
Seated (l-r 1st 2nd 3rd) Denis Stevens, David Sadler (Man United) Ray Parry
Front (l-r 2nd 3rd 4th) Tommy Banks, John Morris, Wilf McGuiness (both Man U)

1993 Charity Bowls day Bolton v Man United. Tommy & David Sadler.

Tommy contemplating if he'd put 7 or 8 spades of sand into the mixer?

1994 Tommy and Rita attending the Musical in honour of Tommy's life.

Showtime; Tommy & Kenneth Wolstenholme walking into Harper Green Secondary School on gala night.

School children Lee Marland (Tommy) & Joanne Hindley (Tommy's mother) act a scene from Tommy Banks the Musical.

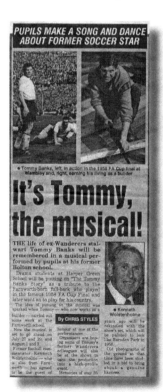

Above: Kenneth Wolstenholme, Tommy & Nat Lofthouse at the reception after the Musical.

Left: Newspaper article promoting Tommy Banks the Musical.

Celebrating Tommy's 80th birthday at Siesta Key. Dave, Catherine (Rita's niece) Lee, Rita, Tommy.

Captain Curt's Crab & Oyster bar in Siesta Key, Sarasota, Florida. Proprietors Brett & Brad Stewart display Tommy's signed shirt.

2005 Legends Night at the Reebok Stadium, Tom Finney, Tommy and Nat.

2008; 50th Anniversary; Reunion of the 1958 F.A. Cup team.
Standing (l-r) Holden, Stevens, Banks, Edwards.
Seating (l-r) Alcock, Gubbins, Lofthouse, Hartle.

Burnden Park 1997; The changed face of the ground environment since Tommy's 1950's era.

25th April 1997, the last game at Burnden Park. Bolton beat Charlton 4-1.

Reebok Stadium; The home of BWFC since season 1997-98.

Summer 2012; Ian Seddon & Tommy Banks inside the Reebok Stadium.

Ah'm tellin thee.

Chapter 20

Other Sports

Outside of family, work and football, cricket was Tommy's big love from being a child, with the sport of crown green bowling growing on him from his twenties to fill his summer evenings.

May to August he can regularly be spotted at weekends amongst the cricket crowds in the "do or die" Bolton League local derbies between his beloved Farnworth Social Circle Cricket Club duels with Farnworth C.C. just over a stone's throw away. The other contest not to be missed by the followers of F.S.C.C.C. was a tad farther away at Kearsley C.C. a couple of bus stops to the east.

Over numerous decades the Bolton League and sister competition the Bolton Association weekend cricketing matches have been fiercely contested by amateurs of no mean ability plus a professional. The professional, a hired gun of status, is often flown in from the various cricket playing nations of the world.

Countless well known aces have plied their cricket trade over the years in the Bolton leagues.

West Indian Sonny Ramadin spun his web at Little Lever C.C. in the early 70's. Pakistan's all rounder Mudassar Nazar made good use of Horwich's sporting wicket a decade later. Young teenager Aussie Mark Waugh was arguably the most elegant bat ever seen in the league collecting runs for fun at Egerton C.C. in the mid 80's before striding the famous grounds of the cricketing world representing Australia alongside his brother Steve.

In the mid 70's, whilst then part of the Bolton Association, Tommy's own club Farnworth Social Circle C.C. engaged the services of a towering West Indian opening bowler. The professional was a Barbadian called Sylvester Clarke an ox of a man whose sheer pace put fear into opposition batsmen. Here was a 21year old barrel chest 6'4" young man who later went on to shell shock international cricketers (never mind Bolton's amateurs) with many a steeple bouncer whilst representing the West Indies in contests around the world.

Before Surrey secured his services for 10 years in County cricket after watching him perform for F.S.C.C.C. Syl's missiles against local Bolton lads were just as fearsome as a Tommy Banks's tackle, trouble was there were six of them every over.

Tommy marvelled at Syl's awesome pace, athleticism and competitive desire for the team. He found him to be a typical laid back West Indian, extremely polite and social off the field unwinding after matches or cricket net nights with a few drinks.

Tommy recalls one cup match when the light was fading, it was with the bat that Clarke excelled that evening.

"It tuk im five minutes t'geet t'wikket draggin ee's bat but bawls wer soon awe'l oer roads areawd ground seein uz wom."

(He took him an age reaching the wicket but he made up for it by quickly dispatching balls far and wide out of the ground to win the game.)

In one tense local derby an umpire told him to bowl a few less intimidating bouncers, Syl replied "Dis, no ladies game man".

Sylvester was tall, but when he invited his international team mate fast bowler Joel Garner (Big Bird) at 6'8" along to the "Circle" he had to duck to get through the door leading into the club.

Most sportsmen seem to mix easily with men of other sporting creeds, one such occasion arising in 1960. Ken Grieves introduced Tommy and other Wanderers to a youthful Gary Sobers one Sunday afternoon at a testimonial cricket match in Stockport. Sobers, even then was a West Indian international cricketer spending five summer seasons from 1958-62 inclusive as the professional of Radcliffe C.C. in the Central Lancashire League.

Gary and Tommy bonded well with Sobers admitting to standing on the Embankment End at Burnden Park whenever possible to cheer the Trotters on, almost making Tommy blush by naming him his favourite player.

In the late 1960's Farnworth Social Circle Cricket Club obtained a license to sell alcohol. A bar was built and the original old army recruitment shed suddenly became the district's very own London Palladium / Wheeltappers and Shunters Club.

Now Tommy and Ralph were larger than life characters as it was, and regular Saturday night attendees and performers.

The atmosphere was unique and trust me seats on a Saturday night were at a premium. In no way would the building pass any Health and Safety legislation these days...a totally wooden hut, no designated fire exits and this in the days when chugging away on a couple of packets on Player No. 6 cigs was the accepted...no expected standard......and that was just for the women!

The usual Saturday night format was the same as most social and labour clubs in those days. There would be an opening artist, a house of bingo followed by what was commonly known as the "main turn". The "main turn" was a total stereotype, someone approaching or already middle aged, a crooner in far too tight trousers with a nom-de-plume of "Rubin Chatterley" when in reality he was probably a bin man from Burnley called Alfie Smith.

It was always after the "main turn" had finished that a very early version of Karaoke would commence backed by the resident organist and drummer.

Various male regulars from the attendees would take turns in singing Sinatra/Dean Martin standards to an appreciative audience by this time now well doused in Lion Bitter with the ladies supping Babycham or Cherry B.

Tommy is a decent singer...but Ralph was a cut above anyone who performed and also had the stage presence and swagger.

However it was first and foremost a cricket club and during the summer months the teams would gather at the bar, usually talking about events that had occurred in the day's cricket match. This was much to the annoyance of some pure social members who were hanging onto every last chord of the karaoke crooners.

Occasionally club officials would have a word with Tommy's old mate Barry Stansfield and his team mates who would be stood at the bar chatting excitably and laughing disturbing the "turn".

One night this went too far and blows were almost exchanged because Ralph's version of 'New York, New York' whilst in full flow was being drowned unintentionally by the cricketers to the annoyance of a few social members.

A "committee" man intervened resulting in much pushing and shoving although it was no Muhammad Ali and Joe Fraser contest, just handbags. Sadly the alternative "main turn" the "pasties" that had been so precariously placed on the bar went overboard along with the peas and gravy.

When Tommy was not relaxing at Piggott Street home of F.S.C.C.C. enjoying a pint and watching others sweat and strain on a summer's afternoon in the Wanderers close season, he would be testing his hand/eye co-ordination and picking his wits on the Crown Green bowling greens of the area. Here was a summer sport where he would or should not damage his hamstrings. A sedate game played through the 20th century by working men in the north of England.

Back in Tommy's twenties, golf was still very much the sport of business men and professional people, solicitors and lawyers. Public golf courses were difficult to find and golf clubs tended to be private expensive clubs only accessible by invitation often with long waiting list. A couple of his Bolton team mates, notably Dennis Stevens and Ralph Gubbins took a liking to the game which remained with them long after the end of their football careers.

Crown green bowling was everywhere in Tommy's younger days most public parks had a green maybe two. Every public house worth its salt had invested in attracting the multitudes of pitman or factory men to taste its best bitter by laying a green. Greens come in all shapes and sizes, undulating land, no two ever the same mainly with a crown hence the sports name and literally played in all weathers by male and female of all ages. No restrictions, bowl the jack where you like, anywhere within the restraints of the playing area. Any distance minimum 19 metres on the green, bowls crossing paths as bowlers of different pairs sort to find a "mark" that their opponent may find difficult to play.

Flat Green bowls is played mainly in the south of the country competing up and down the same patch inside lanes.

The two games do not really bear any comparison, when you play crown green bowls you are playing your opponent plus also the contours of the green whilst concentrating and controlling the delivery of your bowls.

Tommy's bowling hobby started around 1956, he would put his baby son Dave in his pram and push him up to Farnworth park where father Banks would then pull his woods (bowls) out from under sleeping Dave's blanket and join the pensioners for a roll on the green.

He joined the evening bowls teams at arch cricket rivals Farnworth Cricket Club only because they had a green and also the second team at The Royal, a local Farnworth public house on the main road from Walkden through Farnworth to Bolton.

Tommy loved to compete but he was not good enough to "bow" in the first team at The Royal. These lads could lay up to the jack with their "bows" every end just like Stanley Matthews could weight a pass where he wanted it to go.

Many competitions are contested for throughout the greens of Lancashire for decent prize money. Numerous likely lads came from far and wide to The Royal a favourite competitive bowling haunt which was very well supported and thus sold gallons of ale to the joy of the proprietor.

After Bolton's 1958 F.A. Cup success the pub landlord thought it would be novel to invite Tommy and John Higgins along to play a curtain raiser on the grand finals night. The Bolton stars enjoyed a competitive game, with Big John being a handy lad having played now and again when returning home in the summers to Buxton. It was no walkover for Tommy the atmosphere was brilliant generated by a crowd that must have numbered upward of four to five hundred stationed around this mini coliseum.

A young Alan Ball (Blackpool FC) and Tommy did similar crown green battle on a few occasions with the summer of 1966 registering vividly owing to Alan's prominent role in England winning the World Cup.

In the mid 70's Tommy was in the same competition on merit, finding himself in the last 32 after an easy victory over a "bus driver" (a term for a poor bowls player) in the preliminary round. Next up was the then sport's No. 1 Brian Duncan a winner of trophies all over the county and also major competitions in Yorkshire. A good sized crowd was keenly awaiting the contest and whilst waiting to play Tommy sauntered over to Brian and whispered in his ear.

"Neaw thee be careful Brian tek thee time theers umteen folk 'ere un ah deawnt wesh t' luk a foo un mi own doowerstop."

(Brian, be careful, go steady there's plenty of spectators watching who have associated with me through the years and I have no wish to look a fool by losing heavily.)

Brian just grinned at Tommy and they took to the green!

Tommy found himself 23-18 in front in the chase to score 31 points. Bookies around the green had dramatically dropped Tommy's 100-1 odds to a more realistic 25-1 as they started to sweat on the unlikely happening due to a few bob being placed on the Farnworth football legend as the game progressed.

Brian turned to Tommy at this point and said,

"Is that alright Tommy?"

Tommy was on his home green, the contours he knew well, but he never scored another point, Duncan moved up a few gears and took control of the game winning 31-23.

Duncan won the "Waterloo" the pinnacle event of crown green bowling five times in the period 1979-1992. This skilful line and lengthy game calls for a good eye and a rock solid temperament is a must. Anyone reaching the last eight at the Waterloo has done exceptional well each year with over a thousand competing. The green connected to the Waterloo pub in Blackpool is known as the Wembley of Crown Green Bowling and it has given over a hundred years of service to this annual prestigious competition. Tommy's watched a few of the Waterloo final's days which are staged in September; Tommy says that it is easier to buy tickets for the F.A. Cup Final.

Waterloo organiser Jimmy (Pieman) Parker is manfully battling on in these difficult economic times to maintain the venue and ensure the event survives with the history remaining in tack.

Although you win or lose by how well or poorly you bowl in your one versus one match the overall outcome of the inter club bowling contests is how the team of eight or ten bowlers has fared. It's an individual sport (unless you play doubles).......but you're part of a team.

Tommy enjoyed the banter and the team camaraderie plus the challenge created often in a bear pit like environment. It was like being back in the Bolton dressing room on a Saturday afternoon.

One bowls night around 6pm back in the summer of 1967 Tommy was locking the gates to a 'Banks and Banks' compound in Bolton when a concrete wagon pulled up.

"Banky can you use any concrete" said the driver,

"A site down the road ordered a mix for a house base, I have been delayed and now they are all locked up."

Both the driver and Tommy knew the concrete could not be left because it would harden and do untold damage to the large concrete mixer on the wagon.

Forever the negotiator Tommy informed the driver that he was just locking up to go home for his tea, however seeing he was in a difficult predicament Tommy offered a plausible suggestion.

"Thee mekkit a sloppy mix un ah'll tek it ut heawf price fer yon footin"
(I have a footing ready for concrete, add plenty of water so the mix will run easier and I will take it for half the usual price)

Caught with no other option a deal was struck, the driver reversed in and added water to the mix and Tommy began to drag the concrete around the footprint of the house eventually obtaining a true level.

Time was now very tight.....Tommy had no intention of missing his league bowls match. He now had to go straight to the venue, with no chance of any tea, no time for a wash and change of clothes, and no bowls. Tommy's opponent was on the verge of claiming the game due to his no show, but fortunately he sneaked in just before the deadline, if he had not he would have had to forfeit the match.

"You cannot play in those clogs with or without concrete coating" a committee man shrilled at Banky.

"Ah roll'd mi wark britches up t' mi nees un tuk of mi clugs un sokks" said Tommy
(I rolled my trousers up to my knees and took off my clogs and socks)

He borrowed a set of bowls from a mate there was "nowt" in the rules about playing barefooted. Fortune favours the brave, Tommy won his game. Visually he was just short of a knotted handkerchief to complete his beachwear image on the green that night with the smell of his feet apparently being the deciding factor in distracting his opponent.

Tommy played over forty years in the Bolton and Farnworth crown green bowls leagues, but when a good mate passed away in 2001 he retired from regular competitive bowling.

He still turns out for Bolton Wanderers ex players who compete on a number of occasions each year against Wigan and Chester old boys plus the veterans of "Dobbies" Sports and Social club in Breightmet, Bolton. His words of wisdom from the greenside regularly ring out loudly to his novice team mates in his familiar Farn'urth accent,

"Mek sure thi reychs thee block wi thi next bow theers nowt fer short,"
(You need to be sure you reach the jack with your next bowl, you have no hope of winning if you do not.)

When Tommy's "bowwin" on the green he still "tawks" to his bowls demanding they follow his instructions. After his football career he found that he could redirect his competitive nature into this leisurely sport. He could even chase his bowls across the green just like he was back at Burnden repelling visiting forwards.

Sadly a legacy of Tommy's past life The Royal's green now sees weeds and refuse where men once played. The dilapidated overgrown area is virtually unrecognisable from the days of the clatter of woods and chatter of watching folk. It is an indication of the contribution that the overall loss of the pits and demise of the cotton and engineering industries in Bolton, and surrounding regions, has registered on everyday events over a number of decades.

Known as a "drinkers pub," redundancy for the local man rebounded on this (and other) pubs which now had no spare cash to maintain the green's upkeep, plus with additional social changes playing a part the venue fell into disrepair.

One day who knows "The Royal" could return to its former glory similar to "The Valley" the home of Charlton Athletic F.C. Here was a ground back in 1985 that lacked the finances to bring the infrastructure up to the required football league standard and fans thought the doors were locked forever.

Charlton embarked on ground sharing with near neighbours Crystal Palace until the strong will and efforts of the supporters of Charlton brought about a vast revamp with "The Valley" re-opening in 1992.

Has the bowling green of The Royal, a place that holds many fond memories for Tommy over a few decades, still a chance to return to its former glory or is it gone forever like Burnden Park?

The green's detached from the pub by a fair way and to date it has not been smothered with tar macadam for a car park or found a niche for a few houses. It does not yet possess a Wacky Warehouse dining arena or such a building of a similar ilk; the chance is slim but...never say never.

Recalling Burnden Park.....the curtain had finally come down on the 25th April 1997 when Bolton hosted Charlton Athletic prior to the club's move to the fabulous Reebok Stadium at Middlebrook, Horwich, on the outskirts of the town.

Since Tommy's 1950's playing days ongoing off the field changes had occurred to give a vastly different picture of Burnden Park when the doors were closed for the last time pre demolition.

In the late 60's a Supporters Club had been built on legs fronting the main entrance and the waste land and factory lodge behind the Burnden Stand now saw traffic flow via the St. Peter's Way bypass.

The notorious "Gravels" rough small sided pitch area also behind this stand now housed a purpose built 5-a side court. In the 1970's the rail link high above the Embankment End had been closed thus seeing the track ripped up and the Signal Box pulled down. With the rail bridge over Manchester Road also dismantled, little evidence remains of bygone times that now see a supermarket and shopping complex replace the historical ground.

To assist fund the club's finances in 1986 a Normid Superstore was allowed to be built jutting out over the Embankment End on the site of the 1946 disaster.

Prior to the kick off on the last game at Burnden Park numerous former players from throughout the eras had been invited to parade the perimeter of the pitch. They warmly acknowledged the generous applause of the rapturous 22,000 crowd who witnessed this momentous day in the club's history.

The most vociferous greeting though was reserved for the 1958 F.A. Cup heroes.

Tommy Banks welcomed the opportunity to tread the Burnden turf one more time and remember with fondness some great matches, the epic Wolves quarter final tie being very much to the forefront of his mind.

Charlton threatened to spoil the party by taking an early lead. Thankfully in keeping with the occasion Bolton hit back to win 4-1 through goals from Alan Thompson, Gerry Taggart and two from fans' favourite John McGinlay.

It was fitting that "Super John" a Bolton Wanderers legend of modern times should score the last goal on Burnden Park.

Chapter 21

'Papper' Shop

In 1981 at the age of 52 Tommy had to have a replacement hip due to arthritis.

Arthritis is a common legacy for professional footballers who have played and trained daily at pace for 10-15 years during the fittest time in their lives.

His days of carrying bricks and mortar up ladders on building sites were naturally curtailed for the foreseeable future with Tommy having to look and veer out of his comfort zone for a living.

For a few months he received a pittance per week from the Welfare system but he was forever receiving letters being threatened with the withdrawal of his meagre fee. The "Social" claimed he should by now be fit to start work again however his local doctor told him if he received any more such letters to throw them in the fire he would let the government know when Tommy was fit. A desk job was all he could have managed at the time he had always been very active. The operation certainly took the wind out of his sails taking around six months to settle down and give him the confidence to resume a normal life.

Tommy married his second wife Rita in November 1981 residing at Elsie Street with Rita selling her home in Bolton, Tommy's second son Lee now 21 made up the trio in residence.

He wanted to work outside in some capacity and applied to become a postman but there were no vacancies and other options to work in the fresh air were scarce.

A newspaper shop 100 yards away on the corner of Kildare Street was put up for sale by Mrs. Marland the wife of the owner due to his passing. It was a steady business selling papers, cigarettes and toffee, built up over some twenty five years. Tommy took the plunge and bought the business and the premises reckoning he got a bargain for the price he paid. He soon realised that working in his shop seven days a week was taxing on his free spirit but committed every ounce of energy to engender success. Throughout his working life he had always enjoyed the company and camaraderie generated by men in a physical working environment.

"Ah wer leek a caged lion,"
(I was like a caged lion)

The small floor space of the shop enveloped him, he felt tied down which he was far from being used to. Looking back Tommy's glad he has never had the privilege of ever being locked up in a prison cell.

Tommy registered within the Bolton Associated Newsagents, a wholesale outlet which was situated just off Great Moor Street in Bolton town centre where he used to collect his Daily Papers.

At twelve years old the call had come to earn a living to help the family and ever since he had been an early riser, often nowadays existing on only a couple of hours sleep at night. Some mornings he would be waiting outside the newspaper wholesalers at 3am for the papers to arrive!

The gaffer of the wholesalers spoke to Tommy basically saying that if he turned up any sooner he would be waiting for the news to be made before the newspapers could be printed.

Being early helped, he could always drop a few through letter boxes on his way to opening up the shop around 6am; there were always the early birds calling on their way to work. Tommy organised morning newspaper deliveries, via school children, just like he had done himself in his youth. If the paperboys did not show or were late it could cause issues with his regular customers as they would have to leave home without their paper.

Over the years the outside of the shop had been a meeting place for all the kids from Kildare Street and other local streets...Mrs. Marland used to tolerate them but Tommy was not quite as affable. He swears he was a "victim of crime" when some young lads had the gall to snatch a couple of packets of Players No. 6 cigarettes, but Tommy could not prove it! He would chastise the gang forming outside telling them,

"Git on thee bikes, goo un play onth' fee"
(Move along, go on play on the field)

Tommy was basically a one man band, although he was grateful of the assistance of a lady called Margaret, who stood in for him for a couple of hours in the afternoon. Tommy's direct workaholic approach helped to ensure the business ticked over, he was renowned for expressing his views, no beating about the bush with this Farnworth lad. Occasionally whilst in the shop he would spot customers he knew passing by who had bills outstanding for the newspapers they had delivered by the paper lads.

Opening the door he'd bellow,

"Aye thee, geet thisell bakk 'ere un geet thee hond in thee pocket thi's well oer due wi thee papper munny"

(Excuse me, will you return to my shop so that you can settle your outstanding paper bill)

Tommy's shop serviced a whole estate with papers and once he thought outstanding debtors had received enough rope he would stop their papers.

Son Lee back then in his early twenties takes up the story;

"My dad would not go and knock on these doors demanding his money he just left it. Much as the house holder was in the wrong for non payment my father never wanted to look or feel that he was begging. All his life he has never asked a favour off anyone, and felt if you received goods common courtesy should prevail to pay for them. If they did eventually consent to venture into the shop to settle up they would then be subject to the full fury of dad's moral views and leave with their tail between their legs."

After 12-15 months he was confident enough in his new hip to start to exercise again through the gift of an old bicycle a customer was throwing away. Margaret would look after the shop whilst he took to his pushbike late afternoons delivering the Bolton Evening News to the homes of his regular clients on the estate.

Rita more than played her part in helping the wheels turn smoothly, up and out by car to work in Manchester by 7am she would return home to cook tea about 5pm. With Lee catered for, Rita would then take the shop reins from Tommy for the last couple of hours, also delivering a meal for her mother who now occupied the flat above the shop.

The routine remained in place for five years, Tommy knew he was fortunate that the shop just about gave him a living and he was not responsible to any other man. Even though he was his own boss he personally found the general shop refinement difficult to handle and was never really comfortable being lord of his own manor.

By chance he bumped into Francis Lee, who by now was a very successful self made businessman.

"Nethen Francis thee's inth' papper gam dust thi wannter bey a papper shop"

(Hello Francis you're in the paper business would you like to buy a paper shop?)

218

"Hello Tommy, no thanks my business makes paper tissues" replied Francis.

"Ah'm tellin thee, if theers sum mon tha hates, really hates un thi weesh's t'gi um a shoein bey um a papper shop"
(I am letting you know that if there is someone you really detest or despise and you wish to see them suffer buy them a paper shop)

Sunday night was the only time in the week he slipped out to the Moss Rose at Kearsley for a couple of pints with his old mate Alan Longworth who was part of the bricklaying gang before Tommy's operation. "Longy" as he was known to all and sundry was another die in the wool northerner who had also endured his own health problems needing a triple heart by-pass. During their usual chin wag over any subject under the sun that took their fancy, Tommy broached the subject of them joining up again and going back on the tools.

Shop keeping was driving Tommy nuts he was desperate to do something different, less restrictive. Apart from football and the pit....... bricklaying exploits were all he knew. Longy agreed to Tommy's relief, he sold the shop on in 1986 and for the next eight years they enjoyed practically seven days a week of non stop work.

Tommy bought a pair of working boots to do the job in; it was the first time since starting on the building sites that he had never worn a pair of clogs.

The industry was changing, Tommy used to be capable of carrying four fly ash blocks up a ladder. Now the heavier concrete blocks were what sites required, and they eventually began to take their toll on this ageing hod carrier. Tommy started to have ongoing trouble generated from nerves in his back, carrying a hod is really for young men so at sixty five he had to call it a day, he retired.

Many people cannot wait to stop working and draw their pension this was not the case for Tommy he enjoyed being occupied.

He would have liked to have done a lighter job for someone, he always enjoyed being busy but Tommy was too proud to ask anyone.

Chapter 22

Showtime

We have all heard the saying;

"Being in the right place at the right time" and how it can and does on occasions have a bearing on events/fortunes in your or someone else's life.

Tommy was in such a place back in late 1993, the place in question his old secondary school of Harper Green close to his house in Farnworth the district being the only home he has ever known.

Tommy's bricklaying gang were playing their part in building some link classrooms for a local contractor which would assist the school in their quest for additional much needed teaching space.

English teacher Chris Chilton was crossing the schoolyard one dinnertime when one of the boys asked him

"Sir, do you know who that is over there?" pointing in the direction of a sturdy guy loading bricks into a hod.

Chris a Londoner by birth had only taught in the school for a couple of years and on studying the face replied;

"Sorry, I don't, who is it?"

"Tommy Banks, he was a former pupil at this school, he won the F.A. Cup in 1958 with Bolton Wanderers and played for England" said the knowledgeable scholar.

Chris wrote a monthly newsletter for the school, so a day or so later he approached Tommy. Chris introduced himself and politely requested a few words that he could put into print information associated to his football past and link with the school.

"Nah problem lad, wor dust thee weesh t'yer" said Tommy loading the mixer.

(Not a problem what would you like to hear)

Chris listened with interest to events in Tommy's life in particular leading up to and including Bolton's Cup triumph at Wembley in 1958.

A short time after Tommy's words appeared in the next school newsletter another teacher Ian Smethurst was on the lookout for a likely subject for the schoolchildren's next musical production and quizzed Chris over any possible ideas.

Chris without any hint of hesitation said;

"Tommy Banks, let's do Tommy's Story."

It was a somewhat sceptical Tommy Banks who agreed to meet Chris in a local pub, the Bradford Arms, for a pint and to "chew the fat" over exactly what Chris had in mind?

Chris outlined his thoughts and once Tommy realised that Chris was serious and it was not an exercise in 'taking the mickey' he was more than willing to give the thumbs up.

For five nights in the summer of 1994 the Harper Green building was filled with music and laughter as the school produced a spectacular celebration of the early life of Farnworth's famous son Tommy Banks building up to the crescendo of Bolton's 1958 F.A. Cup success;

The show was completely home produced with Chris writing the script and lyrics.

Ian was prominent in the music department and many contributions were made by staff through costumes, choreography, sound and set designs that made for a bespoke production.

Kenneth Wolstenholme another local Farnworth lad who had made his name in sport by his television commentaries, generally on football, agreed to pre-record some voice overs for the show from his London home. He is best remembered for his now famous words on television in the dying minute of the 1966 World Cup Final at Wembley when England's Geoff Hurst broke clear to shoot at the West German goal with the home team leading 3-2.

"Some people are on the pitch they think it's all over" Hurst pulled the trigger and scored,

"It is now" roared Ken.

Ken did voyage north for the "Gala night" where he would be joined in the audience by Tommy, Rita and Tommy's sons Dave and Lee and their families plus former Bolton team mates, Nat Lofthouse, Dennis Stevens, Roy Hartle, Ralph Gubbins to name a few.

Rita used all her tact to prevent Tommy walking across the fields to attend the gala night show, she was in a secret.

Phil Dunne the boss of the building firm Tommy had sub contracted to build for at Harper Green's school arrived unannounced to Tommy outside the Banks residence in his Rolls Royce to whisk them in style to the show. Somewhat taken aback by the arrival of the Rolls Royce he was even more surprised to find Kenneth Wolstenholme already sat in the back.

The entire cast of the musical led by leading girl Joanne Hindley (Tommy's mother) and Lee Marland (Tommy) formed a guard of honour to the school entrance and with clapping loudly ringing out Tommy's chauffeur opened his door.

"Wheers red carpet," Tommy said to Rita with a smile on his face.

Over a hundred personnel mainly comprising school children who had featured in the show, teachers who had worked backstage and the local band all joined to applaud Tommy after a show which was never to be forgotten ..... Chris Chilton presented him with a glass decanter. On hearing Chris's words, "Tommy Banks this is your life" an emotional strangely shy true gent for once found words of thanks hard to find.

Was he consciously reminiscing over his happy schooldays at Harper Green?

Was he wishing Mr. Davy had still been around to acknowledge his confident claim at fourteen years old when the history teacher asked the question,

"Where do you see your future?"

"Ah'm gooin t'bi a futbawler"
(I am going to be a professional footballer)

As with all biographically based shows, the script took some dramatic license. The scenes depicting Tommy's time in the army were pure knockabout, and his childhood was populated with a rich array of invented characters. However as Chris explained, it was important to stay true to the spirit of Tommy's story throughout. It was essential to honour the footballer and the man while at the same time recording his extraordinary journey from working class Farnworth lad and coalminer, to the huge success Tommy found at club and international level.

"I felt that Tommy had invested his trust in me though he never said as much" Chris said.

"The most important thing for Tommy was that the portrayal of his life via our musical was done with dignity."

"I would like to think that we managed to do this, not least because beneath his warmth and ready humour, Tommy is indeed a man of great dignity."

Later Tommy was back in good voice enjoying a few drinks at the Pack Horse Hotel in Bolton who had kindly donated a room for the after show buffet and contributed to sponsoring the musical.

"Itwer magic, kids purron a great show, a feel reet honour'd, bet'thur thun munny con bey"

(The show was superb, the children performed brilliantly, I felt greatly honoured, and no amount of money could buy that feeling)

Tommy was particularly impressed with Lee Marland and Joanne Hindley.

Talent spotter Tommy will be delighted to know that Joanne has since forged a career in the music/musical industry. She's performed in the West End show ...Notre Dame de Paris and in 2004 won a competition to sing a duet "The way you look tonight" with a member of Westlife on their album "Allow me to be frank" receiving her own Platinum disc.

Joanne's gone close on the TV show X factor and felt her ability has been recognised by working with the legendary Gary Barlow of "Take That" fame.

Headmaster at the time was Mr. Alan Atherton, father of former Lancashire and England cricket captain Michael Atherton and himself a former Busby Babe before injury prematurely ended his football career.

There was a fitting circularity to the show at Harper Green which, almost eighteen years and three head teachers later, the performance and occasion people still talk about with great fondness.

Rebecca Rushton, the receptionist at the school who took my call when I first made contact about the show pointed out that she had actually performed in the Tommy Bank's Story as a Year 8 pupil all those years ago.

"I recently showed my son, who's currently in Year 7, the video of the show," said Rebecca,

So, this unique musical back in 1994 has already passed on to another generation.

Rightly so, because Tommy's story, especially in today's tough times is an inspiration to young and old alike.

Chapter 23

Retirement

Following many years of physical endeavour, playing professional football ploughing through fields of mud, and running up ladders with a shoulder full of bricks, Tommy decided that his battered body had taken enough, retiring in 1994.

Ongoing bouts of sciatica were the real cause that hastened his departure from the daily physical grind of serving materials to eager bricklayers. Body tone wise he was still fitter and stronger than many men half his age, then as in his playing days he was a formidable character.

For the eight years previous since teaming up again with "Longy" he would regularly work six day weeks some seven on the building sites of the northwest.

Tommy missed not working, he had always been busy but the wear and tear on his body due to the physical endurance in earning a living carrying the hod over the years was telling, realistically this job is for young men.

In 2000 some six years later on after retiring, Tommy now aged 70, received a phone call seeking his assistance and expertise from Andrew Dean (Bolton Wanderers Promotions Manager) regarding an extension to his property. Tommy not only organised the build, he also hand dug the footings which at one corner reached twelve feet.

"I could not see Tommy, just earth that he seemed to be endlessly throwing" said Andrew.

Unfortunately the old fashioned wind up mixer with the iron wheels Andrew owned had also been retired so Tommy had to make do with a modern push button apparatus to churn the mortar.

"He wore his clogs for the duration of the build" recalls Andrew,

"However they were falling apart caked in concrete, I found them on top of the skip when the job was complete."

Andrew thought Tommy was making a statement, 'just one more time' proving to himself he could still do the graft.

Tommy was never one to lie in bed, in fact he hardly sleeps at all, if he has slept for four or five hours a night he has done well. Even now he is always up and out around 5-5.30am to take his trusted bitch Susie on their regular couple of miles pre breakfast hike. Once back he will do two hundred sit ups before enjoying his daily piping hot bowl of porridge. He will walk Susie a couple more times daily occasionally meeting up with old friend Arthur Barnard. Arthur would be on a similar "dug" walking mission but he has waited until the streets of Farnworth were aired rather than Tommy's initial dawn stroll.

Farnworth is the place that has always been Tommy's home and it has been a happy home though football's taken him abroad to many much more exotic parts of the world. Tommy fully realises how his football ability has helped carve a large chunk of his life and he is grateful for the opportunities it offered in his twenties to broaden his horizons.

"Ah travell'd world fer free" said Tommy recalling foreign sorties in Europe and South Africa with Bolton and fixtures in Russia plus the 1958 World Cup competition in Sweden with England.

Children seem to relate to Tommy, a neighbour's young "anklebiter" regularly knocks on his door asking if Tommy and Susie are coming out to play. Another asked him to show him how to whistle, now that the young 'un's' achieved tying his shoe laces under Tommy's guidance.

In between his dog walking excursions he has become an avid crossword conqueror particularly throughout the winters. The change in seasons sees Tommy pottering in his garden which brings him pleasure in the daytime during the warm summer months.

For endless years Tommy and Rita have attended and contributed football items for Professor Moriarty's fund raising events to send poorly children to Lourdes.

Dennis Stevens who has required the surgical expertise of the Professor on a number of occasions to resolve his hip and knees issues, since his playing days ended, introduced the Banks's to Bolton Hospital's tall and swarthy professor.

Tommy appreciates all the hard work and enterprise Professor Moriarty devotes to such a sad but much needed cause for children and backs him whenever possible.

In early spring every year Tommy the President of Farnworth Social Circle Cricket Club always invites other ex Wanderers players to attend the ultimate in pure football quizzes organised by quizmaster Nigel Howard. This once a year event finds locals and business folk pitting their knowledge at Tommy's 'second home' to help fund the club's various expenses.

Over the last decade Bolton's Former Players Association have hosted a yearly Sportsman's Dinner with Tommy the guest speaker on one occasion. The evening Welshman John Charles of Leeds United (1948-57) and Juventus (1957-62) fame sat under the spotlight it was a questions and answers event involving punters from off the floor. John Charles rated by many when at the peak of his career, the best player in the world, was embarrassingly asked if he thought this was a truthful proposition.

John known as the "Gentle Giant" very modestly muddled through stating that football is a team game made up of players with a range of different attributes commenting that realistically the answer was a matter of opinion.

When John had concluded his answer Tommy Banks who was sat in the audience and never one to pull his punches spoke to voice his own honest views.

"Pardon mi John, thi wer reet gud,in fact thee wer great but in mi opinion yonmon deawn road, Tom Finney, 'eewer top dug"

(Excuse me John, you were a very good player, in fact you were great but in my opinion Tom Finney of Preston was the best)

Bolton belatedly gave Freddie Hill the benefit of a testimonial match at Burnden Park on the 15th October 1990 against Manchester City with Francis Lee a prominent organiser. Phil Brown and Sammy Lee led the Wanderers eleven with Peter Reid proudly pushing his ageing legs around the field in the company of Gary Megson and Colin Hendry in the blue of City.

Many former Wanderers players accepted an invite to the game, although the bulk of the lads were by age, now pure spectators. They were glad to be back in a football environment and enjoying the after match banter in the Old Supporters club which was built on stilts outside the main entrance to the ground.

Roy Hartle had moved to live in Spain but he had recently returned to Bolton and he was known to have also developed a troublesome hip. Francis Lee said he was talking with Tommy when Roy was spotted by both former England internationals limping into the room with the aid of a walking cane. Roy looked pale and drained of colour which prompted Tommy into verse.

"Nah Hartle if tha's wor livin in Spain dust fer thee thi con stuff it thi favvors thee's dun six munths in Warby's bakery under floower mixer"

(Roy it doesn't look like living in Spain has agreed with you I think I will give it a miss)

Roy and Tommy although good buddies throughout their lives are from opposite sides of the political divide. Roy has been a Conservative councillor in Bolton whilst Tommy is an out an out socialist who if he had remained in the pits may have been a leading light in the 1984 miners strike.... would history have been changed?

226

In 1996 Alan Ball junior was installed as the manager of Manchester City by former England favourite Francis Lee now the club's chairman.

Francis originally from Westhoughton had blossomed at Bolton Wanderers after joining the club's ground staff making his debut at the tender age of 16 in 1960. He became a prominent member of the team prior to his £60,000 transfer in 1967 to Manchester City.

Francis invited Tommy and his guests along to a home game and they found themselves pre and post match in a plush room enjoying drinks and nibbles. Other guests of the club present in this lounge apparently including family and friends of the match officials.

The referee of the match had a shocker!

After the game son Lee was one of Tommy's party expressing within their group constructive points of view and thus dismay at the referee's poor display on the day.

A lady who turned out to be the referee's wife was sat nearby and on over hearing 'the ref this,' 'the ref that' comments spoke to them,

"I think it's disgusting that guests of the club are openly criticising the match officials."

Lee said Tommy spoke ever so polite when he countered with a few words of his own which ran along these rough lines,

"Excuse me madam, I spent almost twenty years of my life listening to the good, bad and ugly comments thrown at me from the terraces, your husband's paid to be criticised just like the players whether you or he likes it or not."

"If thi connt stund th'eat geet owter kitchen"
(If he's not thick skinned he needs to do something else)

Tommy's lifelong love of jazz, mainly swing jazz has regularly taken him since the late '80's on numerous holidays to the southern states of America. New Orleans in Louisiana is particularly preferred, back in the 1930's his favourite artist Teddy Wilson often teamed up with Benny Goodman who was known as the "King of Swing."

Wilson who died in 1986 aged 74 was a very sophisticated and elegant individual who graced the records of the biggest names with Louis Armstrong and Billie Holiday to the fore. Goodman only wanted to play with the best musicians and African America pianist Wilson was amongst the elite. Their trio including drummer Gene Krupa became very popular commanding respect all over Dixieland which helped break down the walls of segregation.

"If he does not play I will not play" Goodman was heard to say when questions were asked about the colour of Wilson's skin on arriving at venues in the Southern states.

Tommy enjoys a warble although it is not the songs in the Karaoke mould of today's wannabee singers. Tommy's team mates and "Joe Public" have over the years heard many an impromptu rendition via his dulcet tones of old songs, his most popular is from the 1922 Broadway musical "Make it Snappy"

"Yes! We have no bananas"

On the back of a coach, in a hotel foyer, even a nightclub D.J. has had to take an unscheduled break whilst Farnworth's popular soloist belted out his favourite amongst his endless repertoire.

Without question the magic of Siesta Key in Sarasota, Florida, has enticed Tommy and Rita Banks back on half a dozen late season holidays.

Tommy is treated like royalty at Captain Curt's Crab and Oyster bar by local entrepreneurs Brett and Brad Stewart. This stems from a fortuitous meeting in their restaurant premises at Captain Curt's village, over a decade ago, when they discovered his football history.

A signed 1958 BWFC Cup Final retro shirt and Tommy Banks photograph adorns pride of place on a main wall. It is a slightly older Tommy Banks who nowadays sits down in Brett and Brad's restaurant to enjoy his favourite delicacy of oysters on his oversees sorties. The Banks usually link up in the company of American friends Don and Judy Rochester "snowbirds" who fly down from near the Canada border to escape the cold of winter.

In 2007 the Professional Footballers Association celebrated their centenary year by holding a lavish dinner in the Manchester Town Hall, a vast arena with many suites housing towering ceilings.

Gordon Taylor the Chief Executive of the P.F.A. invited Tommy along to the celebrations offering to lay on a taxi thus providing door to door service.

As usual Tommy did not want any favours and thanked Gordon but opted to make his own way.

"Nah tar, No 8 buzz dreighvur wilt tell mi when ah'm theer"
(No thanks, I will catch the number 8 bus and ask the driver to inform me when I am there)

Prior to the speeches Tommy sought the toilets which seemed to be based a mile away. On his return he waited outside the doors whilst words were being said from the stage rather than push his way through the tightly packed tables in the vast hall.

On completion of the speeches he opened the door to the room only to

228

find following his good manners a commissionaire rushing across to block his path,

"Excuse me sir, this is invitation only"

"Slow deawn tha'art gooin't'meyt thisell coomin bakk, ah yer thee ah'm invit'd, ah'ave bin in before tha noes" replied Tommy
(Slow down, I have heard what you say, I am invited and I have been here all night and only stepped out of the room briefly)

"Oh yes" said the doorman rather dubiously giving Tommy the visual once over
"Where are you sat?"

"Neaw stop thee thrutchin ah'm reet o'er theer" retorted Tommy pointing in the distance to the main guest table at the front of the large hall,
(Now stop mithering I am right over there)

"Thee'll find mi name card Tommy Banks reet next t'main mon Taylor"
(You will find my name card Tommy Banks right next to the Chief Executive Gordon Taylor)

"Oh I am very sorry for troubling you sir", said the inquisitor instantly stepping aside.

2008 saw two 50th anniversaries of what can only be described as "Tommy's year" ......football celebrations from the year 1958.
In May 2008, over 300 people dined in the Platinum suite, the largest room at the fabulous Reebok Stadium, to acknowledge the re-united members of the 1958 F.A. Cup winning team sadly missing the departed Hopkinson, Hennin, Higgins and Parry. Many tributes were paid serious and humorous and late in the evening Francis Lee heard a familiar voice,

"Eigh up theer Leeey ast thee awe reet, who's geeten thee ready"
(Hello Francis how are you...you're very well dressed!)

Tommy reminisced with Francis about the time Eartha Kitt came to watch a game which Bolton played in London. Bill Ridding had rushed Tommy back into action after a small operation on his private parts resulting in him having to wear much padding. Thus he took to the field strapped up resembling a batsman wearing a protective box. Tommy thought he must have put a twinkle in Eartha's eye because the Bolton reserve players sat in the stand heard her say,

"Who is that number three in the white shirt he looks a big boy!"

After a good long chat Tommy turned to Francis and said,
"Nethen ah'll sithee agen, ah'll affertguffertbuzz wom neaw Leeey"
(I will see you again, I have to catch the bus to go home now Francis)

"I'll drive you home" said Francis

"Art gooin bi Farn'urth" chirped Tommy,
(Are you going by Farnworth?)

Francis's reply sealed the trip "No I wasn't but don't worry I'll get you home"
Tommy sat in the front passenger seat and was soon rooting in Francis's glove compartment asking inquisitively on finding a box of Havana cigars,

"Thi dustant smookk cigars dust thee"
(Do you smoke cigars?)

"Er, er, well yes, occasionally, would you like one?" replied Francis smiling remembering his early days at Bolton when Tommy was full of advice always looking out for his well being.

"Nah tar, ah'ave nar smokk'd, ah'd feel ruff as a badgers wi thum ah'll stick t'chewwin mi baccy"
(No thanks, I've never smoked I expected I would feel ill with cigars I'll stick with chewing my tobacco)

Rita also received a phone call from a Latin American lady based in London speaking on behalf of a Brazilian film company. After qualifying Tommy Banks was her husband, details were outlined regarding the reason for the call and arrangements were made for her and the video crew to visit Tommy at his Farnworth home. It was the 50th anniversary of the year that Brazil won their first World Cup with the venue being in Sweden. A Brazilian TV programme was being put together that included interviews and newsreels with key members of each of the opposing teams the country had played en route to collect the Jules Rimet.

With Tommy relaxing in his armchair the camera rolled seeking his views on the Brazilian players and the actual match between the two countries back in June 1958.

Tommy conceded that without doubt the best team had won the World Cup.

Little was known of Brazil prior to the tournament, but with good players in every position he had tipped them at the end of the group stage although England had managed a "backs to the wall" draw.

After a few hours and a couple of pots of tea (these Brazilians did not drink coffee) the crew left to continue their investigative European tour. No fees were offered or requested although a promise of a holiday in Brazil was on the table with tickets soon to be in the post along with a CD of the finished TV programme.

The CD arrived ok in late 2008 showing Tommy's English speaking interview with Brazilian words appearing on the screen for the TV but it would not have been easy translating some of his Lancashire dialect phrases.

Even though the tickets are unofficially "lost" in the post Tommy still fancies that stroll along the Copacabana beach.... who knows some Brazilian native may even recognise him from the World Cup clips. Visual recognition perhaps but it is doubtful if they would have been able to imitate Tommy's very own Farnworth drollery.

"Mr. Bolton Wanderers" Nat Lofthouse sadly passed away aged 85 in January 2011. On the day of his funeral thousands of people took to the streets of the town to show their respect for the world renowned local lad made good. Countless football dignitaries attended the ceremony and many returned to the "wake" hosted by Bolton Wanderers at the Reebok Stadium.

Tommy Banks was chatting with former Bolton colleagues when the Manchester United contingent entered the main room close to where Tommy was stood.

Andrew Dean was also in Tommy's company as "Sirs," Bobby Charlton and Alex Ferguson greeted known contemporaries. Bobby Charlton smiled broadly and shook the hand of Tommy, Bolton's finest ever left full back exchanging smiles and a few quick words, said Andrew.

Tommy turned to Alex Ferguson and in his best Farnworthian said,
"Owdo, thee wonnt no mi wilta"
(Hello how are you, you'll not know who I am will you)

"Don't worry Tommy I know exactly who you are" replied the Scotsman with a cheery smile stretching his hand out to make a firm handshake.

In 2005 The Bolton News ran a vote open to the readers of the local paper to identify their all time legends, the most popular players ever to play for the Wanderers through the decades. Nat Lofthouse quite rightly topped the poll followed by that great entertainer the Nigerian, Jay Jay Okocha "so good they named him twice."

Although it had been forty five years since he had donned the famous white shirt, and had thus never been seen playing live by many of the subsequent generations, Tommy Banks took the Number 13 position which was a fabulous tribute to this local lad.

In January 2011 Tommy and Jimmy Armfield were invited onto the BBC's "One Show" due to it being the 50th anniversary of the end of the 1961 Maximum Wage contracts for professional footballers.

Back in January 1961 Tommy had spoken at a mass gathering of Professional Football Association members at a meeting in Manchester. His words from the heart registered with the players of the time about the injustices that they were enduring, due to the control the Football League had regarding the right to negotiate contracts.

The interviewer in 2011 was Phil Tufnell a former England cricketer and now permanent lead resident of a team on the BBC's a "Question of Sport"

Tommy as usual was spick and spank smartly turned out as was Jimmy Armfield in a suit and tie.

Neither former footballer had met Phil Tufnell before but Jimmy said Tommy did not seem impressed with Tufnell's choice of clothes. Tufnell who was dressed in jeans, winkle picker shoes, leather jacket with not a tie in sight greeted the guests warmly.

"Dust thee allus dress leek tha fer telly?" enquired Tommy to a rather startled Tufnell.

(Do you always dress like that when you're appearing on shows on the television?)

Tommy Banks is a true legend both on and off the field of play.

His dialect harks back to hard yet enjoyable times as a young schoolboy, forward a few years growing into a young adult he experienced many extremely difficult days trying to earn a living from the tender age of fourteen. Regrettably Tommy's calling was par for the course in Farnworth unless you were born blessed with a silver spoon.

Can the fourteen year old boys of today envisage leaving school to start filling over a 100 coal bags on a daily basis before driving a horse and cart delivering to homes in all weathers five and a half days a week?

In the 1930/40's education for the less well off usually came to a full stop at this age previously it had been thirteen which was the norm for most families in the industrial north.

He believed in himself and lived the dream of becoming a professional footballer although he only earned a pittance in relation to the wages the current top players are paid today. Money although important was not everything; football gave him a new direction and stopped him returning to the pit.

Tommy was always a player who led from the front.

He is a natural leader, a charismatic man who channelled his ability for the good of team with his astute talent and competitive spirit on the field and a revered spokesman off it.

Tommy constantly stood up for players' rights within the club environment and later put forward persuasive words to assist the P.F.A. fully knowing he was too long in the tooth to profit personally from improvements to players' contracts. He loved the team camaraderie becoming something of a father figure icon to young impressionable junior professionals with his guiding words.

Throughout his years he will sometime act the clown often joking in a teasing way to prove a point or over emphasise his Farnworth accent to relax people in his company.

Tommy is nobody's fool, he is a bright intelligent man with knowledge of how the world turns which has impinged on his personal way of life and sought him to display immense strength of character throughout his years.

Tommy is hugely proud of reaching the pinnacle of any player's career by representing his country in the World Cup tournament 1958 in Sweden. He was also successful earlier the same year at Wembley bringing home an F.A. Cup winner's medal with his hometown team Bolton, his only Football League professional club.

Business failure did not daunt him he worked even harder carrying the hod to grind out a living for the family he cherishes. He has always been employed in work associated with men apart from his spell in the "papper" shop and does not suffer fools or false people.

A well respected humble man who speaks the truth in laughter and sorrow he will not compromise, Tommy says what he means no matter the company he is keeping.

People take him as they find him he does not change.

Tommy earned a pittance from professional football but he has always recognised money was not everything he is rich in friends and retains a million memories. He played with immense pride for his home town football club.... the games were deadly serious but still fun something he says,

"Munny cawnt bey"
(Money can't buy)

Over a long weekend in April 2012 there will be a Banks Family Reunion held in Bolton and district to welcome the many arms of the family some who have never previously met, the current Mayor of Bolton Noel Spencer is a member of the Banks clan. With family travelling from as far a field as Canada a comprehensive itinerary of events has been carefully pulled together with Rita at the helm.

5th April; BWFC Tour of the Reebok Stadium
6th April; Farnworth Social Circle Cricket Club informal gathering
7th April; Bolton Town Hall banqueting suite; The Main Event

Eighty two attendees are expected for the main event at Bolton's Town Hall where family members will be encouraged to say a few words. In the vaults of this grand building Tommy Banks will certainly be at the forefront. He may start by harking back to his early "three in a bed" days wedged between the wall and his brother Ralph; in fact he will most likely open his speech with his well known "Tommyism"

"Nethen .... Ah'm tellin thee"

The Author

Ian Seddon is a former professional footballer initially with Bolton Wanderers making his first team debut at 18 years old in August 1969 (apprentice 1967). He was transferred to Chester City in 1973 and then joined Cambridge United in 1976 under manager Ron Atkinson, gaining promotions with all three clubs.

In 1979 he ventured to Australia to play for Newcastle KB United in the Phillips National League followed by a spell with Bulova F.C. in Hong Kong.

Ian the eldest of five children was brought up to follow the 'Wanderers' in Walkden (Wogdin) some six miles from Bolton. At seven years of age he witnessed standing on a stool beside his father Bolton's epic quarter final cup tie with Wolves at Burnden Park in 1958 on route to winning the F.A. Cup.

Although a 'Wogdin' lad his father Harold's family were all coal miners from Astley a pit village five miles away near Leigh. Harold's two older brothers were already pitmen when their father Jack was brought home on a door acting as a stretcher following a pit accident. Due to injuries sustained Jack never worked again and his wife decreed Harold wouldn't go down the pit. Both Harold's brothers died relatively young due to lung illnesses related to inhaling coal dust from working below ground.

A talented cricketer Ian represented Lancashire Schoolboys and the North of England at fifteen. From 1965 he enjoyed the cut and thrust of Bolton League cricket for a couple of decades with his hometown team Walkden C.C. and a handful of seasons at Astley Bridge C.C.

Joining Golborne Sports and Social Club he captained their cricket team to great successes throughout the 1990's in the Bolton Association.

Retiring from first team cricket at fifty four he now quenches his competitive spirit via the leisurely sport of crown green bowls.

He retains his link with Bolton Wanderers through a corporate host role on match days at the Reebok Stadium.

Ian's embraced the opportunity of relating the words, events and stories that result in the life story of a true Bolton Wanderers legend..... the one and only Tommy Banks.